GLORY
HOUNDS

How A Small Northwest School Reshaped
College Basketball. And Itself.

BUD WITHERS

GLORY HOUNDS
Bud Withers

ISBN: 978-0-692-77607-0
Also available in Kindle & ePub formats

Cover Photography & Design: Rajah Bose / Factory Town
Bulldog Sculpture by Vincent DeFelice
Layout & Pre-press: Lighthouse24

www.gloryhounds.net

CONTENTS

INTRODUCTION

LATE IN FEBRUARY 2015, in the idle time before the chaos of March in college basketball, a scenario was making the rounds that threw many followers of the University of Kentucky into a froth.

It seems John Calipari's Wildcats were having a season for the ages. Flush with the usual cast of one-and-done, whistlestop-in-Lexington ballers, the 'Cats were deep into an assault on the record book. They were undefeated, only rarely tested, and bearing down on the distinction of becoming the first team since Indiana in 1976 to negotiate the season without a loss.

February is the time when prospective seeds and NCAA-tournament subplots begin to crystallize, and it's when that happened that some Wildcat fans got their blue-and-white panties in a bunch.

Out west, a Gonzaga team that had only an overtime loss to Arizona in December was getting serious mention as a possible No. 1 seed. If that happened, by principles of the NCAA basketball committee, it appeared logical that Kentucky would see in its quartile of the bracket a dangerous Wisconsin team – prospectively seeded No. 2 – that had played in the 2014 Final Four and had most of those players back. Kentucky's road to the Final Four would thus be more perilous.

In an instant, denizens of Kentucky message boards turned on the Zags, one keyboard genius calling it a "freaking joke" if

Gonzaga got a No. 1 seed, another chiming in that they were "frauds for sure."

Well, as it happened, Gonzaga dropped a Senior Night game to Brigham Young for its second defeat, ensuring that it got a No. 2 seed instead. And Kentucky wouldn't have to face Wisconsin until the Final Four (at which juncture it was stared down by history and fell to the Badgers – just later than Big Blue fans had feared in their doomsday scenario).

But it was impossible not to appreciate the hilarity of Kentucky fans tied up in knots by a little Jesuit school in Spokane, Washington. By the time Gonzaga won its first NCAA-tournament game (1999), the Wildcats had won seven national championships. In terms of blueblood history, this was like a scrap-yard mutt sniffing his way through a back door and onto the carpeted expanse of the Westminster Kennel Club Dog Show at Madison Square Garden.

When I mentioned to friends and acquaintances in the past couple of years that I was working on a book on Gonzaga basketball, I tended to elicit raised eyebrows. Some of that owes, no doubt, to the fact I had already written "Bravehearts," a book on GU hoops, in 2002. But I took some of the reaction as surprise that the subject was worthy of any deep exploration.

To which I would suggest: It is.

Not only have the Gonzaga men continued to perk with astonishing consistency, the school's women's program also bobbed into the national consciousness – detailed within these pages – partly because fans couldn't get tickets to the men's games.

Certainly there are nuances to the men's prominence. It's a national championship, or even a Final Four appearance, short of a Hollywood saga. But I'm convinced the Gonzaga story remains underappreciated, perhaps because it's a tale of consistency and stability and sameness. The Zags are simply a part of the woodwork in college basketball, to the point where it seems unthinkable they wouldn't be included in the NCAA-tournament bracket.

The following is the list of top 10 streaks of consecutive appearances in the NCAA men's tournament. It's worth noting that only since 1975 have teams other than conference champions been allowed into the tournament, and that still-exclusionary list expanded in 1985 to the 64-team field – or what is essentially today's tournament. In other words, it was more difficult to assemble such a streak in earlier times, evident from the roster below.

1. (tie) North Carolina 27 (1975-2001)
    Kansas 27 (1990-2016)
3. Arizona 25 (1985-2009)
4. Duke 21 (1996-2016)
5. Michigan State 19 (1998-2016)
6. (tie) Wisconsin 18 (1999-2016)
    Gonzaga 18 (1999-2016)
    Indiana 18 (1986-2003)
9. Kentucky 17 (1992-2008)
10. UCLA 15 (1967-81)

My research also produced this list of streaks of schools having won games in the NCAA tournament in successive years. (Note that it's not merely a streak of wins in opening-round games; it requires making the tournament field each year.)

1. North Carolina 18 (1981-98)
2. Kentucky 16 (1992-2007)
3. Kansas 15 (1990-2004)
4. UCLA 14 (1967-80)
5. Georgetown 11 (1982-92)
6. (tie) Duke 10 (1985-94)
    Stanford 10 (1995-2004)

    Duke 10 (1997-2006)
    Kansas 10 (2007-16)
10. (tie) Syracuse 8 (1983-90)
    UNLV 8 (1984-91)
    Arkansas 8 (1989-96)
    Cincinnati 8 (1995-2002)
    Gonzaga 8 (2009-16)

NCAA basketball statisticians don't keep lists on every category of potential interest, so it sometimes takes some investigation to put perspective on Gonzaga's place in the hoops hierarchy. A few years ago, about the time Zags coach Mark Few noted that his son A.J. had never known a Selection Sunday without his favorite team in the bracket, I began to wonder what the standard was for streaks by head coaches making the tournament to start a career.

By comparing schools' streaks of tournament appearances against the coaches' careers who authored them, it became possible to produce a record for consecutive years making the tournament to start a coaching career. I ran the methodology by NCAA statistician Gary Johnson, and indeed, it turns out Few holds that record, at an ongoing 17 – though, like the streak of consecutive years winning in the tournament, you won't find that one in the NCAA record book. (North Carolina coach Roy Williams could have had a career-opening streak of 21 years, but he began his Kansas tenure in 1988-89 with the Jayhawks on NCAA probation and ineligible for the tournament, courtesy of the school's handiwork under Larry Brown.)

But the Gonzaga phenomenon might be better addressed in conceptual terms, rather than numerical. Think of college basketball programs that sprang up organically, seemingly from nothing, to steady success with an established order around them, and it's difficult to find a comparison to the rise of Gonzaga.

Georgetown, under John Thompson, might be a parallel, except that the Hoyas actually were NCAA runners-up in 1943. And unlike

Gonzaga, the school had the advantage of being in a major metropolitan area, and by the 1980s, was a member of the emerging, titanic Big East Conference.

Connecticut women's basketball? The Huskies had a generally dreadful history before coach Geno Auriemma's arrival in 1985, and the program is now monolithic. But the landscape of that sport was sparse and widely unsupported when UConn began building a colossus.

Over a seafood dinner in Spokane, Jerry Krause pondered the whole phenomenon. Krause was GU director of basketball operations until 2015, when he switched to an administrative role in the women's program. He was a head coach at Eastern Washington, has authored 30-odd books, and once did a five-year civilian stint as a professor of sport philosophy at West Point. Human behavior fascinates him; he generated a paper at West Point in which he surveyed 1,000 graduating cadets on moral and ethical values.

"I'm not a person that believes in simple explanations," he says. "Generally in human behavior, and especially group behavior, there are probably a lot of plausible explanations.

"But how do you sustain success that long? It is highly unlikely. Not many schools have ever done it. When we started all this, honestly, I remember we were comparing salaries of all the other West Coast Conference schools. We were absolutely at the bottom of the heap, in almost everything, from athletic administration to coaches – and by a margin.

"To go from that, it's like, 'What the hell, how did that ever happen?'"

What happened is that, in addition to the wins, the Zags pulled down men's basketball revenues of $12,185,320 in the year ending May 31, 2015, on expenses of $7,362,669, a profit of $4,822,651, according to U.S. Department of Education equity-in-athletics data. The revenue from men's basketball is more than $2 million greater than its state neighbor, the University of Washington (Gonzaga spent about $1 million more), and more than twice that of Washington State.

Still, in college basketball, those aren't high-rolling numbers. Suggesting the Zags are getting considerable bang for their buck is a study done annually by Ryan Brewer, an assistant professor of finance at Indiana University-Purdue University Columbus. Brewer assesses the valuation of college basketball programs – what they would be worth if they could be bought and sold like pro franchises – and puts Gonzaga's at No. 42 at about $48.6 million, up six places and $6.9 million from 2015.

Louisville was No. 1 at $301.3 million. Among schools in the neighborhood of Gonzaga's estimated financial worth were a number with lesser profiles competitively – Missouri (36), St. John's (37), Oklahoma State (38), Auburn (43), Washington (44), Virginia Tech (45), UNLV (46), South Carolina (47) and Florida State (49).

But to a noisy faction of fans and media, none of it seems to matter – the wins, the money, the phenomenon. They don't want to hear it. For some reason, Gonzaga inspires an unusual amount of vitriol.

As Jerry Krause might say, I don't think there's a simple explanation.

Start with this: Societally, we want resolution. We want a clear picture: Winners. Losers. Overachievers. Chokers. Savants. Fools. In some quarters, the Zags are confounding: Yes, they win consistently, and they win on a national level. No, they haven't won a national championship or gone to a Final Four.

So it produces wildly disparate opinions. After the Zags lost a grinding overtime game in December 2014 at Arizona (which made a second straight Elite Eight appearance that season), Myron Medcalf of ESPN.com blistered the Zags, writing in part, "Another year, same story, it seems. This is Gonzaga . . . the talent's there for Gonzaga. So perhaps it will ultimately validate the early hype. Or maybe we've seen this Gonzaga act before. And we all know how it ends."

Less than two weeks before that, Gary Parrish of CBSSports.com wrote by way of counterpoint: "But isn't Gonzaga's consistent success proof that the 'breakthrough' came years ago? And, either way, would four wins in a single-elimination tournament often determined by a lucky bounce here or there really validate Few and his program on a national level any more than the 15 consecutive seasons of at least 23 victories already have?"

Just as the NCAA tournament is, for most Americans, a bracket-driven exercise, the benchmarks of achievement in the tournament are chiefly media-driven, delineated by weekends. The Sweet 16 is one step, the Final Four another. The Elite Eight gets some run as a milepost, but one victory in the tournament brings hardly a whisper. As a measuring stick, nobody says, "They've never made it to a championship game before."

The Final Four, granted, earns its participants a whole extra week of publicity and adulation. But to get there requires a single victory after the Elite Eight. How ludicrous would it sound if a Gonzaga critic wrote, "Well, they've won three games in the tournament, but never four."?

For some, making it to 18 straight tournaments without a Final Four is a deal-breaker. This is the reality: In that span, perhaps three or four times Gonzaga had a team that was an appreciable threat to make it. And it didn't. Nor did it get there as a darkhorse. Until further notice, it's the program's itch left unscratched.

Which brings us to the league. To its detractors, the West Coast Conference is the default setting for criticism, the all-purpose explanation for why Gonzaga succeeds. It's true that there have been seasons, including 2016, when Gonzaga needed the fallback of the league tournament to win an automatic bid. But it takes only a check of its annual non-league performance to recognize that those years represent a clear minority.

If it's so easy to do this year after year, why hasn't anybody else in their peer leagues done it? Virginia Commonwealth puffed out chests in 2016 for having made the tournament six straight years. Butler, which has far exceeded the Zags for high-end achievement with two runner-up finishes in 2010 and 2011, has a school-best streak of five straight. Wichita State's also is five, but with a Final Four appearance in 2013, greased when the Shockers upset Gonzaga in the round of 32.

The striking counter to Gonzaga's absence of a Final Four banner is the school's crazy-good record early in the tournament. Since 1999, Gonzaga is 15-3 in first-round games, 11 of those as a No. 7 seed or poorer. Some of the game's best coaches – Duke's Mike Krzyzewski, Michigan State's Tom Izzo, Kansas' Bill Self – have experienced nightmare first-round surprises, including Duke and Michigan State losses to a 15 seed.

No matter. Critics don't want to hear any of it. Just as there was an operative term around Gonzaga in reference to its WCC brethren – Zag Envy – I think there's another phenomenon among detractors: Zag Fatigue. Some get tired of the story line, nagged by the consistency, beaten down by the winning, even if it's at less than Final Four level.

Overrated? That's a term that occasionally applies to Gonzaga, but only in the narrow sense of poll mechanics, not as a pejorative. The Zags' familiar M.O. of a competitive pre-conference showing against a strong schedule, followed by a domination of the West Coast Conference, lends to advancement in the polls. They're winning, and others are losing in more rugged leagues, and the polls overreact to success and failure.

If it weren't for the fact Gonzaga's streak of NCAA appearances is so mind-warping and worthy of preservation, I'm convinced the Zags would be better off occasionally out of the tournament. You're out of sight, out of mind, shielded from rocks thrown by those who think you don't go far enough or you're not tough enough, even if you're regularly outrebounding those who are.

When I described in the Seattle Times Gonzaga's 2014-15 season as "groundbreaking" – a school-record 35 wins and an Elite Eight appearance for the first time in 16 years – that elicited predictable catcalls.

"Crappy conference, average team if they were in a power conference," read one comment.

"The Zag story was good years ago when they came from nowhere and went deep in the tournament," another reader wrote. "There are many examples in the NCAA of small-college teams being successful every year."

He didn't name them.

Others bristle at what they perceive as an attitude copped by Gonzaga. Chris Standiford, GU deputy athletic director, concedes it can seem like that. Talking about other WCC schools, he says, "I don't want it to come across as arrogant. The thing I have heard a lot is, 'We're in LA, you're in Spokane. They don't have anything but rodeos once a month. As soon as you guys pave the streets and people can drive somewhere, they'll have something to do other than watch basketball games. We have professional teams in our town, so you can't compare us.'

"There a whole lot of 'Why we can't beat Gonzaga.' I think it's probably more rationalizing than anything else. And frankly, it's their reality. They've made it so. I would like to think that if the tables were turned, we'd find a way to overcome that."

If they could, it undoubtedly would owe to something Ray Giacoletti noticed there in a six-year tenure as assistant coach. Giacoletti has been an aide at several places – Oral Roberts, Illinois State, Washington – and a head coach at North Dakota State, Eastern Washington, Utah and Drake.

"Most places talk about family, and that's all BS," he said two seasons after leaving Gonzaga. "This place is truly family, and they live it. You can feel it just being on that campus. The professors, the administration . . . it just seemed like everybody was pulling rope in the same direction. I never felt that before in a college setting."

From that place – oneness – emerged a great American success story.

– 1 –
IN THE BEGINNING,
OR THEREABOUTS

FATHER ROBERT SPITZER was buoyant as he entered a meeting room at Gonzaga's stately Bozarth Mansion in north Spokane. It was early in the summer of 1998, and he was embarking on a formidable professional challenge.

Spitzer, 46, had arrived from a faculty position at Seattle University and would soon become president at Gonzaga. He had gathered the university's deans for a retreat to discuss his mission and to listen to their concerns.

Then Spitzer noticed members of GU's corporate counsel, with thick binders on their laps.

"What's this all about?" Spitzer asked.

"Well," one of the attorneys responded, "we've got a little problem."

Yes, they had a little problem. The National Collegiate Athletic Association would soon be rendering a judgment on a confounding chapter in Zags basketball history. Dan Fitzgerald, the longtime basketball coach and athletic director, had been suspended by GU almost a year earlier. Months after that, he resigned under pressure for misappropriation of almost $200,000 in university money that went into a private account.

Shortly, the NCAA would rule on the severity of Fitzgerald's – and the school's – indiscretions. For several reasons, that created considerable apprehension at Gonzaga: Athletically, it was a mom-and-pop operation that didn't have a lot of history dealing with the NCAA monolith; and, as events of the 21st century would prove time and again, the consistency of NCAA penalties can be a head-scratcher. Moreover, this case didn't fit into a neat box of extra benefits to recruits or improper academic help to players. So the range of possible sanctions was wide.

"I didn't even realize how important this would be for the future of athletics at Gonzaga," Spitzer says today.

For athletics, and for Gonzaga University, period.

To put it kindly, the Gonzaga University of the late 1990s was a raging five-alarm fire. The Fitzgerald affair was only one of three parts of a growing malaise plaguing the school.

First, there was a financial shortfall, caused by declining enrollment. Student tuition is the lifeblood of a private school, and enrollment was down.

Second, the GU administration became embroiled in a power struggle that ended with a president's ouster – and augured the arrival of Spitzer. It seems that the Rev. Edward Glynn, Spitzer's predecessor, had ideas about the reach of his office. The Gonzaga trustees thought otherwise, believing they held sway. Somehow, those philosophical differences weren't vetted in the interview process, and in less than a year, a Jesuit president was fired by Jesuits.

And then there was the Fitzgerald crisis, all of which made Gonzaga of that era a hot mess.

"It was bleak," says Spitzer.

That could be an understatement.

"Looking back, oh my God, was it bleak," says Chris Standiford, deputy athletic director. "I don't think I realized how bleak it was."

The place had always been of modest means. Chuck Murphy, university vice president for finance, recalls the austerity of the early 1970s, "when the school was just about ready to go under."

It was hardly the Park Place of athletic departments, either. Until the 1958-59 season, Gonzaga competed in the lower-level National Association of Intercollegiate Athletics, playing mostly small Northwest schools. It went to the NCAA Big Sky Conference in 1963, and 16 years later, to the West Coast Athletic Conference, but it perpetually ran on a shoestring, and stories of its frugality became legend even as the 20th century wound down. Coaches would bunk up in hotel rooms with recruiters they knew from other schools, and the Zags kept a used automobile in San Francisco's Bay Area to avoid pricey rental cars.

This is how lean the program ran: Even in the summer of 1999, when new head coach Mark Few set about luring Leon Rice from his post as head man at Yakima Valley College – and they already were well acquainted – it wasn't a slam-dunk that Few would succeed.

"It wasn't a no-brainer," Rice says. "I was making like $50,000 at Yakima. I'm like, 'You've gotta get me to $55,000.'"

But in the summer of 1998, as athletic director Mike Roth puts it, "We were imploding institutionally."

Spitzer says the budget outlook became tighter when the GU faculty stumped for pay raises "and were willing to cut $2 million out of the budget to get there." What was hatched was the Budget Reduction and Reallocation Process – inelegantly, yet fittingly, known as BRRP – and it became the scourge of campus.

The idea was that academic departments could study the resources of other departments and suggest where they might make cuts. The philosophy department could thus chisel out fat from the accounting department – or so the theory went.

Athletics, naturally, was particularly under siege, being an often arcane world to academicians. There was talk about Gonzaga receding to NCAA Division III, and Roth was dodging bullets from several sides. One proposal was to get rid of an assistant basketball coach – Bill Grier was the target – so it was with some satisfaction that Roth, after he had staved off the wolves, could later point out that Grier was the chief scout who mapped out opponents' strengths and weaknesses during the glorious Elite Eight run of 1999.

"It was a terribly divisive process," says Standiford.

But that was Gonzaga, circa late 1990s. Exacerbating it was the fiasco around Glynn, which effectively forestalled a badly needed capital campaign.

"I would describe it as just a difference of opinion of the role of the board (of trustees) and the role of the president," says Murphy, who has a four-decades-long association with the school, including as student and senior staffer. "Father Glynn was much more, let's say, old-school on the role of the president, that the president was primary and the board was secondary. And the board was saying, 'No, the board is primary and you work for us.' That was something that unfortunately didn't surface when we were doing the initial vetting of him."

Oops.

But nothing polarized the community and underscored Gonzaga's woes like the Fitzgerald saga. He was a hard-charging Irishman, a product of San Francisco's Mission District. He had a short stint as an assistant on the Gonzaga staff in the early 1970s, then was hired as head coach in 1978.

He became just "Fitz," and he could get a team to compete, and when it was done, he could drink a beer and tell a story with the best of them. In the back half of his coaching days, he would hire first Dan Monson, then Few, then Grier, and they would tell stories about somehow surviving having worked for him, about overanalyzing every out-of-bounds play and every jump ball through the long night after a loss, and when the sun came up, Fitz hauling them out to breakfast to commence another day's grinding.

Over time, Fitzgerald grew to be synonymous with making do with less. He told about traveling 1,200 miles to Los Angeles to recruit while saving money sleeping in his car. Out of league, he would schedule teams like Whitworth and Seattle Pacific, and if he could urge the Zags to an 8-6 record in the WCC, that was golden.

When, sometime in February, Gonzaga would clinch an overall winning record that season, he would stage a big, celebratory dinner, even as the ambitious young assistants rolled their eyes. In Fitz's view, they'd stayed one step ahead of the posse. Years later, when they became head coaches, the former GU assistants would calculate each other's schedules and call to offer facetious congratulations on clinching a winning season.

Fitz was all about fighting the good fight.

He got the 1995 Zags to the school's first NCAA tournament, where they were beaten soundly by Maryland with All-American Joe Smith. Not long after that, after considerable lobbying of the Gonzaga administration, Fitzgerald succeeding in orchestrating a plan to have Monson replace him on the bench after the 1996-97 season.

But one day, the first loose thread in a great ball of yarn protruded. A Gonzaga staffer couldn't place the whereabouts of checks from the West Coast Conference that were routine reimbursement payments for WCC games. For more than 15 years, dating to 1981, Fitzgerald had maintained a personal account in the name of "Gonzaga University athletics."

From 1990 through 1997, Fitzgerald misappropriated $199,874 of university money into the personal account. Through the decade before that, he acknowledged having put other checks into the account, but the NCAA was unable to locate those records.

In part, this is how the NCAA would parse Fitzgerald's possible motives in its report made public in midsummer 1998:

> It is important to note that the director of athletics also deposited personal funds into the private account. He contends that in order to recover the portion of the deposits that were personal without revealing the existence of the private account, he would pay his athletically related expenses out of the account and then obtain reimbursement from the university for those same expenses. He contends that he only used the misappropriated funds to supplement the university's athletic program. However, in part because he routinely destroyed the bank statements for the private account, only limited documentation exists as to how money in the account was spent.

Fitzgerald insisted that none of the athletic funds went for personal use.

The first shoe fell in early July 1997, just a few months after Fitzgerald had coached his last game at Gonzaga. The school announced it was putting him on administrative leave, with pay, while it sorted out the tangled bookkeeping.

Then, on Dec. 22, 1997, the bombshell struck. Fitzgerald resigned under pressure as athletic director, spurning an offer to be reassigned within the university. The school's acting president, Harry Sladich, announced the move at a news conference at the administration building, but refused to take questions.

And that formed the dynamic of what was to come. Nobody at the school would comment, while Fitz's legion of loyalists, emboldened by his denials of wrongdoing, attacked hard. It was a wrenching time in the community.

John Blanchette, the respected, veteran columnist for the Spokane Spokesman-Review, blistered Gonzaga for its "abominable" handling of the affair, for letting Fitzgerald twist for five months while it decided his fate, for its lack of explanation, for its failure to stand by someone who had stood by them. He wrote:

> For 19 years, Dan Fitzgerald dragged this school kicking and screaming into the Division I arena. He gave Gonzaga its single best athletic moment just two years ago, when the Zags reached the NCAA tournament, and generated an enthusiasm that – for better or worse – cannot be duplicated anywhere else on campus. He pushed for better facilities and got them built. He enhanced the quality of life on campus with his leadership and advocacy, and with the people he hired and the students – yeah, students – he recruited. He put the place on the map.
>
> And the school did nothing to salvage those contributions, aside from an insulting offer of re-assignment.

For posterity, the facts were left to the imagination. Did Gonzaga merely offer up Fitzgerald as a sacrificial lamb to facilitate a better outcome with the NCAA? Or did the school fall on its sword and keep mum to protect Fitzgerald?

The vast expanse of possibility made opinions easy to come by. Roth, in particular, was brutalized, having succeeded Fitzgerald as athletic director during the suspension, and before that, having had a presence in the compliance office.

"There were multiple low points," Roth says. "To be honest, I can't tell you them. They would be . . . I just can't. There were some really personal attacks that were really painful."

Says Standiford, Roth's longtime lieutenant, "He took shots from people that should have known better. Some of them were from people he respected. Some people turned on him viciously, and it was wrong, really wrong."

The artillery fire was intense. Sladich was hit as well. At a downtrodden, desultory time in the school's history, the episode was one more body blow.

In his office years later, Standiford acknowledged that a faster resolution on Fitzgerald would have counted in the court of public opinion. He framed the dissent over his ouster like this: "Fitz was a kick in the pants. You couldn't help but love him. When you start to have that impression of somebody, and the reality is presented as something else, you don't want to believe it, and that's what there was a lot of – not a lot of rational discussion or discovery of fact. It was, 'Don't ruin my reality.'"

School officials hewed to the vow of silence. Roth would encounter a Fitz supporter at an event, greet him, and often be ignored, save for a stony stare.

"Everybody loved Dan," says Murphy in his office in the GU administration building. "For those of us that knew the inside story of what the facts on the ground were, we obviously couldn't say anything because it's an employee matter."

About a month after Spitzer took the president's office, the NCAA handed down its verdict: Gonzaga got whacked for lack of institutional control and for "unethical conduct," owing to Fitzgerald's "provision of false and misleading information to the institution in order to prevent detection of misappropriated revenues" and "failure to disclose information to an outside accounting firm retained by the institution to conduct annual NCAA-mandated fiscal control audits."

The finding documented unaccounted funds for meals to host recruits, but nothing in excess of NCAA rules governing recruiting expenditures. The lack of institutional control thus tagged the school's oversight of Fitzgerald as well as Fitz himself. There was no post-season ban, but rather, a four-year probation.

Nobody at Gonzaga could know, nine months later, how monumental that demarcation would be.

Blanchette scorned the school once more, writing:

> Gonzaga, however grudgingly, must have been satisfied
> the money didn't go into Fitzgerald's pocket or else it
> would have him in court this very minute . . . in the
> meantime, remember this: Confronted with his 16-year
> deception, Fitzgerald admitted everything. What he
> confessed – and what he denied – are exactly what came
> to light in the NCAA's report 13 months later.
>
> Meanwhile, confronted with either their own
> ineptitude or involvement, other principals went into full
> dodge. That should put an end to whatever quaint
> notions we've ever had about Gonzaga University.

Of course, the NCAA decision only served to stoke the debate's
embers. A cartoon in the The Spokesman-Review portrayed
Fitzgerald with two hands and a foot in cookie jars, which brought a
printed rebuke to the newspaper from Father Bernard Coughlin, the
school chancellor (and former president), attesting that Fitzgerald
had gained nothing personally from his malfeasance.

At least the NCAA ruling helped move the Fitzgerald melodrama
along to a conclusion, however tortured. But as the decade and the
millennium neared an end, Gonzaga seemed mired in a bottomless
bog. Spitzer would propose a five-point capital campaign called
Momentum 2007, but nobody knew then whether he was kook or
visionary. The gloom on campus was palpable.

Then – wondrously, providentially, fantastically – came March
1999.

Maybe somebody had a premonition. Several athletic department
operatives – Roth, Standiford, associate AD Mike Hogan, publicist
Oliver Pierce, Monson as head coach – decided in 1998 Gonzaga
needed a new look. Part of it, no doubt, was an attempt on some

level to break away from the doldrums created by the NCAA investigation and forge a new identity.

The Gonzaga logo had been a bulldog adorned with a sailor's cap – sort of a benign bulldog, if you will. The blue in the school colors was a soft, sky blue. Now the canine would have a decidedly truculent look, and the blue would become a deeper, bolder blue.

Truth be told, that was only a footnote to more substantive things happening with the basketball program. The young coaches – Monson, Few, Grier – pushed for a tougher schedule and targeted better recruits. They learned a lot of things from Fitz – some good, many bad – but none of them would ever be staging dinners to mark the certainty of a winning season.

Monson's first season of 1997-98 began famously, with a tournament championship in the Top of the World Classic in Fairbanks, Alaska. In the title game, the Zags thumped No. 5-ranked Clemson, 84-71. Alas, there would be too many blemishes along the way, and when Gonzaga lost to San Francisco in the final of the WCC tournament, it was relegated to the National Invitation Tournament. GU lost to Hawaii in the first round.

Still feeling the burn of missing the NCAA tournament, the 1998-99 team opened with a loss at eighth-ranked Kansas, then dispatched Memphis and lost to Purdue. In contrast, just five years earlier, the non-league schedule had included Whitman, Western Montana, New Hampshire and Samford. But there was no true luminous victory for Monson's team, even as the Zags won their second straight regular-season championship. They entered the WCC tournament at Santa Clara with a 22-6 record.

There, they romped over Portland and Saint Mary's, but now, with the tournament berth on the line, they had to face the host team for the title. Roth walked into the gym at SCU and immediately realized there was no pretense of impartiality. The Bronco athletic staff had passed out pom-poms on each seat, and they weren't in the new Zag colors.

"I was so pissed," says Roth, who went hunting for WCC commissioner Mike Gilleran. "We, of course, aren't who we are today. We may have had 100 people. It wasn't like we had a couple of thousand people like we do now. We win the league and all we get to do is wear the white uniforms, and they get to host and turn this into a circus?"

Not to worry. Gonzaga came out dunking and draining threes – making 18 of 31 – and rocked Santa Clara, 91-66. And a stupefying run was about to begin.

You know the rest of the story: How Gonzaga was sent to a friendly sub-regional site in Seattle, and how its first-round opponent, Minnesota, became the subject of a disturbing story in the St. Paul Pioneer Press about academic fraud, causing the Gophers to suspend four players, including two starters.

How the Zags won that game, and the next against physical Stanford, somehow pounding the Cardinal on the boards, 47-33. How Casey Calvary slapped in the game-winning tip to beat Florida, putting the Zags on the doorstep of the Final Four.

Naturally, Roth remembers all that. But he also remembers Hotel Hell.

The Zags got to Seattle and were lodged in a hotel that was undergoing a renovation. You walked right into an elevator that took you to the fifth floor, which impersonated a lobby. Never mind, as Roth insists, that the NCAA was supposed to ensure that no host hotel was doing construction.

It figured. After all, they were the bumpkins from Spokane who had never won an NCAA-tournament game. It continued a tradition launched in 1995 in Salt Lake City, when, legend has it, Fitzgerald's NCAA virgins were bivouacked in a motel where you walked outside to go room-to-room.

So the '99 Zags were off to Phoenix for the Sweet 16, and the athletic department cobbled together a band and cheerleaders, and, Roth says, rode their first chartered aircraft.

"They put us in Mesa," he says. "We're not even in Phoenix."

They got to their hotel, and instead of double rooms, the team was assigned single kings in smoking rooms. And the band and cheerleaders, well, there was nothing for them; they ended up down the street.

"It was a total debacle," says Roth.

In every way, the Zags were Cinderella. Here they were on the day after Florida, and it was getting down to cases. They were one victory from the Final Four, and the NCAA staged its routine "transition" meeting, an advisory for what logistical challenges lay ahead for the winning program. Required to be at the meeting were the athletic director, sports information director, travel coordinator and ticket manager.

"Well, guess what?" says Roth. "We had two of those, an AD and an SID."

The Zag contingent walked in and saw maybe a dozen suits from Connecticut. Afterward, NCAA basketball committeeman Carroll Williams, the former Santa Clara coach, buttonholed Roth and said, "If you guys win, you're going to need a *lot* of help."

Of course, they didn't win. They took UConn to the last minute before losing, 67-62. And the ride was over.

No, in reality, the ride was just beginning. What came later, what continues to come, is a thoroughly improbable American sports story, one of consistency and growth and fulfillment. If the basketball team didn't outright save the university, it at least went a long way toward propping it up.

Immediately, the Gonzaga enrollment office began to notice changes. The "yield" rate – students registering compared to the number granted admission – jumped up. The total of 569 freshmen that enrolled in 1998 increased to 979 three years later. From the opening run in 1999 to 2016, enrollment surged 67 percent, from 4,500 to 7,500.

The expansion on campus has been transformative; the school lists more than a score of buildings that have been constructed or undergone major renovation in that period. Spitzer laughingly called it "Gonzaga's Edifice Complex." He points to seven new academic buildings, including law, business and engineering. Of course, the McCarthey Athletic Center went in, as did the Patterson Baseball Complex.

At about $27 million, the new basketball arena was Gonzaga's spendiest structure in history. That was blown out of the water with the $60 million John J. Hemmingson Center opened in 2015, a gathering place bringing together a variety of student development and club programs in addition to retail outlets.

Since the Elite Eight run, Gonzaga's endowment increased from $108 million to $240 million.

They call it the "Flutie Effect," after the phenomenon that took hold at Boston College when quarterback Doug Flutie threw his famous Hail Mary pass to beat Miami on his way to the Heisman Trophy. It isn't, however, universally accepted, as skeptics point out that other factors might be behind increased enrollment and donations.

Mina Kimes, in ESPN the Magazine in March 2015, wrote that "college applications, like donations and ticket sales, are influenced by complex forces ranging from costs to marketing. But complexity often falls by the wayside in stories about the transformative power of sports." Kimes quoted a Boston College professor of sports sociology as saying that enrollment at BC had been rising steadily even without Flutie's magic, and attributed to Butler a mere three-percent rise in donations after its 2011 run to the NCAA title game, as opposed to 18 percent for the same drama the year before.

Be that as it may, you won't find a lot of people around Gonzaga suggesting the basketball program hasn't been a driving force in the revitalization of the school and the *joie de vivre* on campus. That includes Spitzer, who stepped away from the presidency in 2009.

His Momentum 2007 campaign, he says, was essentially realized in 2004. "Instead of a $150 million campaign," he says, "we got a $250 million campaign. Every single piece that needed to be there, it was there. There went little Gonzaga, in this momentous synchronicity."

Spitzer, energetic and personable, was the perfect helmsman to help lift Gonzaga from its manifold doldrums of the late 1990s. But he is only too willing to recognize that he had help.

"Essentially, our basketball team worked a miracle," he says. "I'll just be honest."

– 2 –
A VISION AND
A VENUE

TO BEGIN TO COMPREHEND Gonzaga's ascension from nondescript Western outpost to national player on the college-basketball stage, think about this: John Stockton crafted his thesis on the physics of basketball in a gym that seated somewhere in the 2,000s.

Or this: When, in 2002, Gonzaga placed Dan Dickau on the AP All-America first team, alongside players from Maryland (Juan Dixon), Kansas (Drew Gooden), Duke (Jay Williams) and Cincinnati (Steve Logan), it did so while playing in a place that housed crowds more on the order of your average Costco.

Capacity at the Martin Centre was short of 3,000. The exact figure fell somewhere between the boundaries of certitude and chutzpah. It's a number lost to history, as elusive as the culprit behind the inflation. Somebody back in 1965 believed a capacity of 4,000 buffed the image of the program.

"That was what was published," says Chuck Murphy, the school's vice president for finance. "It was never as published. It was really only in the 2,200-to-2,300 range."

Mike Roth, the athletic director and a three-decades employee of the school, indulges the old Kennel only slightly more. He puts the capacity at 2,600 to 2,800.

In any case, small wonder that cable giants weren't rushing to land naming rights on the Martin Centre.

This was the place where Dan Fitzgerald roared up and down the sidelines, treating every possession as if it were a biennial plea for clemency before a prison parole board. This was where the Kennel Club grew to full throat. This was Gonzaga as innocent.

Alas, it was also one of the chief descriptors that defined the Zags unfavorably: Minor league.

All that changed early in the new millennium, but not easily. The story of the McCarthey Athletic Center is one of fits and starts, resolve, whimsy, and ultimately maybe, inevitability. The Zags simply became too good to be playing in a 2,000-something-seat crackerbox.

The Martin Centre thus gave way to a 6,000-seat jewel that became the touchstone for a campus building boom. It housed electric winter nights with Saint Mary's, as well as events as routine as post-season banquets for the crew teams. Even at a relatively modest capacity by college hoops standards, the place developed sufficient gravitas to attract blue-ribbon programs like Michigan State, and in a seven-day period in 2015, Arizona and UCLA.

Finally, in 2004, in addition to coaching longevity, program chemistry and an ever-better collection of talent, the Zags had a showpiece to call home.

On a chilly March morning in 2013, Tom and Phil McCarthey welcome a visitor to a graceful older home that serves as their office on South Temple Street in Salt Lake City. Once known as Brigham Street, the thoroughfare oozes history and class, site of century-old mansions that have been home to governors and senators. In fact, kitty-corner to this structure is the governor's mansion, donated to the state of Utah in 1937 by Jennie Judge Kearns, great-grandmother of Tom and Phil McCarthey.

Snow is flurrying along the broad avenue. Otherwise, the brothers say, Phil would have been out, mounting his Gonzaga flag in front.

The house is exquisitely appointed, with wood-inlaid walls and detailed moulding, Oriental rugs and a carving above a fireplace. Oil paintings of the brothers' mother and father adorn a wall in an anteroom.

But it's not all stately. Mounted on one wall is a pair of electric guitars, one signed by the Rolling Stones. One room is reserved for Gonzaga basketball memorabilia, and Phil shows off an artist's rendering of the NBA's top 50 players, autographed, including John Stockton's signature.

The brothers are descendants of Thomas and Jennie Judge Kearns. Thomas Kearns, their great-grandfather, was a U.S. senator who made his fortune in the mining business and then partnered to become owner of The Salt Lake Tribune in 1901.

Through three more generations, the newspaper stayed in the family. Thomas Kearns McCarthey, father of Tom and Phil and three siblings, was a rank-and-file advertising salesman at the paper but a powerful stockholder.

In the heavily Mormon enclave of Utah, the McCartheys were good Catholics.

"We had our own friends and our own community and played CYO basketball," Tom remembers. "But we knew there was something different about it. And you could tell it on occasion. But it was such a good place to live and we had good friends and enjoyed the community so much, that it didn't seem as weird."

And, as he points out, the family had its own deep history in Salt Lake City. Their great-grandfather "had established himself and we felt we had as strong roots in this community as any LDS person did," Tom says. "Our dad always instilled that in us and said, 'Don't forget, you're an Irish-Catholic family, a mining family, and you belong in this community.'"

As kids, Phil says, they were relatively oblivious to the religious differences. What mattered was whether you could compete on the ballfield. Later, when they were going off to college and LDS friends were headed for two-year missions, the distinction became more apparent.

They rooted for the University of Utah. Phil relives two Utah Final Four appearances of their youth, in 1961 and 1966, headed respectively by Billy (The Hill) McGill and Jerry Chambers. Tom recalls their dad taking them to their first Final Four at the Los Angeles Sports Arena in 1968 during the height of UCLA's dominance.

The brothers went to prep school in the East. Tom applied to a number of colleges, but his mother was impressed by Gonzaga, whose president had come to Salt Lake City on a recruiting trip, and after she encouraged him to apply there, he enrolled. Phil took a different path, with a two-year start at Georgetown before transferring to GU.

Both fulfilled the Gonzaga-in-Florence study-abroad program, and, says Tom, "That had a big impact on my life."

Phil would go on to work in the insurance business, while Tom became the journalist of the family, working for decades at the Tribune, where he was popularly seen as the future publisher. He would be the steward of an enterprise that would continue what the boys knew of Salt Lake newspapers growing up.

"It was divided into thirds," Tom recalls. "You have a third LDS that would only read the other newspaper (the rival LDS-owned Deseret News), that would never touch the Tribune. You have the other third that were staunch anti-LDS; they would always read the Tribune. And then you had a third in the middle that were mostly LDS, but they wanted the truth, so to speak."

In 1997, the business dynamic of the Tribune changed. Tele-Communications Inc. bought the Kearns-Tribune Co., parent of The Salt Lake Tribune, for $627 million in TCI stock. That set in motion events including a "reverse merger," by which the McCartheys had the option to buy the newspaper five years later. But AT&T acquired TCI, the Trib was sold to MediaNewsGroup, and what ensued was "a very ugly legal dispute for seven years" for control of the paper, Phil says.

"One day," he recalls, "we woke up and said, 'We're fighting to get back in with somebody that really doesn't want us in an industry that's changing.'" He says they accepted a substantial settlement and gave up the battle.

Well before that settlement, several hundred miles to the Northwest, the little program Tom and Phil knew as undergrads at Gonzaga had taken off. No more was it playing in the Big Sky Conference (its address for 16 years), no more was it scheduling non-league games with St. Cloud State and Parsons College, the opponents of their youth.

When the Zags turned the college-basketball world on its ear with the 1999 Elite Eight run, some of the brass began thinking big. Roth and head coach Dan Monson requested a meeting with Spitzer, the school president, at the Jesuit House on campus with an audacious notion – a new building.

Spitzer's response: "No," says Roth. "Just a flat-out no."

Much as the Zags' March run was a bolt out of the blue, so the idea of a new arena was seemingly borne of fantasy. Years later, Roth is able to play Spitzer's devil's advocate.

"It was going to be millions of dollars," Roth says. "Why did we need it? Were we selling out every game? Was there really that demand? We were taking somebody athletically that had just experienced a first-time [phenomenon], he only had one experience, and we were trying to convince him that we could continue to do this – when *we* didn't know we could continue to do this. He viewed it as very businesslike, in my mind.

"It just didn't pencil out. Where was the money going to come from? It was going to be multiple-millions of dollars, we knew that, at a time when the university was coming out of this dire-straits [existence]. And now we're talking about building a new building? How crazy were we?"

So it was left for the basketball program to continue taking up the flag. Monson left for Minnesota, but the good times continued under Mark Few; the Zags went to the Sweet 16 in 2000 and again in 2001, and now the momentum was onrushing.

In Salt Lake City, the McCartheys were taking notice. They had begun to reconnect with Gonzaga basketball back in 1995, when the Zags made their first foray to the NCAA tournament – in Salt Lake City, fortuitously – and they went out for a drink at a hangout called Green Street with president Father Bernard Coughlin and Fitzgerald.

"So this is what this tournament is all about," Coughlin said mischievously. "This is kind of fun. I could get used to this a little bit."

Later, as they grew into trustee and regent roles, the brothers would get to know Monson, Few and their assistants, and they would be impressed at the value Gonzaga was getting for its basketball investment. Tom McCarthey says they were "astounded" when Spitzer and Coughlin told them how little they were paying the head coach and that they at least ought to match the West Coast Conference high.

"If you need something," Tom recalls the brothers telling Spitzer and Coughlin, "we'll be glad to step up. You ought to make it clear to these coaches they deserve it."

Father Robert Spitzer might have been the perfect president to shepherd Gonzaga out of its pervasive gloom of the late 1990s. He was charismatic and quixotic, brilliant but not stuffy. The conservative element among the GU trustees occasionally had to keep a wary eye on him and his sometimes-fanciful notions, but without question, his impact at the school was prodigious.

Recalling the era when Spitzer began his 11-year tenure as GU president – he took over in September 1998 – Few says, "We needed a visionary then. We needed somebody who dreamed, not somebody who worried."

Gonzaga had worried enough. Now it was time to grow, to spread wings, to be what it could be.

Spitzer was born in Honolulu and got his undergraduate degree from Gonzaga in business in 1974. He followed with philosophy and theology degrees, which led him to two teaching stints at Seattle University. The latter of those, from 1990-98, preceded his appointment to the presidency at GU.

It might not be stretching the truth to say there was just the faintest loopy element to Spitzer's makeup, seemingly enhanced by his poor eyesight. People around the athletic department came to adopt a term – "Spitzerian math" – for some of their leader's calculations.

"You could give him a five and a six," says Standiford, the deputy athletic director, "and it would be 14."

He also didn't know much about athletics, but, unlike a lot of his presidential contemporaries, knew enough not to try to pretend that he did.

It was Spitzer who had been in office only 10 months at Gonzaga when Monson finally succumbed to a personal tug-of-war and accepted the job at Minnesota in the summer of 1999.

"Father, it's done, the decision's been made," Roth told Spitzer, who was attending a conference in Washington, D.C. "They're going to announce this afternoon that Dan's taking the job."

"Oh, Mike, what are we going to do?" Spitzer said disconsolately.

"Father, it's done," Roth replied. "We're hiring Mark. We'll hold a press conference on Monday and announce Mark as our head coach."

"Oh, great," Spitzer said enthusiastically. "Which one is he?"

A couple of years into Few's tenure, Spitzer well knew who he was. The Zags had tacked a pair of Sweet 16 appearances onto the Elite Eight breakthrough under Monson, and it was becoming obvious this whole basketball thing wasn't merely a flash in the pan. However, they were still playing in the Martin Centre, the bandbox with the highly inflated official capacity, which meant that Gonzaga really hadn't done much to capitalize on the surge.

It was time to act. Spitzer knew Phil McCarthey from their GU days, and he set up a meeting with the brothers in Salt Lake City. He would bring his basketball coach to help it resonate.

"It was one of those deals where they just fly me down there and don't tell me what's going on," Few recalls.

The stories diverge here. Spitzer says the first advance on the McCartheys was to ask for three to four million dollars to set up an endowment to underwrite some of basketball's operating expenses – coaching salaries and recruiting, for instance. Few says Spitzer wanted to pitch a new student fitness center.

On the morning of the meeting, they gathered for coffee to plan their presentation – Spitzer, Few and Coughlin, who was now school chancellor.

"Fitness center?" Few sputtered. "We need a new arena."

"Really?" Spitzer said. "OK."

"This was literally like nine in the morning," Few say. "And at 10" – meeting with the McCartheys – "we need a new arena."

Whatever the fine details, the Zags were flying by the seat of their pants. Recalls Phil McCarthey: "We see them coming up the steps, and there was this pause for a minute. Father Spitzer, you never saw that kind of expression – the raised eyebrows – and Mark looked at him and nodded. So they came in and we sat down and we're kind of going through all this. We said, 'What exactly do you think we ought to be talking about? Is it something to do with scholarships or the coaches?' Father Spitzer said, 'No, Mark and I were talking on the way up here: We're going to ask you for a new arena.'"

And he did. But $3 million wasn't going to be enough to launch a $27 million project. Nor would it be sufficient to establish naming rights. (You know, Spitzerian math.) Coughlin hedged on Spitzer's proposal, indicating they might need a little more.

The McCartheys agreed, leaving Spitzer simultaneously cheered and sobered. He had a gift, but this was going to be a marathon, not a sprint. At one point, with a looming question of whether fund-raising would carry the project, he entertained the idea of doing it on the cheap – busting out two walls of the Kennel and expanding it.

During a break at a trustees meeting one day, a trustee named John Stone steered Spitzer to the side and lobbied him to scrap the notion of remodeling.

"I know you're a little scared of the money," Stone told him. "But that's really a bad idea. I'm just going to be honest with you. That place is irredeemable."

"*That* irredeemable?" Spitzer asked.

"I don't care what anybody tells you," Stone said. "You've got to start all over again and build a really fine facility."

Says Roth coyly, "I may have had some people get in his ear to tell him it was a really bad idea."

So not long after came the second proposal to the McCartheys – once again, with its own side story. This time, they came to Spitzer in Spokane for what they believed to be a luncheon meeting. Spitzer says it would hike their investment in the project to $7 million.

Once more, the McCartheys were amenable to Spitzer's request. But the clock passed 1 p.m. toward 1:30. The brothers were getting a little fidgety. Finally, Phil said, "What time are we gonna eat?"

Ohmygod. Somehow, Spitzer had never communicated the details of lunch. "So he sends somebody out and gets these ham sandwiches," says Phil, who has always added that it was the most expensive ham sandwich he'd ever had.

"As I recall," says Spitzer jauntily, "it was a turkey sandwich."

Of course, the golden run of NCAA-tournament success ended rudely against Wyoming in the first round in 2002. But with players like Blake Stepp and Ronny Turiaf heading a second wave of talent to keep the phenomenon humming, it became increasingly apparent the Zags were here to stay and the arena issue demanded consideration.

Not to say there wasn't a considerable level of administrative angst about it all. Here you had a school that had had trouble finding two nickels to rub together less than a decade earlier – not an unprecedented plight at the place – proposing the largest capital project the university had undertaken.

"Do we want to invest that kind of money in a particular sport, a basketball program?" asked Phil McCarthey, sounding the concerns of the day. "Two, it's going to tear up our campus a little bit, and make that the centerpiece. And third, is there something else we should be doing with the money?"

The skeptics recalled a couple of other Catholic schools' basketball stars that had burned brilliantly before flaming out, not to be heard from again. Loyola Marymount was a raging national attention-getter from 1988-90 but then faded into obscurity. DePaul went to the Final Four in 1979, and was ranked No. 1 two years later, but since 1992, has been to only two NCAA tournaments.

Still, the momentum for a new arena was unstoppable, although Spitzer says he was given pause by Tim Welsh of Garco Construction – the firm that had built Spokane Arena – who advised him that fabrication of steel beams was a long process, requiring financing to be in place far in advance of assembly.

Oh, and there was one other hiccup. Preposterous as it might seem today, there was a question about whether the facility would have new locker rooms, or merely fall back on the existing ones in the Martin Centre.

Back, then, to the McCartheys one last time. Spitzer says it was a push for as much as another $2.5 million, which would bring their generosity beyond $9 million. The request came, he says, on the weekend of the Zags' 96-95 near-miss, double-overtime screamer against top-seeded Arizona at the 2003 NCAA subregional in Salt Lake City.

"Let me take you out," Spitzer offered.

"Anytime you pay," they responded wryly, "we pay."

"They had agreed to meet with us after the game," says Spitzer, who beseeched a higher power for a final assist on the floor, figuring it couldn't hurt his case. "I'm begging God, please give us a victory."

The victory didn't materialize. But the donation from the McCartheys did, and a month later, ground was broken. Today, Tom McCarthey looks back on the times with Father Spitzer and says, "He didn't know a basketball from a watermelon. But he got on board."

Tomson Spink tours the McCarthey Athletic Center with no less pride than an expectant mother showing off a nursery. Through an unlikely slice of serendipity, he gets to hug the MAC to his bosom almost like nobody else.

He was the middle of the three Spink brothers, between Scott and Mark, both of whom played at Gonzaga. So did Tomson, after a fashion. Fitzgerald allowed him to walk on to the roster in the mid-1990s, and Gonzaga picked up his expenses for a semester, but Spink freely admits his mind was sometimes as much on partying as it was practicing.

He became an unofficial head of the hedonistic Kennel Club – which meant one of his functions was to close the tap on the keg at his place on Desmet Avenue and hustle over to the games before tipoff. Eventually, he hunkered down and got a civil engineering degree, worked in construction in Seattle and landed back in Spokane at Garco Construction. Fortuitously, that placed him in a trailer as the on-site engineer for the McCarthey project, overseeing change orders, billings and quality control.

It's obvious the project means far more to Spink than some faceless monolith would.

"You're so used to going and working out in a dirt pile with ugly and dirty tradesmen, and you're ugly and dirty," says Spink, now GU manager for facilities, maintenance and grounds. "You get an opportunity to come back and work on a campus that was super-vibrant, next to the bar you grew up drinking at when you were in college. And it was a super-important project for Spokane."

He knows the MAC like a museum curator. He recalls how it took 200-ton cranes to section together the long girders in pieces. How there were decisions made on the fly, because financing for some of the auxiliary structures, like locker rooms, wasn't yet in place. How one hunk of concourse had to be ripped out and re-poured because in the heat of summer, too much retardant – designed to slow the setting process quickened by hot temperatures – had been applied at the concrete plant, creating a gooey clay.

He remembers the anticipation building for the place, remembers John Stockton poking his head in the trailer outside the construction and in a low voice, asking, "Can I go in?"

He remembers the concern about bolts and nuts and washers that came pinging out from under the student section, jarred by staccato, bouncing feet. (He says the section passed structural tests and is examined regularly.)

But mostly what he remembers is the good vibe around the place, the camaraderie, and the fact that it attracted the best subcontractors around, who knew this wasn't just another office building or apartment complex. He remembers the beers after work and the laughs and the process.

And he remembers this: He didn't have a lot of money at the time, and his wife was pregnant, and his tab for tickets in the new place, combined with the requisite donation, was going to be in the neighborhood of $2,000. He couldn't afford it, so he asked Roth and Standiford if he could be at the head of the line to purchase when he could.

"They said, 'Toms, don't worry about it, go pick your seats,'" Spink says. "After that season, I bought in. That was Chris and Mike being super-kind to me.

"I love working here. There's good people. That's part of the reason they win."

The first backhoe's plunge didn't silence debate on several fronts. Arena size was an issue, for instance. Was a 6,000-seat capacity big enough? The Zags were advised that for a program of their size, in the Spokane metropolitan area, it was.

"And the cost of going from 6,000 to 8,000 increased the cost out of proportion," says Murphy, the GU vice president. "All of a sudden, it put another $10-15 million onto the project. We were already looking at: We're going to struggle to raise money just to fill 6,000. It ended up being sort of an economic decision."

Besides, as Roth points out, for some who knew that the old Kennel didn't actually seat 4,000, but 30 to 40 percent less than that, the number 6,000 was daunting.

Roth also recalls upper-level campus dissent about whether his proposed system of seat purchase on a priority-points system was a house of cards.

"Some trustees were saying, 'You're not going to be able to do that,'" Roth says. "'You're not going to be able to make this happen.' There were multiple debates, especially with some very powerful people on campus having strong opinions. I literally had to tell them more than once, this is what you pay me for as an athletic director.

"There was more than one time, coming back with Chris (Standiford) from a meeting, I'd have to ask: 'Is my name still on the door?'"

Then the Zags decided to stage a time-intensive but consumer-friendly campaign – spearheaded by former associate athletic director Mike Hogan – in which prospective ticket-holders could come in and choose their seats within the range of their contribution. One trustee told Roth the idea was a disaster, bound to cast a bad light not only on Gonzaga athletics, but the university.

Roth says the same trustee witnessed the process several times, backtracked and called it a great move.

Not that everybody walked away satisfied. One couple surveyed their seat options based on their contribution and turned them down, leaving a woman in tears.

"One thing everybody found out," Roth says. "If you didn't get in in short order, you weren't getting in at all. Or the price went up significantly."

Is it possible something was lost with the move out of the old Kennel? Of course. No doubt some supporters in the McCarthey are there merely because it's the hot ticket in town, a place to be seen, as opposed to the cognoscenti in the Martin Centre. But that seems a small price to pay for progress.

"We had sold the coziness in there and how loud it was, and we'd won [34 straight games there from 1992-95]," says Few. "The Kennel Club was starting to take hold. But at some point, it became, 'Come on, you've got to do something here.'"

The MAC became a place where the Gonzaga men have carved out a 172-12 record. The women's program began flourishing there as well, launching deep NCAA-tournament runs in 2011-12 at home.

It was the place of Courtney Vandersloot's wizardry, of Adam Morrison's frenetic game.

There were graduations, lectures, banquets. There was Death Cab for Cutie. Bright and bouncy, the arena seemed to radiate good vibes.

"That's what makes you feel so good, that these two guys from Salt Lake came in and just kind of lent a hand and helped all these other people who worked day and night for 18 months to build this really beautiful arena," says Tom McCarthey. "The dividends have been amazing."

Financially, the arena is held to a higher standard. Because of concerns that the building would be a drain on the university finances, its operating expenses are contained within the athletic budget. It has its own gas and electric meters and sewer costs separate from campus ledgers.

"In many ways, that's allowed us to do things a little differently, because we have so much ownership in the building," says Standiford. "We're able to make improvements on the basis of where our revenues are and not have to stand in line and wait for centralized funds to become available. It's been an empowering thing rather than a burdening thing."

So the arena is a hit at the upper level of campus. Early in 2015, Murphy said, "After 10 years, we've essentially accumulated enough revenue from the building to cover the debt that remains on it now. So it's essentially debt-free. And then, we've used the revenue from the program to help fund not only enhancements in the men's basketball program but also in the women's program and other programs."

But the effect didn't stop there. "Particularly as it relates to facilities, we were able, with the success of the basketball program, to get people interested in other sports programs," Murphy says. "With soccer, baseball and now tennis, we have some really great facilities."

Who could have foreseen the value of a ham sandwich?

"I still get that rush when I go in there and see those kids," says Tom McCarthey. "And I go, 'You know, this is big-time basketball.'"

− 3 −
THE LOYALIST

ON AN EARLY-SPRING DAY IN 2009, Mark Few had a mission. He had an important business meeting at an unlikely venue. In fact, it's safe to say it's the only time in the history of a nondescript rest stop off Interstate 84 in north-central Oregon that the place has hosted a negotiation that would materially affect the trajectory of two college athletic programs in the Northwest.

Few's Gonzaga basketball team had just lost to North Carolina in the Sweet 16 and now the routine of postseason housekeeping was upon him. For Few, that frequently has meant entertaining inquiries about vacant jobs. They seem to be nothing he cultivates; the approaches are made to him, by athletic directors – in recent times, more commonly by middlemen – interested in seeing if they could pry Few from his comfortable roost at Gonzaga.

More than half a dozen times, Few has been romanced by programs that have hung national-championship banners. It's difficult to know definitively how many times he has been those suitors' No. 1 candidate, but those occasions have been multiple.

By 2009, a decade into Few's head-coaching tenure, this had become a rite of spring. Front men for Arizona, Indiana, Stanford and UCLA had nosed around, and somehow, Few had rationalized staying at Gonzaga. But now a different force loomed, one with assets unequaled by the others, and this might just be the one to shake Few loose.

The University of Oregon had been trying for some time to uncouple itself from Ernie Kent, in a relationship that reflects the fragile nature of coaching. Kent had been a beloved Oregon player in the Dick Harter era of the 1970s. In 2007, Kent had taken Oregon, a school with a sparse basketball history, to a second Elite Eight in five years. But he had surrounded that latter burst with some fruitless seasons, capped by a last-place, 2-16 finish in the Pac-10 in 2009, and the wolves were baying ominously in Eugene. Through those uneven years, Kent had exhausted capital with boosters in the lingering innuendo related to some personal issues off the floor.

To the northeast, there was another Oregon alumnus who looked like a prime candidate to replace Kent. Few grew up in Creswell, just 10 miles south of Eugene, he had graduated from Oregon, playing pickup games on the courts and ballfields on the UO campus. His parents, Barbara and Norm, had lived in Creswell for half a century.

And then there was the Pat Kilkenny factor. Kilkenny, who made himself a millionaire in the insurance industry in San Diego, was the Oregon athletic director. But he had taken a booster's route to that chair, and by chance, he had also formed along the way great friendships at Gonzaga, owing to its several coaches with Oregon connections. Kilkenny was sufficiently beneficent to donate to their salaries, and so steadfast that when Zag assistant coaches departed the program to begin their own head-coaching careers, he donated significantly to them, too.

"He's just an unbelievably benevolent guy," Few says. "If he didn't have a cent, he'd be a great friend."

Behind the scenes, of course, there was Phil Knight, the Nike founder, who had long since befriended Few, and of whom Few says, "Phil, and Nike, really propped this program up. They've treated us like the national program it was long before other people came around."

Even head-slapping happenstance seemed to argue for Few to be headed to Oregon. His Gonzaga team, a No. 4 seed in the 2009 NCAA basketball tournament, was sent to Portland for first- and second-round games, where the host school was none other than Oregon. So as the Zags were toppling Akron in their first game, there at one end of the scorer's table as one of the regional's hosts was Kilkenny, stationed close enough to the Gonzaga bench to hear Few mapping instructions during timeouts.

It all seemed perfect, too perfect not to happen.

Until it didn't.

This wasn't like many of the advances on Few by other schools, which don't get past Brad Williams, the Spokane attorney who acts as his agent. This was Kilkenny, and he deserved a more personal hearing.

So they drove, Kilkenny and Few, to meet at a predetermined spot. For Few, it was a four-hour haul, west on I-90, down State Route 395 and then west on I-84. It was as clandestine as clandestine gets – "sunglasses and hats on," Few says.

At a turnout off the freeway, Few had his come-to-Jesus meeting with Kilkenny. They talked and they talked some more – three hours' worth, as Few recalls. In front of them, the Columbia River surged to the sea, flush with the winter's record snowpack.

Kilkenny tried. Oh, how he tried. But in the end, what seemed so right . . . just wasn't right.

The Fews' fourth child, Colt, was only three months old. The other kids were settled in their schools. Marcy Few, his wife, was busy with a prominent role in the local Coaches Versus Cancer campaign. But more than anything, the way Mark Few viewed Oregon was the same as he viewed all those other opportunities. He had a better gig.

"I just wasn't feeling it," Few says.

Few couldn't pull the trigger. In his mind, it just never lined up. Yes, there was a new arena on the way at Oregon, but it was going to be a 12,000-seat-plus hulk difficult to fill to capacity, a factor with its own pressures.

Yes, Oregon was fueled heavily by Knight's largesse. But as a basketball force, it could get lost among other Pac-10 schools like Arizona and UCLA. There was no consistent talent pool in the lightly populated state.

"I never, ever felt that job was better than this one," Few says, sitting behind his desk at the McCarthey Athletic Center. "Still don't."

In the end, Oregon, the place that was finally going to lure Few, became like all the other schools that approached him. In the end, Few made the decision to live in a place where his rustic home on 10 acres has mountain views to the northeast; where the drive to work is a skosh over 10 minutes; where rivers and lakes abound for his fishing jones; where, every year, you go to the NCAA tournament; and where your public obligations to boosters are under control.

The money could be greater elsewhere. But what can you do with four million dollars that you can't do with two?

It seems inescapable: Dude's got it figured out.

One time, returning to his hometown, Mark Few asked his dad Norm how long he and Barbara had lived in Creswell, Oregon.

"Fifty-four years," Norm replied.

"I've got a couple to go to pass you," his son acknowledged.

Exploring Creswell, getting a feel for this little town off Interstate 5 and the Fews' place in it, you develop a sense for one of the reasons Few cultivated a culture of family at Gonzaga. And why he hasn't left. The population of Creswell is a little more than 5,000, and it was less than half that four decades ago when Few and his three siblings were growing up. It was a place of old values, where family was important, and few families were as integral to the pulse beat of the town as the Fews.

In the middle of Creswell, on Fourth Street, sits the white-painted Presbyterian church, Norm Few's destination back in 1957. He drove a 1955 Oldsmobile north from seminary in California and became minister there. For half a century, he would give sermons, perform baptisms, officiate marriages and funerals, act as father confessor and become one of the town's true characters, mixing Biblical verse with biting wit.

He didn't have far to go to work. For a couple of decades Norm and Barb, a nurse, lived in "The Manse," the church's attached minister's home, where they raised four kids. The grounds, including a large yard, appear cast from a Norman Rockwell painting.

Kathy Few, one of Mark's two younger sisters, calls the town "Mayberry." Like that setting for "The Andy Griffith Show," it had its quirky characters, and the Few family saw a lot of them close up.

"My parents were very active in the community," Kathy Few says. "So there were lots of people stopping through. As I look back now, my gosh . . ." She lowers her voice. "People needing money, which is fine . . . my dad isn't a real good filter as far as who he'd let into the house, or the car. Very trusting."

The Few parents read to their kids every evening, and they soaked it up. Barb Few remembers Mark reading things at four years old, poring over the sports pages of the local Eugene newspaper, The Register-Guard.

Sports, and games of all sorts, came to define his youth. Incessantly, there was a game of some kind going on. The church hall was a third building on the grounds, with its own recreation area. Outside, Norm and the boys built a treehouse and installed a zip line.

Kathy Few remembers – fondly – being terrorized by her older brothers. "Throwing me in a garbage can, and I couldn't come out until I kissed the neighbor boy," she says, laughing. "But the worst was when, 'Hey, you have three seconds to run,' and you never knew what was coming. It could be a hard ball of clay. It meant run as fast as you can, and get out of the way. Mark was very confident, a good heart down deep, but ornery a little bit."

They'd visit one of Barb's sisters up in Grand Ronde, west of Salem. There was a treehouse, and when the girls were playing in it, the boys would take the ladder away and toss up garter snakes.

Kathy Few is leafing through a scrapbook on the family property outside Sisters in central Oregon. Years ago, there wasn't a lot of money for vacations, so the Few family had a favorite campground not far away. Mark and his brother Dave would pull trout out of a stream there.

Back in Creswell, sports – organized or pickup games – progressively became a bigger part of Mark Few's life. Years later, when he was old enough to drive, he kept a baseball and bat, a basketball and football in the car, prepared for whatever game might come about.

Organized baseball, naturally, began with Little League. On those fields, one of the umpires was Norm Few, who for three decades, was also a member of the local school board. But to hear Kathy Few tell it, the disciplinarian of the family was her mother. "She'd quietly pull you aside," she says, "and then the hammer fell. That's tough, with four kids, and a couple of wily ones in there."

Nearby, the college basketball teams provided plenty of juice for youngsters to emulate. Oregon and Oregon State developed a nasty rivalry in the 1970s, each school with some notable successes. The reigning local hero in Eugene was guard Ronnie Lee, and Few had a little figurine of him that he kept by his bed. He was among the crowd once at the Eugene airport, greeting the Oregon team on its return after a benchmark road victory.

Up the road, Oregon State, against all odds, ascended to a No. 1 national ranking through much of the 1981 season, and when Creswell High began assembling its own memorable run, some of the locals sensed a parallel.

"Yeah, we thought we were the high school version of Oregon State," says Randy Schott, a friend and teammate of Few since grade-school days.

Few played shortstop for Creswell High's baseball team, point guard in basketball, and after coaxing Barb Few, running back and defensive back for the football team. She came to have some misgivings about that decision on an autumn night in 1980, when Creswell was playing a late-season game against South Umpqua High, an hour's drive south. There was a harvest dinner at the church that night, with turkey and the trimmings, and Few's parents weren't planning to go to the game. But Barb Few suddenly felt one of those maternal tugs that only mothers seem to feel, and it told her that they needed to be at the game.

"We won't get there until halftime," Norm protested.

They piled in the car, drove south, and when they got to the field, somebody asked them, "How's Mark?" They found him sitting in an ambulance, whose driver said he couldn't leave because, well, there would be no ambulance remaining. Mark was propping up a shoulder that had become dislocated after he slipped on a muddy field.

The Fews asked for directions to the best hospital, and after going to the wrong one first, located the one with a specialist on call.

"This is not going to be easy," the orthopedist told them. Then they heard the sound of ligaments grinding, and bone on bone.

"I about passed out," says Barb Few, the nurse.

The injury was going to make for a slow transition to basketball season for their son. And it was supposed to be a basketball season to remember.

From the time the kids of Few's age group had been in grade school, it appeared big things could be in store for Creswell's basketball team. It had Few's leadership and playmaking skills at guard, it had a big guy in 6-foot-8 Todd Buerk, and it had the 6-3 Schott, a sturdy forward who couldn't be rooted out down low. Schott grew up on a farm three miles south of town and became country-strong. Nobody really lifted weights then, but Few and others, especially Schott, spent some summers bucking hay.

"You start hauling 200 tons of hay when you're in the seventh, eighth grade, you get strong," says Schott, now sitting in his office in Vancouver, Washington, where he is an executive for a gas company.

The first thing they had to do was stay together. Doug Orton became basketball coach at Creswell in the late '70s, and says he was told by the school superintendent that he needed to be wary of kids gravitating to a private school in Eugene, Marist High School.

"I can tell you one boy that's not going to Marist High School," Norm Few promised Orton.

That, naturally, was Mark. And as it turned out, no other Creswell Bulldog of that time frame did, either, and Orton, over coffee in Eugene, says, "I think Mark was probably helpful in that process. I know Norm was."

In 1979, Few and Schott, as sophomores, helped the junior varsity team to a 17-2 record. A year later, employing Orton's fast-paced system, the Bulldog varsity went 20-4. They ran a patterned fast break, played mostly man-to-man defense with a little 2-3 zone, and used Orton's wiles to overpower teams. If defenses overplayed to one side, he had a mirror-image attack on the other side that invariably worked.

Late that season, after Creswell ran away for a 35-point victory in a playoff game, the lead in the Register-Guard's story read, "The one thing you don't want to do when playing Creswell is get into a running game."

Alas, the Bulldogs were denied a trip to the state tournament in a playoff loss to South Umpqua, and that experience might have been valuable in 1981. As it was, with the nucleus of their team returning for the 1980-81 season, they were clearly the cream of the state's Class AA teams, ranked No. 1.

Few recovered from his shoulder problem, but only partly. Says Orton, "He really couldn't shoot. He did a really good job of hiding it. He'd shoot just enough jump shots so the scouting report couldn't say, 'This guy'll never shoot.'"

Few thus relied more on guile than gunnery. He was the proverbial coach on the floor. One time, Orton called timeout and Few asked why he had done it.

"Well, we've got to switch or something," Orton said.

"I was just going to do that," Few said.

Few averaged six points and 8.5 assists in the regular season. Says Orton, "Mark had the ability to talk to the officials in the heat of battle and not get anybody upset – just planting the seed. His style was, 'I know when to push it, and I kind of know no, no, no' without a coach having to tell him. It was not out of character for him, not in a yelling way, to say, 'Schott, you've got to get your head back in the ball game.' In school or out of school, he was the ringleader. He absolutely called the shots for the whole group."

That's precisely how Schott recalls it, saying, "He was the floor general, and he would reel you in if you were getting out of hand, which I did a lot. He got the ball down the floor, he had great ball skills. With entry passes and lobs, he was excellent. I was mostly on the receiving end of his passes. His demeanor was the same as it is now."

The Few household was often the nexus of the action. Teammates would gather for an impromptu pregame dinner, and Barb Few remembers the instructions: "We need a high-carb meal, Mom."

For the players, it was the time of their young lives. They were piling up victory upon victory. They played in a quaint gym, with a slightly vaulted ceiling, exposed wood beams and distinctive wood paneling at each end. After another win, the Bulldogs sometimes would gather to listen to a nearby radio station's rebroadcast of the game, reliving the night's successes. The next night, they might be making the short trip to Eugene, where "dragging the gut" – cruising South Willamette Street – was all the rage.

"Once we could drive, it changed everything," says Schott. "We weren't like partyers or anything. We stayed focused and committed. I think we had a commitment to each other, to stick together. It was all business. We just knew each other very well. We'd been together since fourth grade."

Seemingly, the only thing that could stop them was time – there was no shot clock, so they became Goliath, susceptible to defeat only if somebody could successfully hold the ball against them.

There was no staying with Creswell in a conventional game. So when the opponent tried – and succeeded – in putting the brakes on the Bulldogs, the games became a splitting headache for Creswell and its supporters.

"Slowdown, slowdown, slowdown," says Orton, remembering the exasperation. "It had us all frayed. It frayed everybody, from the head coach down to the manager and every parent."

In the final game of the regular season, nearby Marist brought proceedings to a screeching halt, holding the ball and leading 6-2 at the half before Creswell rescued a 16-15 victory. That was win No. 22 for the Bulldogs, the only Oregon team in Class AAA, AA or A to get to a state tournament unbeaten that year.

"Must have been a miserable game to watch," Schott said.

Schott won the Sky-Em League scoring title at 21 points per game and Buerk averaged 11 points and 10 rebounds. As Creswell's streak lengthened, its quest to go the distance consumed a town of a couple of thousand people. Schott says he and his classmates had the "mentality that we were going to put the town on the map through sports. There was just a real tremendous urge to be successful for the community."

As Orton tells it, it was a respectful group. "The times I heard them talking about other school events, or maybe teachers in the building, even if they weren't happy with a particular instructor, they weren't disrespectful – and I heard a lot of that over the years," Orton says. "They had their backs. Everybody had their backs. It was a really, really tight group socially. It was the highlight of a small town."

With the state Class AA tournament looming at venerable McArthur Court in Eugene, the highlight would only grow bigger. So the script said, anyway.

The week of the tournament, The Register-Guard ran a sports cover story on Creswell's prospects to win a state championship. Underscoring the country roots of the team, the piece was accompanied by a color photograph of the starters – joined by a cow. Bob Rodman's story noted the possible parallel between this team and the 1969 outfit that won the state championship; it scored 100 points in the title game that year.

"We've been winning like this since we were in the sixth grade," Few told the newspaper. "All along we kept saying, 'Wait until we're seniors.' Now we are."

The Bulldogs got past an athletic Grant Union team in the first round, and then stifled Astoria, 53-27, in the quarterfinals. It was a blowout victory – keyed by a zone defense that held Astoria to a tournament-record-low 16.3-percent shooting – yet it still wasn't vintage Creswell. "Not too good," Few told the Register-Guard. "We may still have the jitters. I know we can still improve."

That brought a semifinal game with La Salle, whose coach, Jack Cleghorn, had been around the block, winning a couple of state championships in the 1970s with Scappoose High. Ominously for Creswell, it also meant having to survive another opponent holding the ball.

Even at the plodding pace, Creswell led 30-22 after three quarters. Then everything went south on the Bulldogs, who weren't even in foul trouble entering the last period, as Buerk had two and

Schott three. But suddenly the whistles began sounding and La Salle mounted a comeback, scoring 10 straight points to take a 32-30 lead. Buerk collected three fouls in three minutes and was gone at the 2:47 mark.

Creswell tied it at 32 on a pair of free throws with 41 seconds remaining, and after a late La Salle turnover, Few had a chance to end it but his 35-foot desperation shot hit the back iron and the game went overtime.

Soon, Schott had fouled out, too. Each team wedged out a mere two points in overtime before Creswell's J.R. Bonebrake missed a long jumper, the rebound caromed out and Mark McLaughlin of La Salle retrieved it with three seconds left, raced to the other end and laid the ball in for a 36-34 upset at the buzzer.

It crushed a team. It crushed a town.

"A slow, ugly death," says Few, recalling the night 34 years later. "We didn't play very good."

Schott remembers how it slipped away from them. There was no "pause" button to hit. "You could just not slow everything down and regroup," he says, "especially when it's getting away from you."

Those around Creswell will always remember marginal foul calls that weighed heavily on the game. Indeed, the Register-Guard story said, "A few of the calls, especially two of the offensive fouls against Buerk, might have been debatable."

When he wasn't heartsick, Orton was furious. He contends neither Schott nor Buerk ever fouled out of a game before or after that, and both played in college. "They were some of the most phantom calls I've ever seen in the last four minutes of that game," Orton says. So angered was Orton, he didn't speak for a decade to one of the officials, whom he knew well.

This would be a high-achieving bunch, for whom there were much bigger things in life. One became a hugely successful college basketball coach, another a doctor (Buerk), another (Schott) a prominent businessman. But for some of them, that La Salle loss created a hole that could not be cemented. Says Schott, "I don't think about college losses like I do the La Salle loss. It's still there."

Orton speaks similarly, saying, "I've never been able to address that game. It just took everything out of me."

In the years that followed, the Bulldogs of '81 would gather in the Few kitchen, home from college for Christmas break, and inevitably go back to the heartbreak they felt that night at McArthur Court, play by agonizing play.

"Finally, the third Christmas, Barb said, 'Norm, you're going to have to do something about that,'" Norm Few recalls. "I said, 'Guys, there's no way you're gonna win. Forget it, it's over. The future's that way.'"

For their final night together in the third-place consolation game, what they really needed was a climactic run-and-gun exhibition, something to help get their minds off the La Salle loss, a performance to draw them and their town back to their best nights at Creswell. What they got, for the fourth time that season, was . . . Marist. Creswell took only 23 shots, scored a mere 10 second-half points and Marist won, 29-27.

"We didn't show up," Few says. "It seems like it was 16-14."

"We had so many kids who were so mentally out of it, I don't even know if they wanted to play," says Orton. "That was probably the poorest coaching job I ever did."

With that, the Bulldogs soon went on with the rest of their lives. More than three decades later, the 1981 team was named to the school's hall of fame on the strength of its undefeated regular season.

Few went off to Linfield College in McMinnville, given a small amount of scholarship aid. But something was missing. The close-knit community he knew, the reliable friendships – the sort of culture he would promote years later at Gonzaga – weren't the same. That, and the expensive private-school tuition, pushed him back down to Eugene, where he transferred to Oregon and studied kinesiology. Coaching was far off his radar; instead, he entertained the idea of becoming an athletic trainer.

He fell in with an athletically minded group that included Kory Tarpenning, a future Olympic pole vaulter; Tim Bright, a decathlete/vaulter who also became a multiple Olympian; Greg Bell, a basketball guard at Oregon; and eventually, two others with whom he would have a long professional relationship, Bill Grier and Leon Rice.

They would stage decathlons of a different kind. The idea was to pack as many events into one day – golf at Laurelwood in south Eugene or Emerald Valley down in Creswell, tennis, 2-on-2 basketball, 2-on-2 baseball between McArthur Court and the west grandstand at Hayward Field. The competition progressed in subsequent years when Few would herd a group of 10 or so to the family vacation place near Sisters, and they added a fishing derby and bar games like shuffleboard.

His first incursion into coaching came when Orton sought somebody to head up the freshman team at Creswell. Few was still well short of his degree at Oregon, but he accepted the part-time role and found coaching intriguing.

"His mental capacity was super," Orton says. "He really liked going to Seattle or Portland for the Nike clinics."

He put in a couple of more seasons as an assistant at Sheldon High in Eugene and when Orton stepped away from his position, Few went after it, unsuccessfully. The myriad schools that have sought to unhinge Few from Gonzaga would no doubt find that ironic.

Today, Norm Few revels in repeating the story of how his son didn't land that job. Kent Hunsaker was young in the superintendent's position then, later to become an administrator of Oregon school boards. By way of self-deprecating introduction, Hunsaker would tell those boards that he had an uncanny ability to foretell success or failure among aspirants.

There was a coaching applicant one time, Norm Few says, repeating Hunsaker's story. "He was an excellent player," Hunsaker would tell the boards. "But I just don't think he had a grasp of the game to be a coach. What the heck was the name of that kid? Oh, Mark. Mark Few."

So Few's coaching path would have to take a different turn. Working a camp under Oregon coach Don Monson one year, he bumped into a fellow sitting on a registration table and they struck up a conversation. At that time, Leon Rice was an assistant coach at Pasco High in south-central Washington, working for Mike Guajardo, a longtime friend of Monson, himself a Pasco-bred coach.

"What do you want to do?" Rice asked Few.

"I'm trying to get the grad assistant's job here at Oregon," Few said.

So was Rice, and he got it. But about a year later, Gonzaga was seeking a grad assistant. Gonzaga, where the coach, Dan Fitzgerald, had earlier hired Dan Monson, son of the Oregon coach.

"Funny thing was," says Rice, "when Mark was about to take that job, he said, 'Why don't you go to Gonzaga, and I'll have your job at Oregon?' I said, 'No way.' I didn't even know Gonzaga had a basketball program then."

It did. But in three decades as an NCAA Division I entity, Gonzaga had achieved only modest success. In their first 10 seasons in the West Coast Athletic Conference – as it was known then – the Zags finished anywhere from second to sixth. Four times, their lot was fourth place.

On the recommendation of Dan Monson, Few came north in 1989, blissfully unaware of what awaited.

The story of Fitzgerald and the dynamic between him and his young assistants has been told and retold. He drove them, berated them and worked them to all hours. He confounded them with his demand for every minute they could give, yet his simultaneous acceptance – no, embrace – of fourth-place finishes.

He loved his assistants, and he drove them crazy.

"There were halftimes," Few told me in the book "Bravehearts" in 2002, "when we'd go into an opposite room from the players and go, 'Let's sell life insurance. It's a heck of a lot easier than going through this for $24,000 a year.'"

What a seminal moment it was in 1988, when Dan Monson landed a position under Fitzgerald, who had interviewed an assistant at Eastern Washington, John Wade, and come away unimpressed. How the narrative would have been different, how the staff chemistry in the '90s – its constituents – would have been a total unknown. How the imperative to make the place better might have died, stillborn.

Monson knew Few from working camps at Oregon under his father, Don. They knew Grier, whose coaching background was similar to Few's, and who would join them at Gonzaga.

"No, no, it just happened," says Few, disclaiming the notion that anybody had a vision. "I was never a five-years-you-need-to-be-here guy. It was so bad then. You could never have imagined anything like that. We were just trying to survive, working for Fitz. We were just trying to make it a little better every year."

Few made an early mark. As a grad assistant in 1989-90, he was entrusted with six redshirts, who developed nicely and regularly schooled the active roster, which went 8-20 and took eighth in the WCC, then and now the school's worst finish in the league. Three years later, those redshirts would help Gonzaga to second place in the WCC, and in 1994, a National Invitation Tournament bid that marked GU's first postseason appearance since it made the transition to Division I in 1958-59.

A couple of years after Few arrived came Grier in 1991, and he would work alongside Monson and Few for six seasons under Fitzgerald. At a school where continuity became paramount, their own prolonged association was worth something to Gonzaga, in the quest to pursue better recruits, to help build it brick-by-brick – even if that campaign sometime seemed more about collectively surviving Fitz. Monson evolved into sort of a buffer between Fitzgerald and the others, suffering Fitz's whims so Few and Grier could better go about their business.

So close were Monson, Few and Grier that they lived together in Monson's house in north Spokane. Few paid rent, Grier chipped in what he could and the three of them lived a frenetic but happy existence. Soon, though, Few found other companionship.

Marcy Laca was a sophomore majoring in communications, a striking brunette helping with Gonzaga's freshman registration back in 1989 at the Martin Centre. She was from a small town in southern Idaho, Parma, similar in population to Creswell. Her father, of Basque ancestry, was a teacher/coach who rose to the roles of principal and superintendent – and for whom Julian Laca Gym would someday be named. Her mother was a teacher.

Few happened by one day with Gonzaga assistant coach Joe Hillock, and they talked with Marcy and her friends about the possibility of hosting recruits on campus.

"That was my first meeting with him," Marcy said. "It was pretty funny. I didn't think anything of it. I was a sophomore and he seemed way older to me then. He's seven years older. He wasn't on my radar at all."

Their "chance" meetings became more frequent when Marcy got a work-study grant at the Martin Centre, checking student IDs when they would come in to work out.

They became good friends and later began dating. The early one that sticks out to Marcy had to be a costly one for her date, who scarcely had pocket change at that time. The night began at the Spokane Club.

"Someone must have got him into the Spokane Club; no way he could have afforded it," Marcy says. "And then to a musical playing downtown: Les Miserables. I had never been to a musical. I loved it."

Later in the relationship, she remembers a walk they took down by Lake Arthur on campus, when Few waxed soberly about the difficult lives coaches place upon their wives while they try to make their way in their careers. That was true in spades working under his boss.

"What I remember sticking with me is how loyal he is," Marcy says, "and what a good person he is."

By the early '90s, it was more than a friendship. Says Marcy, "Once we decided we could be more than friends, it was like love at first sight. I fell totally in love then."

When they were married in 1994, Norm Few officiated.

Inch by inch, the program moved forward. The NIT appearance came in 1994, with a first-round victory at Stanford, followed by the school's initial plunge into the NCAA tournament in 1995. Safe to say that there isn't a person alive who foresaw that season's novelty appearance becoming the ho-hum regularity it is two decades later.

As the late 1990s approached, Fitzgerald grew concerned that he might lose his top assistant, Monson, so he proposed a prearranged handoff to him after five years. Too long, Monson said, and it was bargained down to two years. Fitzgerald stepped down in the spring of 1997, soon to be awash in the NCAA investigation, and Monson took over.

Whether coincidence or inevitability, the program immediately took a sharp upturn. In November, Gonzaga won the Top of the World Classic in Fairbanks, Alaska, beating Tulsa, Mississippi State and Clemson, far more rugged opponents than the Zags had been scheduling. They settled for another NIT appearance, but then came 1998-99, the year it all changed for Gonzaga.

About then, Roth, the athletic director, moved to make Few coach-in-waiting contractually, ensuring continuity if Monson were to leave.

"I can't tell you what I was thinking then," says Roth. "But I know what I think today if I make that commitment. You do it so you don't lose the assistant. If I remember correctly, Mark was being courted by other institutions. Ben Howland had been at Northern Arizona, he got the Pitt job and he wanted Mark, and he was going to pay Mark more than I could pay, for sure. I don't know if I was thinking this way then, but I think of it this way now. It also keeps the head coach happy, because he sees administratively that we're committed to keeping this staff together."

Having said that, Roth acknowledges there was much unknown about Few, never mind the fact he had been there virtually a decade.

"I knew who Mark was, but I didn't know how Mark was going to be like 18 inches over," Roth says. "Mark didn't know what Mark was going to be like 18 inches over."

The first order of business, when Monson made his midsummer dash to Minnesota in 1999, was to negotiate Few a contract – laughable in retrospect. Monson had been bumped into six figures – only barely, though – after his first team won the West Coast Conference, but now Few was going to have to earn his spurs. The school offered $70,000, and Few's side held out for $75,000.

"It was like this big negotiating thing for five grand," says Few, chuckling at the recollection.

"He was so pissed," says Williams, Few's attorney. "He said, 'They were going to pay Dan $150,000.'"

"Yeah," Williams retorted. "But you haven't won any games. You go win some games and I'll get you the money."

He would represent a change on the sideline, the third coach for some players in the program. Fitzgerald had been almost a cult figure. Monson was hard-driving – he threw the '99 team out of the locker room the week of the Sweet 16; it had to dress in the Martin

Centre bleachers – and now came Few, appealing more to the intellect than the raw fires.

"Fitz was a bar fight," says guard Matt Santangelo. "Monson was more of a football [style] guy. He got you to play really hard, compete in everything and got you to play together. Fewie's more reserved and conservative and analytical."

The unusual timing of Monson's departure added to the swirl of emotions Few was feeling – there was urgency, there was sadness, there was a sense of being overwhelmed. Players were starting school next month. And suddenly, around a program that had won its first NCAA-tournament games only four months earlier, there were expectations.

"Mark had a lot more pressure on him than Dan ever did," says Roth.

Mostly, it went famously. The Zags lost five games before the calendar turned to 2000, but they finished second in the WCC – to Pepperdine – and clocked another No. 2 seed, St. John's, in the NCAA tournament, on the way to Few's first of a half-dozen Sweet 16s. They repeated that advance in 2001, but this time winning the WCC regular season. The school that had never won an NCAA-tournament game until 1999 had now won seven in three years.

Soon, people were writing profiles on Few, which wasn't easy, because he isn't easily profiled.

For Gonzaga's purposes, this might be his overarching characteristic: He never viewed the school as limited. Where some saw a ceiling, he saw sky.

"He has taught me always to look for the opportunity; always look for the reason you can do something, not the reason you can't," says Standiford, the deputy athletic director. "He's made a spectacular career out of it. Mark's never seen a limitation in his life. If you told him he needed to get to the moon tomorrow, you could be sure he'd find a way to get there."

Those who have coached with him say his best attributes are an even keel, a knack for reading people and an ability to push the right buttons. In a profession where the highs and lows are precipitous and unavoidable, Few manages to minimize the sky-is-falling moments.

"I'd be hard-pressed that there's maybe anybody in college basketball that's as good at keeping things in proper balance," says former Gonzaga assistant coach Ray Giacoletti.

That includes curbing urges to overwork his team. Probably as a reaction to working long, sometimes empty, hours under Fitzgerald, Few evolved into a believer in wise use of time. His former aide Rice, Boise State's head coach, hired an assistant who was sometimes surprised at the lack of workload at BSU.

"The Gonzaga way," Rice calls it. "Let's not grind our players into the ground. Let's not grind our coaches into the ground. Sometimes the best answer is to do less."

"He doesn't watch a ton of game film," says Few's assistant, Tommy Lloyd. Nor does he overanalyze practice. "Why would I re-watch practice?" Few will tell Lloyd, declining another film session. "I just lived it."

Some of his relationships with ex-players tend to be more respectful than close. Yet he is the central figure in an enterprise that attracts an inordinate number of players back to the city where they played college ball.

He has his players' backs. Former GU center Richard Fox was early into a stint as color commentator on the Zags' radio broadcasts, when he found himself being critical of guards Jeremy Pargo and Derek Raivio during a Battle in Seattle loss to Nevada in 2006.

"If Gonzaga's going to reach its potential, both those kids need to figure it out," Fox said on the air.

At a commercial break, he looked at play-by-play man Tom Hudson, who said, "That was a little strong."

At the time, Fox was getting his master's degree, but still hopeful of playing professionally. He would use the Gonzaga training room, the locker room, he would share training-table meals with the team.

One day soon after, Few told Fox, "I'm really good friends with (ESPN's) Jay Bilas. Jay sometimes gets on us. He's critical of the program. But you know what he never does? He never eats at training table."

Says Fox, "He was right. If I want to be objective and critical, I need to be removed."

Those who have known Few longest are the ones with whom he has the deepest friendships, which might hint at why he gets skewered on some Seattle talk-radio shows. The quick-hit nature of sports-talk radio is not a platform which flatters – nor interests – him.

"I have a few guys that I like and trust like Colin Cowherd, that are better platforms for our program," Few says. "I'd just as soon stay out of that whole mix." Referring to jousts with Seattle media people, he says, "I don't have to deal with those guys. This position is beyond that now. I just tell these guys [at Gonzaga], I'll go on with guys I trust and guys I think are credible journalists."

Few does not suffer easily the ill-considered question, a fact inexperienced reporters sometimes learn the hard way.

"I've never had an instance where he's been bad to me," says Spokane sportscaster Dennis Patchin, who has known Few since the coach's assistant days at Gonzaga. "I've never had an instance where he's made it harder for me to do my job."

But Patchin adds, laughing, "Among the electronic media, we call it 'The Mark Few Shootdown.' It's kind of a running joke: Who got shot down today? Who asked the stupid question?"

His willingness to play devil's advocate often leads him down a Lou Holtz path when discussing Gonzaga opponents with the media, sometimes flattering them beyond recognition. In 2013, the Zags played South Alabama in the Battle in Seattle, and because it's a stand-alone event that has often drawn powerful teams, advance stories tended to focus on the modest profile of the Jaguars.

Few defended them, though, and after the Zags won a hard-fought 68-59 victory, he emerged from the locker room and said, "I told you guys."

Shortly after, South Alabama lost 12 of 13 and finished 11-20 that season.

Picture this: Few and some fishing buddies, headed south on the first Monday of March in 2013 toward the Clearwater River in Idaho. They're listening to ESPN radio, and the host is barbecuing Few for not being in the office to field interviews on the morning the Zags are voted No. 1 in the country. Few's friends are cackling with laughter at his displeasure.

"You gonna tell me what to do on my day off?" Few says, still incredulous. "Does he get a vote in my life?"

Ah, fishing. For Few, it's a passion with religious fervor. Former GU assistant athletic director Joel Morgan has plied Northwest rivers with Few – Deschutes, Grande Ronde, North Fork St. Joe, Coeur d'Alene, Methow, Missouri, the Kvichak in Alaska – and describes sort of a power-fishing mindset in which "you're leaving in the middle of the night and getting back in the middle of the night" and nobody talks about work and you're apt to forget you haven't eaten for eight hours.

Two things happen: Few competes hard in that arena, and he also clears his head. And if, say, he's the one doing the best that day, he might bring out the needle. Almost as much of a stock-in-trade as Gonzaga's NCAA-tournament appearances is his penchant for engaging in the wry dig – with friends, fellow coaches, the people he knows best. It's the currency of his conversation. It's him.

"He'll push, and he'll push, and then he'll acquiesce," says Mike Burns, a coaching friend from Eastern Washington and WCC days. "But he likes to needle."

Of course, he gets needled back. His closest coaching friends will jab him that his world isn't theirs. Says Burns, "He's been insulated by a cocoon of his own making. He's had nothing but success. He hasn't gone through adversity in his coaching career. There's times when we look at him and go, 'Oh my God, it's Camelot.'"

The needle emerges without warning. Discussing how he concluded he had a better job at Gonzaga than the one Kilkenny offered at Oregon, he told me dryly, "I know you Pac-12 guys have a hard time wrestling with that in your head."

As much as the needle – or in accordance with it – Few, as his wife Marcy says, "loves a good debate, for sure."

He revels in playing the contrarian – absolutely fitting for somebody willing to spurn programs like Indiana and Arizona and UCLA to stay at Gonzaga. When convention says zig, Mark Few tends to zag.

"A normal conversation with Mark is a small argument," says Lloyd. "He plays a little bit of devil's advocate. But he's always listening. You can walk out and think, 'He ain't even listening to a word I'm saying,' and then he'll go in front of the team and literally regurgitate the same thing you said."

He doesn't tweet, doesn't do the whole social-media scene. A little whimsically, he says, "I'm kind of thinking it's going to pass, just like everything else." He adds: "I don't want people knowing where I'm at or what I'm doing or what I'm thinking."

What he does is a lot of good things that go unnoticed. In 1988, his old roommate, Tim Bright, was going to be competing in the Seoul Olympics, and Few and Bright's girlfriend (and future wife), Julie Goodrich, and her sister scraped together enough money to go there. A friend set them up for a stopover night at a traditional home near Honolulu.

Their hostess was replacing kitchen floor tiles, but the project was proceeding slowly. "I swear, Mark stayed up all night and laid the whole thing for her," says Julie Bright.

He got to know the proprietors of a café not far from his Spokane home years ago and showed up, pre-kids, to help with a construction project. Unfamiliar with his background, Celeste Shaw, the owner, said, "I can pay you if you need a job." No thanks, he already had one.

More than once, he and Marcy have spent significantly to help out a family member. When his sister Kathy went to Kampala, Uganda, to finalize the adoption of her daughter Shanitah, third-world red tape stretched the trip unexpectedly into three months.

"I'd get plane tickets to get out and they'd postpone it two more weeks," Kathy Few says. "You'd go to the Delta office and they'd say, 'Nope, you don't get any of this money back.' You have to pay for two more tickets, which is thousands of dollars."

He's hardly a regular at monthly athletic-department staff meetings. But if he gets a pass there, surely there's payback for all in the peripheral benefits of Gonzaga basketball. He's been known to offer his time to GU coaches if they need a conversation with a recruit to help clinch a letter of intent.

The priorities seem unchanged. HBO spent months shadowing the Zags for its 2016 series, "Gonzaga: The March to Madness," interviewing players at apartments and in hotel rooms, filming Few walking Stella, the family German shepherd. But when it came time for the team to make an annual visit to families at the Ronald McDonald House in Spokane, it was done on the down-low, without the accompaniment of TV cameras. He didn't want that occasion to turn into a photo op.

During the July, 2016 recruiting-evaluation period, CBSsports.com's basketball writers asked 100 coaches this question, as part of a series it calls "Candid Coaches": "Which college coach would you most like your son to play for?" Few was the seventh-most-named coach, behind, in order, Tom Izzo, Tony Bennett, Bill Self, Mike Krzyzewski, Lon Kruger and Shaka Smart.

Few works hard at living in the moment. Kathy Few describes a guy who tends to be late and let the gas gauge veer toward empty. His high school coach, Orton, recalls what might be a definitive Mark Few moment at Kathy's wedding in central Oregon. "Where's Mark?" somebody said, as the appointed hour grew close. "There was a place to fish over the hill," Orton says. "All of a sudden, he's coming over the hill, got his hat on, got his pole."

Nobody quite remembers exactly when the Mark Few Fishing Derby – the seemingly annual quest to lure him from Gonzaga – began. Roth thinks it might have started with Oregon State, probably when Eddie Payne gave way in 2000 to the lamentable two-year regime of Ritchie McKay.

Roth is asked how many schools have shown serious interest.

"I would guess at least 16," he says.

A good many don't even rate consideration, usually because of locale or potential. Few will also tell you that coach-hunting season always comes at a difficult time emotionally, when you've just been eliminated from the NCAA tournament, and you're licking wounds and thinking about how to prepare for a better ending next year, rather than feeling inclined to jet off to interview with somebody else.

Says Roth, "I do know over the years, some schools have been shocked by his lack of response to their inquiries. There was a very prestigious school in recent years [that said], 'He didn't even call us back. We're XYZ, and you're telling me, he didn't even call us back.'"

For Brad Williams, who handles several other coaches' contracts, the virtually annual approaches to Few by other schools became a thick portfolio of experiences representing a hot-commodity coach. The once-accepted protocol for initiating contact – first getting permission from the athletic director – has evolved during Few's regime to the practice of dealing with the agent, often by a head-hunter firm retained by the school. But Few and Roth have a good relationship, and the GU athletic director says he's confident he's kept up to speed on suitors.

One of the last advances made the traditional way – through the AD – was by Washington's courtly Barbara Hedges in 2002 after she explored the interest of Missouri's Quin Snyder. Few was her No. 1 target at the Final Four in Atlanta that year and in an ironic and fateful turn of events, after he said no, she eventually offered the job to Monson, who accepted it on the day of the national-title game. But by dawn the next day, he had a change of heart, stayed at Minnesota, and Hedges ultimately settled on Lorenzo Romar.

A year later, Williams called UCLA athletic director Dan Guerrero to gauge his interest in Few when the Bruins fired Steve Lavin. He says Guerrero called back five minutes later, but Howland was known to be pushing hard for the job and landed it. UCLA would approach Few when it fired Howland 10 years later.

"He was involved in both Indiana searches," says Williams, referring to 2006, when the Hoosiers hired Kelvin Sampson, and two years later, when Sampson ran afoul of NCAA violations in Bloomington.

In 2006, Few told Williams that Indiana athletic director Rick Greenspan was as much a part of the scenery at the Zags' subregional in Salt Lake City as the nearby Wasatch Mountains. The Hoosiers happened to be at that site as well, losing to Gonzaga in the second round.

"Mark said, 'Every time I turned around, he was there,'" Williams says. " 'He was at all my press conferences, he was at all our practices. I saw him in the hotel every morning.'"

But Indiana is one of those high-profile, life-in-a-fishbowl jobs that don't seem to suit Few. Another of those is Kentucky, with which his name was floated in 2007. The job ended up swallowing Billy Gillispie whole.

"The thing I told him about Kentucky is, it's a great job, unbelievable, one of the greatest basketball jobs there is," Williams says. "But if you don't win, they're going to be burning you in effigy in your front yard. Mark's very intelligent. He and Marcy know who they are. They know how they want to live and raise their kids."

Something instinctive always told Few to be selective. This is a guy who won't be rushed, who has an old-school foundation. Whose mother, if she didn't attend the game, always calls him afterward.

The year the Kentucky job was open, the Wildcats' search was conducted by Dan Parker, who headed an Atlanta search firm and called Few directly. Parker, says Williams, also was directing a search by Arkansas, which had fired Stan Heath.

"You're not going to get Kentucky," says Williams, repeating what Parker said to Few. "But I think you'd be great at Arkansas."

"I'm not going to Arkansas," said Few.

A year later, says Williams, Stanford athletic director Bob Bowlsby called, having just fired Trent Johnson. Bowlsby eventually had a long talk with Few – whatever happened, he told him, they needed to go fly-fishing sometime – but nothing materialized. Eventually, Duke coach Mike Krzyzewski put the squeeze on Bowlsby to hire ex-Blue Devils aide Johnny Dawkins.

The tipping point for Few's future – the sign that he might indeed stay forever at Gonzaga – seemed to come around the year 2009. Before the full-court press by Oregon, there was Arizona, trying to find itself after the 2007 departure of Lute Olson and eventful, one-year gigs by Kevin O'Neill and Russ Pennell. The place was fractured, with the shadow of Olson looming over it.

"It was just a mess, just a total mess," says Few. "It was done through intermediary guys. In fact, we talked way back when we were in Orlando [winning the Old Spice Classic] in November."

Among the components of the mess: There was little talent on the roster. Then, after the Wildcats hired Sean Miller to climax a protracted search, Tim Floyd resigned amid allegations of wrongdoing at USC. That led to the release of three recruits, including Derrick Williams and Solomon Hill, who landed at Arizona, and would have been, effectively, a pot-sweetener for Few had it happened months earlier.

"That was one I probably looked at harder than the other ones," Few admits.

In short order, along came the Confab on the Columbia with Oregon's Kilkenny.

"They ratcheted up the pressure hard on that," says Williams. "They had Phil Knight calling. Mark had been on their radar for a long time."

Other stray feelers come unexpectedly. In the spring of 2014, Few picked up the phone one day and had a message from Glenn Sugiyama of DHR International, running the point for Cal's search to replace Mike Montgomery. Few called Williams and told his attorney, "There's no way I'm taking Cal."

Sugiyama said he was at the Spokane Airport. Williams and Few gave him the courtesy of a meeting at a local restaurant, but his initial manifesto held up: There was no way he was taking Cal.

Well into spring 2015 Few got a call from Duke Werner, basketball trainer at Florida and someone with whom he had developed a friendship through USA Basketball. Few's friend Billy Donovan had finally taken an NBA job with the Oklahoma City Thunder, Werner was on a search committee, and would Few be interested in pursuing the job?

"Bad timing," Few says. "They come at you right when your season ends. Those are horrible times to approach coaches."

It was a few years after Few had made his mark as a head coach that Gonzaga hit upon a way to upgrade its appeal to him, putting him on 10-year rollover contracts. The school couldn't compete with annual deals now topping $5 million, but it could exchange cash for security, and that resonated with a coach not obsessed with money. And he appreciates the effort to grow the product, from the move to chartered aircraft more than a decade ago to a new building that will house a practice facility and academic-support center.

Few's longevity at Gonzaga serves to underscore the complementary folly of so many college-basketball hires, in which the ladder-climbing coach lunges at the biggest raise available, and the school targets the hot property, who has usually just grabbed headlines in the NCAA tournament. Few's checklist has been much more analytical: Are his prospective bosses his kind of people? Could he foster a family atmosphere at this big a school? Would his calendar be dominated with booster activities? Can you win there? Is the location desirable? (Memorably, when he floated the notion of UCLA by his father more than a decade ago, Norm Few snorted, "Well, I haven't seen many record trout coming out of the Los Angeles River.")

"He gets all kinds of weird calls," says Williams. One of them came in 2015 from T. Boone Pickens, billionaire tycoon and Oklahoma State mega-benefactor, increasingly disgruntled with coach Travis Ford. Pickens, among other things, might have been tired of losing to Gonzaga; Few is 6-0 against the Cowboys.

"He said he'd pay him three or four million and build him a new trout stream," said Williams. "These rich guys don't like to lose and don't like to be told no."

Like all the others, Pickens was told no. It never even got to the issue of fatter trout in the Northwest.

– 4 –
TOMMY:
A HOOPS OPERA

IF YOU KNEW that one of the nation's better college-basketball programs was renowned for recruiting overseas, it might be tempting to project what sort of coaching figure would successfully spearhead such an effort. I'm picturing an urbane fellow with a thin mustache, probably educated at an international school on the East Coast, a shadowy, multi-lingual bon vivant who immediately knows the dates and site of the next European championships as readily as he knows who sells the best croissant on the Champs-Elysees.

Spoiler alert: That's not Tommy Lloyd.

Oh, the part about the best pastry in Paris, maybe. After all, he has been to Europe 20-something times in 16 years as an assistant coach at Gonzaga. That means he's visited just about every corner of the continent and places as far-flung as Nigeria and Australia.

This is all on Gonzaga's dime, and you'd have to say the campaign has been worth every penny. Even the 500 or so euros Lloyd had to plunk down on a rental-car drop charge in Cologne, enabling him to call an audible and drive beneath European airspace befouled by ash from the 2010 eruption of the Icelandic volcano Eyjafjallajokull.

"Some crazy number," says Lloyd, referring to those euros. "But at the end of the day, I'm over here, I have to get done what I have to get done. Otherwise, you're spending thousands of dollars and I'm doing nothing."

As far as I know, nobody at Gonzaga has ever quibbled, because Lloyd's contribution to the Zags has been immense, so much that head coach Mark Few calls him "one of the cornerstone guys in the whole run."

As pivotal as Lloyd has been in procuring talent overseas, it would be shorting him to define his contribution as that of recruiter. Few pegs his "Xs and Os acumen" at an elite level, and even as it might seem that the hay is in the barn when a foreign recruit steps on campus to begin his freshman year, Lloyd surely knows part of the program's reputation hangs on the progress of that player in a faraway land.

The first international breakthrough by the Zags this millennium was attracting Ronny Turiaf (they did, however, have fabled 7-foot-3 Frenchman Jean Claude Lefebvre in the late 1950s, Australian seven-footer Paul Rogers was a mid-'90s force, and Aussie John Rillie gunned them into their first NCAA tournament in 1995).

But to hear former teammate Cory Violette tell it, the successful recruitment of Turiaf was only the start of his metamorphosis at Gonzaga.

"Tommy Lloyd, I would credit him almost entirely with Ronny's development," says Violette. "He helped him through all kinds of mental challenges players have – mental challenges of a kid being away from home, having to go to school, culture changes. I mean, Tommy was literally everything to him in that regard."

It seems so unlikely, all of it. Gonzaga, rising to become a national force. The Zags, capitalizing like no other program on the flourishing international pool of talent. And that effort being driven by a guy who grew up in a small town where basketball is historically an afterthought.

Tommy Lloyd's story begins high on a hill above Kelso, Washington, with a hoop, and a driveway, and the light pole that his dad Dale had rescued from its horizontal resting spot down in town, where it was seemingly forgotten.

"My dad just kept his eye on it," Lloyd says. "I don't know if he got permission or whatever. He and a couple of his buddies loaded it up on the truck and painted it and put it up, so I had a really nice city light."

Part way down the hill, where Dale and Jackie Lloyd live now, Dale opens the blinds on a hazy, boiling summer afternoon and lends context. To the right of the sweeping expanse below the dining-room window is Kelso, population about 12,000. Farther to the northwest are the Cowlitz and Columbia rivers, the city of Longview and "the Fibre." Longview Fibre Company, now known as KapStone Paper and Packaging Corporation, has been a key employer in the region since the late 1920s.

Dale Lloyd became a carpenter, and eventually a superintendent, for an industrial contractor. Jackie, after bearing two boys – Tommy is the second – went back to school, earned a master's degree and a certification and became an elementary-school teacher.

"Jackie and Dale are blue-collar people," says a family friend, Bill Bakamus, the basketball coach at Mark Morris High in Longview. "They believe in work ethic, family values. (Tommy) was molded by some pretty outstanding parents. She's a great lady and Dale's one of the most humble and hard-working men you'll ever find – up at the crack of dawn and works late. When you're around that all the time, it kind of permeates."

Most of the work Tommy was putting in then was on his jump shot. He wore out that basket and the light from that city pole. He also had a bit of daredevil in him, and when he wasn't in the driveway firing jumpers, he was out tearing it up on dirt bikes or in the go-kart Dale bought him.

In basketball, baseball and football, he steeled himself against buddies of his older brother, whom he could hang with athletically. And by the time he was in junior high in the late 1980s, word was getting around the area: Between a 6-foot-2 guard who could shoot and another kid, Ryan Chilton, who would eventually grow to seven feet tall, Kelso might at last have something to crow about in basketball.

The place had been destitute in the game for so long. It hadn't been to a state tournament since 1960. It hadn't so much as had a winning season since 1977. Kelso was a football town.

In the late '80s, the Kelso basketball job came open, and a coach named Jeff Reinland began looking into it. Once a player at Eastern Washington for ex-Gonzaga basketball operations chief Jerry Krause, he was coach at Cascade High in the mountains of Leavenworth, and he kept hearing that Kelso was a dead-end place no basketball coach should touch.

One guy took issue with that. Bakamus was coaching 30 miles up the road from Kelso at Toledo, and he had heard about the two kids coming up, Lloyd and Chilton. Reinland took his word for it and accepted the offer.

He was a bit of a wild man. But Kelso needed a wild man. He was Bob Knight without the chair.

"I was a perfect fit for Kelso at the time," says Reinland.

He was also perfect for Tommy Lloyd, who took Reinland's harangues for what they were – a call to work harder, for Kelso to strive for more than its perennial also-ran station in southwest Washington.

About then, Lloyd did something unusual. He quit playing football after eighth grade, although he had promise as a quarterback. A year after that, he quit baseball, although he might have had a future as a catcher.

"It was kind of a big deal," he admits today. "Nobody had ever done that in Kelso."

He was pushing in all his chips on basketball. He was a deadly shooter, but not overly athletic, and Reinland told him if he had designs on playing college basketball, he probably needed to spend more time on the sport.

Lloyd's first games as a varsity player were eye-openers. He had 28 points as Kelso thumped R.A. Long of Longview, 71-57, prompting the Longview Daily News to refer to him as "sophomore gunslinger Tom Lloyd." The paper quoted Reinland: "Tommy helps make us a better shooting team this year. He took a couple of shots too quick tonight, but it's a big step up from Coweeman Junior High to here."

Before the game, Reinland learned that first-hand. Lloyd, arriving early, was hungry, so he visited a concession stand. He was devouring an ice-cream bar and some Gummy Worms when Reinland, ever the drill sergeant, happened upon him in the bleachers and aired him out.

"I should have made it a routine," says Lloyd, noting the 28 points.

W.F. West High of Chehalis strove to shut down Chilton but Lloyd scored 39 points in a 68-59 Kelso loss. Brian Hunter, the coach at West, told the Centralia Chronicle: "He was unbelievable. Guys were draped all over him and he still put on a show."

Alas, Kelso finished 8-13 that year, even as Lloyd was named first-team Greater St. Helens Conference. But with Lloyd and Chilton returning as juniors, the Hilanders seemed on the brink of good things.

"Did he tell you about the trampoline incident, the broken leg?" asks Jackie Lloyd.

That was the day the kid in Tommy won out again. It seems that the neighbors were gone and they had a trampoline in the backyard, and he and Chilton decided to help themselves to the premises. Being the smaller and more lithe of the two kids, Lloyd was the one bouncing the highest. At the top of one of his jumps, he saw something scary: Directly below was Chilton's oversized frame.

"I landed on his femur and snapped it," Lloyd says. "It was so bad, we were hopeful he had dislocated it."

"The first phone call went to coach Reinland," says Jackie, rolling her eyes. "They didn't want to have to face coach and tell him that Ryan had broken his leg and Tom had done it. Funny, neither of the moms got called first, it was the coach."

It was going to be that kind of year for Kelso. Without the towering Chilton, Lloyd had more than he could handle; for example, in a 29-25 loss to Mark Morris in a jamboree, Lloyd scored 19 Hilander points. Then, in February, the season went from bad to worse when Lloyd sustained a medial-collateral ligament tear that torpedoed the rest of his season.

Kelso sank to 6-15 without Lloyd, and at season's end, Reinland was left to tell the Daily News, "About the time he got going good this year, he got hurt. Tom basically leads by example. He's a quiet kid on the court, very coachable. He always attempts to do the things we want him to do. He's a very positive influence on the rest of the team."

Suddenly, what had loomed as Kelso's golden era of hoops wasn't so golden. Notwithstanding the injuries to Chilton and Lloyd, the Hilanders hadn't even approached a winning season. But it all came together in 1992-93.

Lloyd hit for 29 points to lead his team to a win over Fort Vancouver, and 13 days later, he poured in 31 to help beat Evergreen. In a 65-62 victory over Bakamus' Mark Morris team, Lloyd had 30 – 21 in the second half – and the Hilanders overcame an eight-point deficit in the fourth quarter to cinch the school's first winning season in 16 years.

"They kept finding him in the deep corner," Bakamus says. "He got one up on me on that one. I'm still irritated."

Kelso went 20-2, won its last 13 of the regular season, rose to a No. 7 ranking among the state AAA boys and at long last, crashed the state tournament.

It turned out that making the tournament, more than making hay in it, was Kelso's lot. The Hilanders ran afoul of Federal Way and future Arizona standout Michael Dickerson, who had 29 points and 17 rebounds in a 62-47 first-round victory. Lloyd was limited to eight points.

Before the Hilanders exited, however, they won a one-point decision over Olympic High and Lloyd scored 14 points. It was a signal moment in the school's sparse basketball history. Kelso hadn't been to a boys state tournament in 33 years, and it hasn't been back since.

Lloyd connected with Reinland, and it speaks tellingly to Lloyd's eventual calling as a coach that even as a mid-teen, he managed not to take Reinland's hard-bitten style personally.

"He was controversial in our small community," Jackie Lloyd says of Reinland. "He was pretty vocal."

"Pretty vocal," adds Dale Lloyd, "and some of the parents didn't like that."

When Reinland opted to capitalize on Kelso's 1993 success by moving on to an opening at Walla Walla Community College, Lloyd was only too willing to follow. His presence helped Walla Walla's roster adjust to the rigors of Reinland; if he could put up with it, the thinking went, so can we.

As at Kelso, there was a duality to Lloyd's personality. Off the floor, he was bubbly, personable and magnetic. No doubt that serves him well in the homes of recruits.

He was a different figure on the court. In his small office on the Walla Walla campus, Reinland remembers the sunny side of Tommy Lloyd, and then this one: "He was a very intense person. He liked to win. I mean, he was a coach's player. He brought it every day. I was a real intense coach back when I was 26 years old, and Tommy never batted an eye. He could take anything you could dish out. He was very, very tough."

Reinland appreciated Lloyd even more the night Walla Walla played at Blue Mountain CC in Pendleton, Oregon. Walla Walla had a good team, but kicked one away. Lloyd and his Warrior teammates slumped to their locker room and closed the door. Reinland, descending a flight of steps, was behind them when he heard shouting in the dressing quarters. It was Lloyd, reaming out his teammates.

"We're not gonna do this! We're not gonna do that!" Reinland recounts with satisfaction. "That's when I knew he was going to be a coach."

Not that Reinland and Lloyd always found themselves on the same page. In the most oft-told story of Lloyd's playing days, Walla Walla was in Ontario, Oregon at the Chukar Classic, so named for the host school, Treasure Valley Community College.

The first night, Lloyd ran into a ball screen. His eyes flashed and he hit the floor with what might have been diagnosed today as a concussion. A generation ago, not so much.

At shootaround the next day, before the title game with Treasure Valley, the Warriors were working on their quick-hitter plays, and Lloyd couldn't make a shot.

"If you can't freakin' help us tonight," Reinland exploded, "do the right thing and don't play!"

Lloyd remembers dropping an F-bomb on Reinland, vowing that he'd play the game, at which point Reinland threw him out of the shootaround and told him to walk back to the hotel.

"Half a mile, a mile," Lloyd shrugs. "Nothing crazy. You're in Ontario, a small town."

Reinland called Lloyd to his motel room and asked, "What the hell was that all about?"

"I just got frustrated."

"I'm OK if you tell me to f--- off, just don't tell me in front of the team."

Reinland doubted whether Lloyd could play, so they visited a doctor, who cleared him. And Lloyd had the night of his life, scoring a school-record 52 points.

"Nine out of 12 from three, I do remember that," Lloyd says.

His time with Reinland was coming to a close. It had been six years, six formative years that were sometimes challenging.

"I was hard on Tommy his sophomore year here," Reinland confesses. "I remember after a game, I ran into Tommy's father. I was pretty close with the family and still am. Dale had never said a word to me in six years. They're very supportive parents. He said, 'You know, coach, Tommy's not having very much fun.'

"From that moment on, I really changed how I dealt with Tommy. I called him in and said, 'Hey, Tommy, I've been pretty hard on you this year. I just want you to know, that's over. I mean, we've been together six years. You know what I want you to do. I know you're going to do your best to do it. I'm going to quit riding your ass so hard.'

"Tommy would never say anything, but I know he really appreciated it. We had a great finish to our career."

If the years around Reinland represented a certain stability for Lloyd, the next few would be a lot different. He had drawn modest recruiting attention at Walla Walla, but nothing eye-opening. Utah coach Rick Majerus took a look but concluded Lloyd was a step slow. Dan Monson, then an assistant at Gonzaga, made contact, but the Zags went in a different direction.

So Lloyd opted for a scholarship from Southern Colorado. It wasn't a good fit, as Lloyd spent a season riding the bench, deciding before it was over that he was transferring out. The best thing that happened that year, Lloyd summarized in a call home: "Mom and Dad, I think I found the girl." He had met his future wife, Chanelle.

With one year of eligibility left, he landed back in Walla Walla at Whitman College. There, he caught the first whiff of a long relationship with Gonzaga, playing for veteran Skip Molitor, who knew all about Lloyd. When Lloyd and Chilton were helping to revive Kelso High, Molitor was an assistant at Colorado State to fellow 1974 Gonzaga grad Stew Morrill, and they signed Chilton to play for CSU. In doing so, they also saw a lot of Lloyd.

"He may be the only kid in Whitman College basketball history to transfer in as a senior," said Molitor in his office at the school, where he is women's golf coach and assistant athletic director. "Whitman is the kind of place where you don't have all that many two-year transfers. But it worked out really well for him. He stayed around the extra half-year to get enough credits for the degree."

But not before he had to do a little wrangling with Jackie and Dale Lloyd. Academically challenging Whitman is pricey, and he was leaving a scholarship at Southern Colorado to attend a place where he'd be paying his own way. His parents had bought him a Volkswagen Cabriolet when he was in high school, and that became essentially a down payment on his move.

"We said, 'Tom, if you really want to do this, you're going to have to sell that car,'" recalls Jackie. "We knew if he'd sell the car, he'd really want to do it."

He did. And he averaged about 14 points a game for an 8-16 team. Truth be told, there weren't a lot of memorable moments that year for the Missionaries, unless you count the weather-related audible they called in mid-season. Unable to fly out of Portland to get to San Diego for a game with Christian Heritage College (now known as San Diego Christian), the Missionaries flipped a U-turn and headed north. They spent the night at the Lloyds' home in Kelso on the way to a hastily arranged game at Seattle Pacific, where they led Ken Bone's Falcons most of the night before succumbing.

Soon, Lloyd's college playing days were done, and bigger matters loomed: As in, what to do with the rest of his life?

He actually mulled the notion of medical school. He considered becoming a teacher. Coaching also was an option. He and Chanelle, now married, went to Australia, where he played semipro basketball and coached a high school team before he returned to finish up at Whitman.

Then he went home to Kelso to work and put away some money. It was 1998, the year Gonzaga started its mad run to the NCAA Elite Eight. He got in touch with Monson, head coach of the Zags, recalling a conversation they'd once had about the possibility of Lloyd helping out in some capacity in the basketball office, perhaps while attending graduate school.

He also had an opportunity to play pro ball in Dusseldorf, Germany. "You need to do that," Monson said. And then he added, almost hauntingly, "Find us some players over there."

Tommy and Chanelle went overseas. And at the end of the season, they took off on a five-month backpacking trip around the world – to Turkey, Greece, Africa, the Mauritius Islands, Fiji, Hawaii. Of course, while they were indulging their wanderlust, things were percolating wildly at Gonzaga. The basketball team was winning its first games in school history in the NCAA tournament, capturing the nation's attention, and a few months later, Monson was accepting an offer at Minnesota.

Lloyd's naivete was immense. He called Monson, thinking maybe the head Gopher would want to hire him in Minneapolis. Monson got back, acknowledged what a crazy turn events had taken, and told him he'd talked to his successor, Few, and Few had consented to have Lloyd help out in the office. History suggests that what might have been as innocent a decision as Few has made as head coach may have been his most profound one.

As an administrative assistant, Lloyd did odd jobs in the office while fulfilling a student-teaching position at Mead High, where he recalls coming upon a skinny ninth-grader wearing a Pantera T-shirt – Adam Morrison. Tommy and Chanelle were still finding their way, he coaching enough JV football at Mead to know he wasn't good at that, she working a minimum-wage job at Macy's downtown. They had no money, no medical coverage.

He began a gig as a long-term substitute science teacher at Glover Middle School in Spokane. Three days into it, he threw up his hands, decided it wasn't for him and told the principal he was out. Which was fine, except he was tossing away a stable income. He was going to work at being a coach.

"I must have been convincing," he says, recalling how he finessed that decision with Chanelle. " 'This is what we're gonna do, and we're gonna be great at it.' She's just a good person. She trusted me."

To his parents, hard-working people who knew the value of a dollar, it didn't always make sense. Dale Lloyd recalls a trip he and Jackie made to Spokane. Says Dale, "I remember asking him, 'Tommy, are you sure you want to do this?' He goes, 'Yeah, it'll all work out.'"

The next part was a blur. Scott Snider, Zag center of the mid-1990s who was an assistant coach, opted out of the business one day in 2001. Chanelle became pregnant with the Lloyds' first child. A day later, Few offered Tommy the position Snider had vacated. What a windfall: $1,000 a month for nine months excluding the summer, plus $15,000 to $20,000 from camps.

It launched Tommy Lloyd into a world that, 15 years later, he would describe like this in front of a room of Gonzaga boosters: "You've never worked a day in your life, but you're working your ass off every day."

He plunged headlong into the job and loved it. So much of it was incremental – the camps, film exchange, scouting, individual workouts – the workaday stuff that keeps a program's heartbeat pumping. But it fascinated him.

Lloyd was working under Few and alongside Bill Grier, a longtime Few associate, and Leon Rice, another old Few running mate from the mid-'80s who had struck his own path elsewhere before joining the Gonzaga staff in 1998. The chemistry was good, the program was winning, and Lloyd devoured the coaching culture.

"I always remember loving the process of trying to figure it out," he says. "That is what I love to do, putting in that work, and thinking about the game. I wonder now, 'Man, how could I have been a good coach 15 years ago?' Things have evolved and changed so much. (But) I don't remember being overwhelmed. I always remember loving the process, figuring out a way to make guys better."

Of course, you can only make guys so much better. Player development is crucial, but so is recruiting. Lloyd remembers listening one day to advice from Few: "You're a sharp basketball guy. You're doing a great job with player development. But if you want to make a mark in this business . . ." Lloyd mouths the next words slowly: ". . . find a way to get players."

At that time, there was no campaign by Gonzaga to conquer Europe. But the staff got a tip – Lloyd believes it was from Dean Stepp, coach at South Eugene (Oregon) High and dad of Gonzaga guard Blake Stepp – on an intriguing Croatian big man.

Mario Kasun was a seven-foot center who had already played for a professional club in Zagreb. He signed a letter of intent for Gonzaga, but this was an era when the NCAA was trying to come to grips with the tangled issue of amateurism, and Kasun sat idle for a year in Spokane, awaiting clearance. Finally, as Kasun's family struggled financially back home, Gonzaga reluctantly parted company with him. Kasun returned to a long career in Europe, save for two NBA seasons (2004-06) with the Orlando Magic.

Had Kasun cleared the NCAA labyrinth and played at Gonzaga, the program never would have sought – and experienced – the exotic wonders of one Ronny Turiaf, who merely became what many consider the most popular Zag ever to don compression shorts.

Turiaf, 6-foot-10, grew up on Martinique, a French possession in the eastern Caribbean. He attended high school in Paris and trained at INSEP, France's national institute for elite athletes.

The Gonzaga staff studied a video of the European 18-and-under championships in Zadar, Croatia. What caught their eyes was Turiaf, slapping a backboard and the thing shattering. (Deep irony there: In the early Turiaf days at GU, they couldn't get him to dunk. He said it hurt his hands too much.)

Lloyd's work then was strictly low-budget and long-distance. He made contact with officials at INSEP, and with Turiaf's father, Georges-Louis. Ronny was going to college in the United States, and he planned to visit Pepperdine, Saint Mary's, Gonzaga and Miami.

Only by being around Turiaf can you begin to appreciate what happened after that. He has a disarming quality that tends to take his relationships to a level a layer deeper.

"The people that are closest to me know how shy and how afraid of not being accepted I can be," he told me in 2016. "That's a part of me not many people know. For me, trust is the only way I can survive in those relationships. That's why I'm so passionate about every single relationship I have with the [people] I can trust."

Turiaf got off an airplane in Spokane, 4,800 miles from Paris, looking for Lloyd. They had never met.

"I need to know," Turiaf said. "Can I trust you?"

The moment sparked a connection that burns brightly 15 years later. Lloyd became a big brother of sorts to Turiaf, guiding him through cultural barriers, being at his side for his momentous heart surgery in 2005, propping him up at every sign of vulnerability. Lloyd remembers the fine details of how, in the fall of 2001, they were walking on campus – between the library and engineering building – and Turiaf said he thought he should redshirt as a freshman, and Lloyd reassured him, that no, competitively he was going to be just fine.

Years later, Turiaf would say, "With me and Tommy, we have this amazing dynamic, where I can get mad at him, and I can say bad words to him, and he can get mad at me and say bad words to me, and there is not an ounce of judgment or anything other than understanding and appreciation for the other person."

Truth be told, it took all of Lloyd's wiles to ensure that Turiaf would become a Zag. It seems that the visit to Miami was going to piggyback on Turiaf's trip to Spokane, and there were some well-founded fears in the Gonzaga basketball office that once he spent time in south Florida – far closer to Martinique – it would be all over for the Zags.

But Lloyd had done his homework. It wasn't easy deconstructing Turiaf's high school transcript in France to pass muster in an American compliance office, but Lloyd had figured it out. Referring to Miami, Lloyd says, "They couldn't quite wrap their head around his transcript. Basically, they wanted four years of transcripts and there were only three. You only have three years of high school in France.

"I wasn't going to help Miami, because we had figured out his transcript."

Bottom line: Gonzaga engineered a change in Turiaf's plane ticket and he flew back to Paris, never taking the visit to the Hurricanes. To this day, it's a lively point of discussion between Lloyd and Turiaf.

"Best thing anybody ever did for you," Lloyd tells Turiaf, "because if I let you go on that Miami visit, you probably end up going to Miami and don't have this Gonzaga experience."

Turiaf agrees, but not without the obligatory arrow aimed at Lloyd.

"He lied; he lied," Turiaf says before retreating. "Let me just take that back. From my understanding, he did not tell the whole truth.

He knew; he's a smart guy. He knew that if I went to Miami, I probably would have signed there. I think Darius Rice [a big man who averaged double figures all four years] was there at the time. The facilities there . . . being close to my family was very important to me. So I think I would have made the decision to go there. And so . . . Tommy did his job.

"That's why Tommy is so great at recruiting. He understands how the system works. He takes pride in understanding how the system works, what the schooling system overseas looks like and how does that transfer to America. He does his job and I guess Miami didn't do their job."

Now Turiaf turns playful, mimicking a mystery-theater musical riff before posing this question: "What would have happened if Ronny Turiaf had gone to Miami?"

Well, it surely would have diluted the second wave of talent (Dan Dickau, Blake Stepp) that helped define Gonzaga as an emerging, legitimate program. And it would have deprived the program of not only 13.6 points and 6.8 rebounds a game over Turiaf's four seasons, but a whimsical, almost mythic figure.

Back then, there was a ribald TV show called "Jackass" built around frat-boy humor. It featured a character named Party Boy, whose signature move was striptease. "Ronny liked to follow the lead of Party Boy," says former teammate David Pendergraft, laughing. "He used to dance around with not very many clothes on, mostly in the locker room. All of a sudden, it's just out of the shower. It brought a lot of laughter and fun. He knew when to bring it."

Now Turiaf's long NBA career is behind him, and he concedes that – notwithstanding Tommy Lloyd's proprietary maneuvers – he wouldn't change a lot.

"I think I made a good choice," he says. "I think Gonzaga made a good choice, too."

Turiaf reinforced that Lloyd's hustle could work. He was young, his energy was boundless. This was what he wanted to do. Human sales, he called it, selling the opportunity and experience at Gonzaga.

Of course, Lloyd was naïve; there were other people out there beating the streets for players, and sometimes it didn't matter how many phone calls you made or how many hours you put in – *whether you actually did a better recruiting job than the next guy* – the kid might end up elsewhere. As enthralling as it was, it could also be devastating. He didn't always know how to manage his time, didn't recognize when the better option was to cut bait and move on.

"Recruiting is one of those things, you put your heart and soul into it, especially when you're young," he says. "You've got to get used to getting kicked in the nuts. You've got to get back up and dust yourself off."

Those early years, he could beat himself up. If he was convinced the only place for a certain recruit was Gonzaga, and the recruit went somewhere else, he'd wonder: *Where did I go wrong? Why didn't I make him see?* A year after Turiaf came to GU, Lloyd was hot on the trail of Christian Drejer, a Danish swingman who chose Florida instead. Lloyd was crushed.

"I just remember emotionally getting caught up in the recruiting stuff, working at all hours of the night, becoming almost obsessive with it," Lloyd says. "To where your family's going, 'Why are you talking to these teenage boys when you could be hanging out with us?'"

He grew to be more efficient, if no less determined. Instead of spending time with eight people with connections to a recruit, he'd focus on a couple who mattered. When he scouted, he didn't try to watch all 10 tapes of an opponent. He'd pick four.

His recruiting reach was almost ridiculous: Europe, Canada, the States. Sometimes he was the point man on a recruit, sometimes it was more of a group effort. They don't post scoreboards for assistant coaches' recruiting successes, but say this: If they had a plus-minus quotient for coaches like they do player minutes on the floor, Lloyd would be a smash.

Not that they all worked out; far from it. Lloyd doggedly tracked Theo Davis' tortuous path from Ontario, Canada to the United States, but at Gonzaga, Davis got injured, never seemed fully engaged and washed out. Similarly, Zag followers soared and sagged with every new development in the story of Bol Kong, a swingman from Sudan whose family left his strife-torn country and settled in Canada. Lloyd helped shepherd Kong through a long process of obtaining a visa to play collegiately in the U.S., only to discover that, once he arrived, his motor was missing.

All the while, though, Lloyd's network of contacts grew. Dominoes followed after the Turiaf experience, and Lloyd began to be a regular presence at European spring and summer tournaments. A few years later, Lloyd would do the legwork on Elias Harris in Germany and Przemek Karnowski in Poland and Domantas Sabonis in Spain.

Why does it work? Perhaps the earliest roots of Gonzaga's recruiting success overseas go as far back as Jackie and Dale Lloyd's home in Kelso, where the Lloyd boys learned about different cultures from foreign-exchange students. For 10 straight years, they hosted one – a Japanese boy, three girls from Sweden, others from Finland, Germany, The Netherlands and Russia.

Then there's Lloyd's magnetism. Seemingly, he could sell snow tires in San Diego. Says Reinland, his old mentor, "In all the years I coached Tommy, I don't know that I ever saw him down, no matter how badly he played or how things were going."

Bill Bakamus' son Rem learned first-hand about Lloyd's lighter side several years before he became a Gonzaga reserve. He was early in high school then, and the Bakamuses and Lloyd and his son Liam, then in grade school, were going to attend a Seattle Seahawks home game.

Outside CenturyLink Field, there was a face-painting booth. Liam Lloyd wanted a Teenage Mutant Ninja Turtles look, but Rem

Bakamus backed off warily. So Tommy Lloyd assured him that after the kids got painted, their dads would follow suit. Reluctantly, Rem submitted to the artwork.

"Then Tom snaps his fingers, 'Aw, hey guys, looks like we're running out of time, we gotta go,'" says Bill Bakamus, hooting at the recollection. "Tom called Rem 'Donatello' the whole game. It was classic."

Lloyd's upbeat personality might suggest more snake oil than substance, which is inaccurate. When Lloyd goes to Europe, it's not on a flier, but with a plan. Sabonis recalls how Lloyd arrived with video of Gonzaga's former big men from overseas. He had done his homework, and when Sabonis made his official visit to Spokane, hosted by David Stockton, he remembered it for things like a river-rafting trip as opposed to the "meeting-meeting-meeting" agenda he recalled on his other visits.

The history of success overseas – the track record – is pivotal to Gonzaga's inroads there. It acts as an equalizer to the edge in reputation a program like North Carolina or Louisville or Michigan State holds in the States. Overseas, name brand isn't as critical as a smaller enrollment, a superior teacher-to-student ratio or the legacy of foreigners who have succeeded at Gonzaga.

Casting a wide net has become synonymous with Gonzaga, but the philosophy underlying it is even older. Says Lloyd, referring to Few, "One of his greatest strengths is, he thinks we should be good every year. If we can't find a guy, or we miss on a kid, somebody somewhere is what we're looking for. Let's go 'til we find him."

In 2016-17, Lloyd will become the Zags' longest-tenured assistant coach – of modern times, and very likely, through the sweep of history. He got that way by being willing, even eager, to travel to Europe. The number of his trans-oceanic forays is approaching 30.

"Yeah, it is a long trip," he says. "But to go back to the East Coast is a long trip. Hey, if it's where you've got to go to get the players to be competitive, you do it gladly. I've done it so many times, I just deal with it. I love it, actually. You kind of get over there, smell that European air with the cigarettes in it, the open-air cafes . . . it kind of re-energizes me."

So it figures that he travels easily. He knows where to get the best doner kebab. He knows enough German to get by, a little less French. He can solve problems on the fly. Even when Eyjafjallajokull, the vexing and nigh-unspellable Icelandic volcano, blows up.

On that trip, he was seeing two future Gonzaga players, Mathis Keita in France and Mathis Moenninghoff in Germany, as well as a second prospect in France and another in Denmark. After doing the French leg, he was supposed to fly to Berlin, but planes were grounded and he opted to drive to Cologne. That's where he had to eat the 500-euro rental-car drop charge.

Then, a train to Berlin, and another to Copenhagen. He was gassed. He hadn't slept. The train was jammed, bloated by would-be air travelers. He asked a Swedish family if he could crash underneath their seat bench, and he spent the next five hours with his nose inches from his benefactor's backside.

He made it to Copenhagen to get his flight back to Spokane. The woman behind the counter outlined a departure – in eight days. Not good. But there was a flight out of Amsterdam in two days, and he could take a train there, get home and be able to tell another story you won't hear from Rick Steves.

Thus invested, what Lloyd and the Zags got out of that deal were two marginal talents in Keita and Moenninghoff, who had modest careers at Gonzaga. That's recruiting.

Fortunately, the returns are often better, in the U.S. and abroad. Counterintuitively, perhaps, Lloyd believes Gonzaga's relatively isolated locale – almost 300 miles from the nearest metropolitan city, Seattle – has worked in the Zags' favor.

"I think if you put a school like Gonzaga in a major city on the East Coast, and you have a good player, the competition is going to be thick," he says. "Here, yeah, there's competition, but I don't think it's quite as thick."

The flip side of being surrounded by wheatfields and forests is that the Zags have a captive audience. Says Lloyd, "We can show people, 'Look at this arena. This isn't just the big games, this is every game.' You could lie down in the middle of Division [Street], and you probably wouldn't get run over, because they're either at the game, or they're somewhere watching the game. It's a huge deal, and I think kids love that, being a part of something that's big."

Lloyd is the Zags' latest coach-in-waiting, the heir to Few's chair whenever that day comes. When the West Coast Conference underwent its 2016 convulsion with four coaching changes, Lloyd was approached by a couple of schools. Those WCC programs tend to be cautionary tales, but athletic director Mike Roth nevertheless headed off any potential trouble. Says Lloyd, "It didn't hinge on me getting an offer. He wanted to give me what he thought I deserved. He did a great job making it tough for me to consider a lot of options."

"My thought is," says Bakamus, Lloyd's longtime friend, "he wants to be the head coach at Gonzaga."

When that time comes, one thing will be indisputable: Tommy Lloyd will deserve it.

– 5 –
THE OTHER ZAGS

IT'S A SUNNY SPRING MORNING in 2015 after another NCAA Sweet 16 appearance by the Gonzaga women, and the first-year coach is explaining why the Zag program appears to be on the same track it was under the previous coach.

Lisa Fortier has a large cup of coffee in hand, which is understandable, given that nights are short and demands on her time unstinting. Two months after being named to her first head-coaching position, she gave birth for the third time. The kids are still moppets, blissfully oblivious to the NCAA recruiting windows or contingencies like West Coast Conference meetings.

Seated in a chair across from Fortier is one of her assistant coaches who knows all about the crush of juggling a job with three young kids, inasmuch as he's Craig Fortier, Lisa's husband. More than just about any other partners, they're in this together, the competitive, can-do multitasking head coach and the ardent, supportive spouse/alter-ego, who isn't shy about leavening the conversation with a wisecrack.

They grew up in the foothills of the California gold country, where, says Craig, his family moved to the town of Cool. Yes, Cool.

"There's one flashing light," says Lisa. "Think it's still there?"

"The town?" asks Craig innocently.

"No, the flashing red light."

"I left," Craig says, "but the town kept going."

"Imagine that."

One of the Zags' men's coaches' kids is nosing at Lisa's office door, prowling for a handout from the candy jar on her desk.

"Can you give me one second?" she asks. "I think it's Parker."

"As long as it's not our kids," says Craig.

Their bond is palpable, from the ability to manage family and job to the mutual respect necessary in working through a fundamental issue in their professional lives: How do they capitalize on an opportunity for her (or him) while keeping alive the career goals of the other? Can you have it both ways professionally?

That's an equation still to be worked out, but at least it will spring from a strong foundation.

"People talk about, 'I love my boss,'" says Craig. "No, I do actually love my boss."

The best moments of the two-year Lisa Fortier regime almost didn't happen. In the semifinals of the 2015 WCC tournament, the Zags coughed up a 12-point, second-half lead and lost to BYU. Afterward, when she was asked how she viewed Gonzaga's chances to be selected at-large for the NCAA tournament, she struck a pessimistic chord.

But in the week preceding the NCAA selections, Fortier's hope grew, and indeed, Gonzaga got in. And then it proceeded to take down George Washington and Pac-12 champion Oregon State on its home floor. That gifted the Zags the stunning benefit of a round-of-16 game at Spokane Arena against Tennessee, and only after Gonzaga wilted in the late stages after owning a 17-point lead with six minutes left did its season finally die.

For a long time, Fortier wouldn't look at that Tennessee tape. Well, she did sneak a peek at a sequence down the stretch to confirm a suspicion that the Lady Vols got a break on a non-traveling call.

When it was done, the Zags had finished 26-8, they had won the WCC regular-season title at 16-2, they had played into the second weekend of the NCAA tournament, and they had averaged more than 5,300 fans a game.

In other words, they had done a lot of the same things that the guy preceding Fortier had done.

Kelly Graves stretches back in his chair, sporting a black T-shirt with a large yellow "O" on it. Mike Bellotti, the football coach who had a heavy hand in building the University of Oregon program, used to occupy this Casanova Center office, from where you can see part of the south deck of Autzen Stadium.

Months after he departed Gonzaga to become head women's coach at Oregon, Graves was still referring to the Zags as "We." That's the byproduct of his 14 years at Gonzaga, where, if he didn't do it all, he did most of it. Got the Zags to their first NCAA tournament. Took them to seven NCAAs over his last eight seasons. Went to a couple of Sweet 16s and an Elite Eight. Won the West Coast Conference's coach-of-the-year award eight times.

Indisputably, even as he's now awash in all things lemon and green, Graves is the godfather of GU women's basketball.

Referring to that 2010-12 period of Sweet 16s sandwiching an Elite Eight, he says with pride, "In the history of the Pac-12, only two programs were able to have that same kind of success – Cheryl Miller and USC (1983-86) and Stanford on several occasions."

The success of the Zag men had a part in establishing the women's program. Some of Graves' early recruits to GU say the madcap postseason runs of the men from 1999-2001 at least provided a name familiarity. And the scarcity of tickets to the men's games, and the relative affordability of the women's seats, attracted fans to that side.

But Graves cut a far different figure in public than the guarded Mark Few, the men's coach.

"That's one of the things I do well," he says. "I shake hands, I kiss babies. I promote. I'm accessible to people."

And ultimately, more than the stylistic differences, Graves took a career path in sharp contrast to that of Few. Graves began to sense that the women's program was losing – and would continue to lose – too many high-level recruits to conferences like the Pac-12.

Graves recalls being in the southern California home of Kelsey Plum, the point guard who would go on to a fine career at Washington. Graves put forth his best pitch for Gonzaga.

"But," Plum's father said, "it's the WCC."

"It's not the WCC," Graves responded stubbornly. "It's Gonzaga."

Graves would lose that debate. It was one that was increasingly wearing him down.

Washington had reached out to him in 2011 about its coaching vacancy, but he was in the middle of a strong run at Gonzaga, and there was the prickliness of leaving to coach an in-state rival. Oregon was different – a bit out of the area, fueled by Nike baron Phil Knight, and Graves and his wife had cherished his years as an assistant coach at the University of Portland.

So he left Gonzaga having taken the program to places it had never gone before. Back in 1987-88, the Zags, in their second year as a Division I entity, won the regular-season WCC title (under coach Mike Petersen, who, ironically, had been an assistant at Oregon). But Petersen left in 1989, and the program knew only fallow seasons through the rest of the century, save for a 21-10 record and NIT appearance in 1993-94 under Julie Holt.

By 2000, GU athletic director Mike Roth was hosting a coach from Saint Mary's at Spencer Steakhouse in downtown Spokane and telling him, "I want our women's team to be as good as our men's."

"That was pretty powerful," said Graves, recalling that steak dinner. "He had a vision."

Graves grew up in Kaysville, Utah, raised Mormon. "Who isn't in Utah?" he says. "It's a great way of life, though. I loved it. Every Mormon church has a gym."

His father, a teacher at Salt Lake Community College, was a ticket-taker at the University of Utah's Special Events Center, where the Utes would attract nationally recognized programs. Kelly would tag along, and as a junior-high kid in the late 1970s, he was an usher – "the worst usher in the world. All I did was watch the games."

He became a college prospect, although not in the eyes of most of the teams in his beloved Western Athletic Conference. So he committed to Weber State and, back in the era when coaches could sign players in person, the Wildcats promised to dispatch one to him on Wednesday, signing day.

Neil McCarthy was the head coach at Weber State, considered sort of an odd duck in his profession. Wednesday came and went, and no Weber coach. Thursday, nothing. Graves and his first-year coach, Mark Poth, were flummoxed. Finally, they made an inquiry and were told Weber had reconsidered and pulled the offer.

So Graves veered off to Ricks College for a year, put in a church mission in Santiago, Chile, and returned to Ricks for the 1984-85 season, where he caught the eye of New Mexico.

Brazenly, Weber State also knocked on Graves' door. "I told my coach (at Ricks); he knew the whole story," Graves says. "He goes, 'You guys are kidding, right?' They said, 'No, no.' He said, 'Well, good luck.'"

At the time, New Mexico coach Gary Colson was trying to make inroads into Brigham Young's dominance in recruiting Mormon prospects; although not a Mormon, Colson related to their beliefs and their commitment. And, well, he needed a shooter.

While Graves was being recruited, so was Colson. He interviewed for the University of Washington job vacated because the Huskies had forced out veteran Marv Harshman. In fact, *The Seattle Post-*

Intelligencer reported that Washington had struck a deal with Colson that would be announced shortly.

Colson had told Graves he wanted him to join him at Washington if he took the job, but that never came to pass. The Huskies hired Andy Russo, and Colson coached three more seasons at New Mexico.

That was fine with Graves, who had an affinity for the Lobos from the fine teams he had seen them bring to Salt Lake City. This time, signing day was much more pleasant, and when Larry Shyatt, then an assistant to Colson, came to make it official, Graves evinced his trademark sense of humor.

"Where's the head coach?" asked Graves, feigning umbrage.

"He's in Lawton, Okla.," Shyatt said, putting Graves in his place, "trying to sign Stacey King."

On teams that played in the National Invitation Tournament, Graves struggled as a junior, but had a productive senior year, starting all 34 games and hitting 42.8 percent from distance in the debut year of the three-point shot.

"He wasn't as good as Stephen Curry, but he was good," says Colson. "Kelly was our go-to guy on the wing. He brought so much to the table. I don't ever remember him being down. He was always up, always smiling, always positive. If he missed two or three shots, that wasn't going to get him down.

"Kelly and I became more than just coach and player. It was like he was my son."

Once, Graves figured himself to become an attorney. During his senior season, he took the LSAT on the same day the Lobos had a game at Colorado State. But the plan to rush him to the Albuquerque airport got a little too tight, and he skipped the last section and a half of the test.

"I figured, 'Come on, I'm a Lobo star,' so I didn't think that much of it," Graves said. "I wanted to stay at UNM and go to UNM law school."

The dean of the law school, albeit a Lobos fan, wasn't amused.

"Do I have a chance to get in?" Graves asked.

"Not unless you're a Navajo woman," the dean replied. "No way we can let you in with this score."

Graves' interest in law school began to wane and Colson offered him a graduate assistant's position. Colson was gone the next year and Graves had the chance to stay on with Dave Bliss' new staff, but declined. "I felt I should be loyal to Gary," he says. "I didn't think long-term, but I loved Gary that much."

By this time, Poth, his high school coach in Utah, had taken a job at Big Bend Community College in Moses Lake, Washington. Poth made the place sound like Nirvana.

"Kelly, I live on the lake, we only have four-day school weeks, you'll love it," Poth said.

Graves had never been to Washington, the Evergreen State, but he bit on the offer. Driving west toward his new home, he was haunted by a question: "Where are the trees?"

At Big Bend, Graves was going to assist Poth, but the women's coach resigned shortly before the season began and, without time to seek a replacement, the school offered Graves the chance to head the women's program. Thus was a career launched.

"It was an extra $2,500, I was young and we played double-headers, so it just meant I had to show up a little earlier," Graves said. "I loved it."

He joined Jim Sollars at the University of Portland in 1992, and two decades later, he says, "It may be the favorite place I've ever coached." Portland was where he met his wife Mary, where they had their first two of three children, where they bought their first home. In his time there, the Pilots had all four of their NCAA-tournament appearances.

Graves could recruit. Sollars once told me Graves sold himself to the UP head coach by telling him that he bettered all his missionary colleagues in Chile in persuading converts to the LDS church. "He recruits with a religious zeal," Sollars said.

The Portland years augured Graves' first major-college head coaching job at Saint Mary's. From 1998 to 2000, the Gaels had 20-win seasons, spiced by the school's first NCAA appearance in '99.

But there were limitations in Moraga, Calif. For one, there was talk of a new arena to replace St. Mary's small, 3,500-seat McKeon Pavilion, but that's all it was – talk.

"They were going to build this arena," Graves says. "Build it, build it, build it. Well, it's still not built."

Graves and his wife were unable to get their kids into Catholic school, their preference, because it was too full. Meanwhile, Mary had multiple family ties in the Spokane area.

Competitively, the Zags were at the end of the rope. Under former Washington State assistant Kellee Barney, Gonzaga won but 45 games in a six-year stretch from 1995 to 2000, including a 17-67 record in West Coast Conference play. Anybody who could see through that darkness to the glory days ahead would have needed military-grade binoculars.

"They were pretty bad," says Shannon Mathews, a guard who would eventually aid the program's revival. "You can say it."

It was Barney, ironically, who, after her dismissal, tipped Roth that he might want to give Graves a call. He reached Graves, who was in Arizona indulging a passion – watching spring-training baseball with his dad.

Another night, Roth called the Graves home, intending to woo the coach, who was out. So Roth recruited Mary Graves.

The money wasn't great, but it looked a lot better against the inflated Bay Area housing market. Roth offered almost exactly what Graves was making at Saint Mary's.

"We figured out the cost of living," Graves says. "It essentially doubled my salary. Happy wife, happy life. I liked it there (at Saint Mary's) a lot, but we needed a change."

As much as the Graves family might have needed a change, it was nothing compared to the transfusion of energy Gonzaga was seeking. Fan interest mirrored the play on the floor, and it wouldn't change overnight. Graves still has a photograph taken by the father of a player during his first year, blown up, that the coach labeled "The Beginning." Graves is in the middle of a timeout huddle, preaching, while some of his players are looking vacantly around the old Kennel. Which was itself vacant in the photo – "with like three or four people on the other side of the stands," Graves says.

Things would be different, as the dreaded, obligatory culture change had to take place. For one, Graves discovered that players would routinely take five years to graduate. He quickly implemented four-year cycles.

Fortunately, the Zags had had heavy senior attrition upon Barney's departure, so as Graves says, "We had a lot of cap space, so to speak."

And a lot of growing pains ahead.

A couple of headlines on the Gonzaga website that year describe the 2000-01 season. Early in February, it was "Zag Women in Search of First Conference Win." A week later, the headline was, "Zag Women Still in Search of First WCC Win."

With an already short roster depleted by several injuries, Gonzaga limped to a 5-23 record and went winless in the WCC. Graves' go-to joke on that season: "Don't let the record fool you. We weren't that good."

It didn't help that the Saint Mary's program Graves left went 26-6 and won the school's first game in history in the NCAA tournament. The Gaels beat Gonzaga convincingly three times that year, including a 62-36 clunker at the Kennel in which the Zags trailed 32-6 at half, shooting 10.7 percent before intermission.

Part of Graves' abbreviated recruiting class in the spring of 2000 included a guard, Triana Allen, who would eventually coach for him. Graves recruited Allen out of a junior college for Saint Mary's, backed off her when he signed another player, and then beckoned her to Gonzaga. Allen would do a lot of heavy lifting for Graves, a player who would help establish the foundation yet wouldn't realize the spoils of the future.

"It was really, really tough to see that people didn't want it as bad as I did, or Coach did, or maybe some other people did," says Allen, now an attorney in Los Angeles. "A lot of people talk the game but won't put in the work to get the results. Oh yeah, there were fights in the locker room, fights on the court. I got kicked out of practice a number of times. There were certain players that were very much OK with having gotten a scholarship to Gonzaga. That was very, very difficult to deal with. There was some selfishness on that team, because it was a new coaching staff coming in with a new way of doing things, and every player didn't buy into it."

This was a time when the dichotomy between the men's and women's programs was never greater. The men had just come off their breakthrough Elite Eight and first Sweet 16 season, and were about to crash another round of 16. The women were, well, scarcely a rumor.

"I do remember Kelly constantly reminding us," says Allen, "'This is not what it's gonna be.'"

Allen recalls Graves being relatively patient with that first team. There was, after all, little point in beating it into the ground, since its nucleus would shortly be gone and he had plenty of available scholarships. "I think he knew exactly what he was getting into," says Allen. "He had just coached against this team for the past three or four seasons. He was like, 'Well, get through the season, get my players the following year.'"

Done. Graves attracted a recruiting class of six – guards Shannon Mathews, Raeanna Jewell, Delphine Lecoultre and Sara Steblaj, swing player Juliann Laney and up front, Ashley Burke.

That class's impact would be staggering. Burke, from North Vancouver, B.C., would win WCC first-team honors three times,

Mathews twice. Today, Burke is No. 6 on the GU career points list, No. 7 in rebounds, while Mathews is No. 13 in scoring and Jewell 18th.

Mathews was the Zags' career assist leader until somebody named Courtney Vandersloot came along. Recruited from Riverside, Calif., Mathews was WCC player of the year in 2005.

No doubt that class was born of necessity and hard work. But good fortune also played a part. Burke was planning to go to nearby Simon Fraser, but the mother of one of Graves' assistants, J.R. Payne, happened to see her play, leading to interest from the Zags. Burke and her father visited campus, and today, she says, "It sounds so cliché, but I just kind of fell in love with everything about it."

On the drive home from Spokane, Burke told her father, "I think I want to go there."

"He just about drove off the road," she says.

Burke's path at Gonzaga was reflective of the urgency that had come to the program. If you had promise, you played. She had expected to be a bench player as a freshman but on the day of the opener, Graves took her aside and said, "I'm going to start you tonight. You're one of the biggest surprises I've had."

It was sink or swim, and the patience that Graves had exhibited his first year was largely gone. This was the nucleus of what would be the program's turnaround, so habits would either be good or bad.

"There was no mercy because we were freshmen," says Burke. "He needed us to be more than that. I remember practices (where) we just ran. Every time there was a mistake, we ran and ran and ran."

Says Mathews, "He really pushed us. We got heavy minutes. He just threw us in and worked us to death."

Against a soft schedule befitting a fragile roster, Gonzaga started 6-5 before there was a long break between games in the latter half of December. One day, the team entered the practice gym and found an unsmiling Graves, hell-bent on establishing his foundation.

There was a drill in which a player drove full-court with a defender stationed in the key, forbidden to retreat even a step.

"We spent that day doing defense almost exclusively," Mathews recalls. "Personally, I spent about half the practice running. And you weren't just running, you were running with all four coaches yelling at you, that you can't do the drill."

The young Zags tumbled to an 11-18 record, just 2-14 in the WCC. But the cornerstone had been laid, even if the season was fitful.

Allen remembers it as something less. The hard reality had sunk in that she wasn't really part of the future, more like a place-holder.

"That was the year he finally got a full class of his players," she says of Graves. "For me, I always felt I was just a filler; 'Now you got your girls.' It was actually probably my worst season. But I battled."

By the 2002-03 season, the most rugged part of the rebuild was behind Gonzaga. The loss the year before at Washington State with that freshman-laden team turned into a 20-point victory. The defeat at Boise State preceding the memorable Christmas-break practices became a 27-point win over the Broncos at the Kennel.

GU finished 18-12, tying for second in the WCC at 9-5, its first winning season since 1994. The culture had shifted. Players stayed to work out over the summer, taking a cue from mainstays from the men's program like Dan Dickau and Kyle Bankhead. Even John Stockton would come by.

"We really, really jelled," says Allen. "Now we were kind of angry, we had a chip on our shoulder. 'We're not the Gonzaga that was here two years ago, and we're about to show you.'"

More help was on the way, in the form of front-court players like eastern Oregonians Ashley Anderson and Stephanie Hawk. By 2004-05, everything seemed in place for Gonzaga's first NCAA-tournament appearance.

The long process of total buy-in crested in the off-season after 2004, when players made a Lent-like sacrifice, determining they would give up something important to them. Mathews, who would regularly visit a gas-station mini-mart and bore in on a 32-ounce Coca-Cola, opted to forgo soda, a practice she continues today. The change in her preseason conditioning was apparent.

The Zags incurred blowout losses early at New Mexico and Arizona State, but in December, they launched a 23-game winning streak, sweeping the 14-game WCC schedule and flattening five league opponents by 20 points or more.

But disaster struck in the semifinals of the WCC tournament against Pepperdine. Mathews sprained an ankle midway through the first half of a 58-40 victory, and despite considerable stimulation, icing and massage treatments, was severely limited in the finale against Santa Clara, playing 18 minutes. Meanwhile, Santa Clara bombed from outside, hitting 14 of 26 threes, and won 77-67 on its home floor. If the season had been a magic-carpet ride, the Zags just had the rug pulled from under them.

"We hurt, not having Shannon," says Burke. "She was such a big presence for us. We ran a lot of stuff together, a lot of pick-and-rolls."

Selection Sunday remained. Could the selection committee snub a team that went 28-3 and lost only to squads headed to the tournament?

As it turned out, it could. No matter how ascendant the arc of Gonzaga women's hoops, that day holds a place in infamy.

"I still get bitter about it," says Mathews.

"It was tough," says Graves. "This is their senior year [for his foundational class], and I just really wanted them to be rewarded. I actually talked to somebody on the committee a couple of years later, and she admitted they'd made a mistake. But we had no history."

Soon enough, they would.

The breakthrough wouldn't come in 2006. The foundational class that entered Gonzaga in 2001 was gone, and after a 3-9 start against a daunting schedule, the Zags finished 16-14, even as they tied with Santa Clara for the WCC regular-season title.

A year later, the planets aligned. In November 2005, Graves and his staff had signed another bellwether class that included forwards Heather Bowman of Spokane's Lewis and Clark High and Vivian Frieson of Garfield in Seattle. Bowman would go on to have a prolific career at Gonzaga, rising to the top of the scoring list with 2,165 points, becoming a rare four-time all-WCC performer, while Frieson finished as the No. 3 career rebounder who twice landed on the all-league team.

Just as a competitive lag in the programs at Washington and Washington State had helped launch the Gonzaga men around the turn of the century, the GU women availed themselves of a similar regional opportunity. Under June Daugherty, Washington went to the Elite Eight in 2001, but in the next six years, won only one NCAA game, and Daugherty eventually fell out of favor, giving way to the lamentable regime of Tia Jackson. Washington State, after an NCAA-tournament appearance in 1991, wouldn't get back in the next quarter-century. Oregon and Oregon State had winning league records in 2002 but struggled most of the rest of the decade.

"We were starting now to attract kids who had BCS-school offers," Graves says. "We became kind of that option in the Northwest."

In Portland at the WCC tournament, Gonzaga crashed its first NCAA with an exclamation mark – the Zags thundered past Portland, San Francisco and Loyola Marymount, beating all three by double digits. Bowman, Hawk and sophomore guard Jami Bjorklund made the all-tournament team and GU held LMU to 29-percent shooting in the final.

But March Madness is a fickle temptress. Gonzaga's first advance into an NCAA women's bracket ended ghoulishly with an 85-46 loss to Middle Tennessee State, a game in which the Zags committed an unthinkable 37 turnovers.

On a post-game interview podium, Graves tried to see past the immediate carnage. Nothing is so conflicted as the losing side after an NCAA-tournament game, bringing together notes of achievement, regret, pride and melancholy all in one unholy little package.

Near the end, Graves said, "I anticipate this isn't going to be the last people see of Gonzaga."

He got that right. Four months earlier, Gonzaga had signed Vandersloot, a player who would render nil the danger of a 37-turnover game, one who would change the face of the program.

On the evening that Gonzaga lost to Middle Tennessee State in its first NCAA tournament game in 2007, a forlorn figure listened over the Internet in northern Colorado, dropping her head to a table and groaning. For much of the game, Gonzaga turnovers outnumbered points.

The outcome cut deeply for Lisa Fortier, who knew the Gonzaga program intimately, having spent two years as its director of basketball operations. She was in a different time zone, on a different job now, but part of her was still riding the highs and lows of the Zags.

She grew up in Grass Valley, Calif., a town in the western foothills of the Sierra Nevada. Lisa Mispley was always a high-achiever – a basketball and track performer and a student who would earn magna cum laude honors in college.

Mispley began at Bear River High in Grass Valley, but, projecting a greater role at Placer High in Auburn 24 miles away, she transferred for her senior year. There, a guard named Craig Fortier was carving a circuitous route in basketball: Cut as a ninth-grader, JV player as a sophomore, cut again as a junior, all-league as a senior.

They found themselves hanging out with each other the summer before college, which was going to take Lisa to Butte Community

College in Oroville 90 minutes north, and Craig to Sierra Community College in Rocklin, 14 miles from Auburn.

Mispley pointed herself toward a career as an English teacher and coach. She was the hardest worker on the basketball team, so it wasn't a surprise when, one night in a game at Porterville College, she took off in pursuit of a Porterville breakaway, landed wrong and tore an anterior cruciate ligament.

She rehabilitated the knee in Auburn, which served to increase the occasions when Mispley would see Fortier. She sat out her sophomore season recovering from the injury, returned for a third year and helped Butte to the state tournament. She played off-guard, but also swung to front-court positions where her grit allowed her to compete, though undersized. Her signature act was charges taken; she recorded upwards of 100 in junior college.

"She's a grinder, not afraid to do the dirty work," says Joddie Gleason, her coach at Butte. "You never had to worry about her going to class or being dumb off the court."

By Mispley's third season, Craig Fortier had moved on to Cal State University-Monterey Bay, a service-based school founded in 1994 after the shuttering of the Fort Ord Army base. By then, the two were dating but hardly inseparable.

"I was recruiting her a little," says Craig. "I don't think she came because of me. I don't think it hurt."

"I was trying not to make that decision based on him," says Lisa, conceding that "it didn't hurt that he was there."

She chose CSUMB. The two played college basketball at the NAIA level, hard by the Pacific Ocean. She could see the water from her porch, and one year, she took a surfing class. Craig, meanwhile, had designs for a time on becoming a sportswriter – "He's a really good writer," Lisa says – but veered into believing he wanted to coach.

They got degrees in human communications from CSUMB, they dated, and they faced a happily uncertain future. Then came a stroke of pure luck, one that would ultimately rearrange the women's coaching offices at Gonzaga.

In Monterey, there was a publisher named Jim Peterson, one of whose pursuits is a series of books and videos called Coaches Choice. His business employed lots of CSUMB students, whose job was primarily to affix stickers to VHS tapes describing what was inside.

Peterson had more luck hiring players from the CSUMB women's program than the men's. So it was that Lisa hooked on part-time at his business, and she managed to persuade Peterson to hire Craig as well – soured though Peterson was with the work ethic of many of the men's players.

"It was more about just not being an idiot," Craig says.

Mispley and Fortier won Peterson's respect, and in time, they came to learn of Jerry Krause.

Krause is the fellow who bookishly tracked analytics on the Gonzaga men's bench in recent years as its director of basketball operations, had a presence on the game's rules committee, coached at Eastern Washington, advocated for a campaign to enforce a standard tension on basketball rims, did stints as a civilian professor at West Point and has conducted clinics in Europe, South America and the Pacific Rim.

Krause has also been a consistent contributor to Peterson's Coaches Choice series, part of a prolific avocation as an author. When I asked Krause a few years ago how many books he had done, he said, "Over thirty-some."

With degrees in hand, Mispley and Fortier were looking for graduate assistant positions.

"Peterson kept saying, 'You guys need to check out Gonzaga, this is where Krause is,'" says Lisa.

Krause recalls the message from his old friend Peterson: "I've got these two young people working for me. They're the most reliable people I've ever seen. They want to go to graduate school. I'm going to fly 'em up from San Francisco if you'll put 'em up in a motel."

Truth be told, Gonzaga didn't seem to be much of a match for either aspiring coach in 2004. The private-school tuition was a killer, Krause explained to them that there was no assistantship program, and money from summer camps would be minimal.

"Of course," Krause says, "that made them more determined."

Mispley found the head women's coach, Graves, receptive to office help. She did odd jobs, from ordering gear to film exchange to supervising ballgirls. The role kept expanding and she got a broad-based introduction to coaching. For his part, Craig Fortier found an immediate role in the men's program with its summer camps.

The existence was spartan, but they were all in. Lisa pulled five-hour shifts waitressing at Chili's three nights a week, and they scrounged a living. Craig fit fluidly on the men's side, if frugally.

"All the guys were great to me," he says, naming assistant coaches then. "They never think you're leaving – Billy [Grier], Leon [Rice], 'You're not leaving; how could you ever leave here?'"

"Well," Fortier recited his standard response, "I'm making no money and I don't really get to coach."

Midway through grad school, the two got engaged, and a year later, just after they were married, came a breakthrough. Northern Colorado was completing the transition to NCAA Division I and the head women's coach, Jaime White, was looking for a young, inexpensive assistant. So threadbare was the budget that the school didn't even fly Lisa Mispley – who had just become Lisa Fortier – in for an interview. It all took place by phone.

Thus began a recurring self-examination by the couple of their respective career goals, and how best to realize them. If both had an eye toward college coaching, could it work? How many locales offer multiple schools with suitable opportunities – and never mind the perfect juxtaposition of challenge and vacancy and timing? Was it inevitable that if one landed at the college level, the other should focus on a high school job?

And oh yeah, where did starting a family figure into all this?

They moved to Fort Collins, Colorado, where Craig Fortier got a job as a video administrative assistant at Colorado State, pulling down all of $3,500. They weren't getting rich, but they were young and in love.

"It was a fun first year of marriage," Lisa says. "A lot of cuddling, because there was no heat."

"We never turned on the heat or the AC the entire year," Craig says.

Dale Layer, the CSU coach, got fired after that season, and Craig worked to get a substitute teaching credential and a high school coaching job. He accepted one at Fort Collins High and was excited about launching his first program.

A few days later, Lisa came home looking ashen. Graves had called, wanting her to rejoin the staff at Gonzaga, where assistant Triana Allen was leaving the program she had helped resuscitate as a player.

"So five days in, I resigned," Craig says. The headline in the local paper was WELL, THAT WAS QUICK.

He called Krause, and then he called Tommy Lloyd, the Gonzaga assistant, who tipped him on a position at Spokane Community College. Twenty minutes later, Lloyd was calling back. There was a vacancy on the staff at Whitworth, the NCAA Division III power in north Spokane. Soon, the Gonzaga men's staff was flooding the phone lines with calls of recommendation to Whitworth coach Jim Hayford.

"Please don't have anybody else call me," Hayford told Fortier. "I've got it."

The Fortiers wedged their belongings into a U-Haul trailer and drove back to Spokane. They went straight to Hayford's home, had dinner and shortly, Craig had a job. For two months, Krause put them up in the guest bedroom of his home on Fish Lake, where they regularly did battle with a large hole in a screened window.

At Gonzaga, Lisa worked primarily with the guards, including four golden years with Vandersloot, and she developed a reputation as a terrific communicator. A few miles north at Whitworth, her husband shaped his playing and coaching experiences to a model without scholarships.

"The thing I thought I could do pretty good was evaluate," says Craig. "I could figure out what they wanted and what he (Hayford) wanted. There is no better recruiting tool, I still think, than winning – and they were winning."

The Pirates continued winning. After four 20-plus win seasons, Hayford moved on to nearby Eastern Washington, and Fortier followed. From a blank canvas, they worked up a program that went to the NCAA tournament in 2015 for only the second time in school history, keyed by an under-recruited guard from southern California, Tyler Harvey.

Fifteen miles east, the Zag women were cutting their own swath, winning seven games in the NCAA tournament from 2010 to 2012. Even if that happened with the frequent backdrop of home cooking – thanks to the host-school perks that remain a part of the women's tournament – that was a height Graves and Roth probably couldn't have foreseen over steaks that night during the 2000 interview.

By then, something novel had taken hold. Gonzaga's women had won fans over, but largely, they were different fans. People who were shut out of sold-out men's games at the McCarthey Athletic Center responded to friendlier ticket prices and an upbeat, enjoyable style. And no doubt, Vandersloot's wizardry was pivotal.

It didn't happen overnight. As recently as 2004, the Gonzaga women ranked only No. 100 in NCAA attendance, and not until 2010 did they crack the top 50, averaging 2,931. But the next two years, they jumped to 25th and then 14th, surpassing the 5,000-fan mark.

Winning is an obvious component. But Graves advances a bold theory for the phenomenon, saying, "I call it 'Our Girls' Syndrome." He notes that nearby programs at Eastern Washington and Washington State, while competitive, struggle to draw.

"But why are we getting it?" he asks. (There's that "we" again.) "People like our players. They're not huge fans of women's basketball. Last year (2013-14), I'll bet 95 percent of our fans couldn't tell you who two of the teams were that went to the Final Four. They're fans of my team, because we recruited good kids, they were good students, they were good citizens, they liked being in the community, they were good team people, they played hard."

Operationally, the Gonzaga women's program didn't always function in a conventional manner.

"I've got to give the administration a lot of credit," Graves says. "There were a couple of years we used all the marketing money for women's basketball. There was really no sense in marketing the men; they were as big as it could get."

Then there was the budget. Or the lack of one. The bean-counters at GU gave Graves a wide berth.

"I never saw a budget in 14 years," he says. "I don't know what we spent. We have one here now [at Oregon]. I've been used to just kind of doing what we needed to do. I mean, we were never excessive. I'm sure we had one. I just didn't really know what it was. We just kind of kept going on trips and spending it."

Graves says that a couple of times before a recruiting trip, he was asked, "Do you really need this?"

"I said, 'Yeah, we really want this player.' They said OK," he remembers. "They were good about that. It was never excessive. A few times, they wanted us to spend money because the men had a bigger recruiting budget and they wanted to justify us having the same. They said, 'You need to spend.'"

But by 2014, Graves was antsy. He needed a new challenge. He interviewed for Oregon in a golf shirt and jeans in Nashville after a long return trip recruiting in Europe, and finally on a Monday in early spring, Graves had an offer in hand. After a visit to the UO campus, he had two plane tickets booked – one home to Spokane, the other to Palm Springs, where his family was vacationing. If he chose the one back home, it would be to tell his team he was leaving.

He picked Spokane.

For a few days, Lisa Fortier's life was a jumble. Would she follow Graves to Oregon? Would the phone interview she had with the University of Portland about its vacant head-coaching position – and the scheduled visit there – result in an offer? Would Roth hew to a familiar pattern at Gonzaga and name Graves' successor in-house?

Late in the week, she had meetings with Roth and GU president Thayne McCulloh, and before the weekend was out, she had her first head coaching job.

Then it got really crazy. The rest of the staff had left. Fortier routinely made the rounds of the departed coaches offices to check e-mails, then plopped down at her own desk. Oh, and by the way, she was seven months pregnant.

"At least it was nice to have a few months to get settled before she came along," Fortier says, referring to her daughter Quincy.

Fortier hired Jordan Green from Idaho and Stacy Clinesmith from Santa Clara, but the last coaching choice was the most intriguing. The Fortiers had talked about coaching on the same staff, but Craig usually ended the conversation with, "Awww, we'll see." Now that the moment was at hand, Lisa was forced to entertain the question: What would it mean for her husband's career?

She sought counsel from an old mentor, Bobbi Bonace, an early athletic director at Cal State-Monterey Bay and later a professor who grew to know both Fortiers from a sports-ethics class she taught. Bonace told her to follow her instincts and her heart.

"Maybe this wouldn't work for a lot of couples," says Bonace, now retired and living in Michigan, "but I thought it would work for them. I love them. I couldn't love them more if they were my kids."

Another source of advice was Gleason, Lisa Fortier's junior college coach. Her husband Skip coached at College of the Redwoods while his wife was at Humboldt State, and they came to learn that the simultaneous highs and lows they were experiencing on the same nights were difficult. Eventually he took a job on her staff.

"We kind of decided to join forces," says Gleason. "I talked to her (Lisa) a lot about it when she was still an assistant. I told her it was not for everybody, but I felt she and Craig had a similar relationship. Not a lot of guys could do that, but Craig doesn't have a big ego."

For Craig, the move simply made sense, exemplified by this observation on his wife: "I've always kind of known she was a superstar." Or as Lisa explains, "We've always been doing this together."

Leaving Eastern Washington could stall a prospective career coaching men's basketball for Craig Fortier. Or it could hasten one coaching women. The possibilities are multiple.

"It was difficult," he says. "But I think all along this is what I needed to do. It's what I wanted to do."

But what about doing this with three young kids?

"She's crazy," cracked Gleason. "Every time I talked to her, it seemed like she was pregnant again."

Those around Lisa Fortier say she's a remarkable multitasker. She must be. "I don't know," Gleason says. "She can just kind of do everything. She's always calm and collected, doesn't get rattled."

They get help. Craig Fortier's mother is in town, and friends pitch in. "The sum is greater than its parts," he says. "We find a way to rassle those three."

Until the kids were about a year old, Lisa took them on the road. On one weekend after we spoke in 2015, Quincy was going to be hauled along on recruiting trips to Virginia, Phoenix and Sacramento for a week. On a couple of visits to recruits' homes, Lisa would line up baby sitters in the area, sometimes an old teammate. Once, as she fulfilled a home visit, her sitter watched as Quincy played on the front lawn.

"Obviously, I can't be in the middle of a presentation and have to say, 'I need more time,'" Lisa says. "I'm not brave enough to take a child into a home visit by myself."

But the Gonzaga women's players have come to learn that this is a big team. Young kids are part of the woodwork. "We hang out with them, draw with them, read to them," says guard Emma Stach.

"They're part of the team," Lisa says. "It's OK with me if somebody doesn't like that. They're not going to come to Gonzaga."

The longest-tenured (by a landslide) women's coach in Gonzaga history, the winningest women's coach in Gonzaga history (by a mile), Graves is now entrenched at Oregon, beginning his third season. The Ducks went 37-28 his first two years, and their 24-11 record in 2016 marked the program's most victories since 1999.

He and Mary settled into a neighborhood of classy older homes only a few blocks south of the Oregon campus. There, he's a popular figure; an irrepressible personality helps to bridge the gap between where his program has been and where he wants it to go.

Meanwhile, around his old school, it can't be said that the parting with Graves was entirely seamless. Surely there are frayed feelings with almost every coaching transition; at their core, they're breakups, and breakups rarely come without some hurt.

Sources say there was more than the expected tension when Graves departed Gonzaga. He and Roth had some differences over the buyout clause in Graves' contract, and there was a disagreement over the use of a courtesy car.

Beyond that, some say Graves didn't win points with his old team when he informed it he was leaving for Eugene. In their eyes, he was too amped about his new destination, too unfeeling about the players to whom he was saying goodbye.

Ask a group of the GU players about that day, and one senses them stiffening.

"It's an awkward thing to come in and tell someone in any job or anything, 'OK, I'm leaving,'" says Lindsay Sherbert, who completed her eligibility in 2015. "It's just awkward. I don't know how else to explain that situation."

However he left, Graves left with a legacy.

"He genuinely cared," says Triana Allen. "Even when I went to law school, he always reached out to me. If there was a phone call I needed, if there was something he needed to do to make sure I was a successful human being, he did it. And I don't think he just did that for me."

Her teammate, Ashley Burke, will remember Graves similarly.

"At times, he was a total hardass, absolutely," she says. "But what great coach isn't? I laughed, I cried, everything at Gonzaga. He's a wonderful person and I feel lucky to have played for him."

Plopping down on a couch in her office, Lisa Fortier apologizes if she sounds a little disjointed. She's been up most of the night at a local hospital, tending to one of her players who was dealing with a kidney infection.

On short rest, she packed hurriedly and got her three kids settled in advance of another recruiting trip that afternoon. She seemed more collected than frazzled.

If anything taught Fortier about adjusting on the fly, it was the 2015-16 season. Her first year as a head coach had been fulfilling and fruitful, bringing a Sweet 16 appearance and the Maggie Dixon Division I rookie coach of the year award from the Women's Basketball Coaches Association. Season No. 2 was a confounding slog of injury setbacks, lineups sabotaged and expectations rearranged.

The Zags might have guessed what kind of star-crossed season was in store as early as their exhibition game, when forward Elle Tinkle, trying to save a ball, got tangled up with a TV cameraman on the baseline and injured cartilage in her knee. A senior all-league player, she elected to have surgery on it in January, taking the chance on the NCAA looking kindly upon her application for a medical redshirt. Indeed, it was granted late in April.

Center Emma Wolfram, a key part of Gonzaga's success the year before, sat out eight games recovering from a shoulder procedure in the off-season. She returned, played eight minutes of an early-December game and tore an ACL. Senior wing Shaniqua Nilles missed the first third of the season as she rehabbed a knee. Forward Kiara Kudron sat out February with a hand injury.

The Zags finished 19-14, 10-8 in league. They lost in the second round of the NIT.

"What can you do?" Fortier says. "You can't feel sorry for yourself. It's not like the 6,000 people that come to games are going to say it's OK if you don't win. Or Mike Roth is going to say, 'It's OK if you don't lose by a bunch.' That's not what we're out here to do. We're out here to get better and play great."

There were other adjustments that reinforced to Fortier that this can be a bruising business.

"We've gone through some situations where the business (side) showed its face, the ugly part of it," Fortier says. "It wasn't easy. When Kelly left, it wasn't as seamless as we thought it was going to be. Some of those kids that didn't end up coming here . . ."

One was Lexi Bando, a guard from Eugene who was released from a letter of intent at Gonzaga to follow Graves to Oregon. Maybe it's the long, productive association with Graves, but Fortier finds that the Zags are frequently recruiting the same players as the Ducks.

So the conversations with Graves, the routine phone calls all old coaching compadres make with one another, tend to be restrained.

"When he left, he's part of another program, so his job is to help another program be successful," Fortier says. "It's not about this program anymore . . . I would say I was his right-hand man. My office is right here, and I swear to you, he spent more time in my office than in this office. And I loved him and he loved me. But when he leaves, it's weird, because you're enemies instantly. Not enemies, but opponents.

"It's awkward a little bit, trying to call and say, 'How's it going? How's recruiting? What should I do here?' You know it's not all being turned around against you, but you just feel guarded. I think both ways – he feels it and I feel it."

As Fortier grows into the job, the battle lines have become sharper. In Eugene, Graves' second Oregon team's 24 wins were one shy of the school record. Meanwhile, Oregon State – another school Gonzaga repeatedly recruits against – and Washington each crashed the Final Four.

Suddenly, the Northwest is teeming with formidable women's basketball programs. But Fortier is 35, and she's trying to sell something the others aren't. Graves is 53, and Washington's Mike Neighbors and OSU's Scott Rueck are each 47. Fortier's job is to sustain winning basketball at Gonzaga, but while she's at it, she can be a powerful example that it's possible to be a mother to three kids and a reliable mentor to a dozen young women.

"I think we're very different from those guys, in university and our approach to the game," she says. "I'm a young, female head coach. [Players] can have a different relationship with me than they can with those male head coaches who are older."

She's young, but after trying years like the last one, seasoning quickly.

"When it happens again, which I'm sure it will, we'll have some experience with it," Fortier says lightly. "I'm going to be coaching at least 40, 50 years, right?"

– 6 –
THE COLOSSAL COURTNEY

AT A COFFEE SHOP in Seattle's Belltown neighborhood, she orders a mocha and two-percent milk and sits down. It's chocolate milk, a kid's drink, and not exactly in keeping with what Courtney Vandersloot says a little later about her maturity as a basketball player.

"I've come into my own, I guess," she says reflectively.

Yeah, in facing down a demanding U.S.-to-Europe regimen and growing her game. In the everlasting campaign to make the players around her better. In interviews, where she is now engaging and expansive, not the reticent undergrad of her early Gonzaga days. In coming to grips with the game at its highest level.

"You know, it takes time," she says. "It's almost like someone can tell you and coach you, but it's kind of like you have to figure it out on your own. Some people do and some people don't. It's tough."

It almost seems startling to think that Vandersloot could find the game a struggle. This was the player who was better than the boys she grew up contesting on the playgrounds. She's the one etched into the NCAA records books for owning the Division I women's season assists record (367) and having the distinction of being the first Division I player, man or woman, to register 2,000 points and 1,000 assists.

She was the player of whom her college coach, Kelly Graves, said, "We'll never see another one like her in our parts."

But in these new parts – the WNBA and Europe following her golden years at Gonzaga – Vandersloot was foundering. At 23, she called home and said she couldn't handle it anymore, that she was ready to be done with the game that she had always shaped so wondrously.

In his office at Lindbergh High School in Renton, Washington, Keith Hennig has mementoes of his basketball past. He played guard at Central Washington in the late 1990s, courted his future wife Wendy there – she played for the Wildcat women's team – and eventually they would land at Kentwood High in suburban Seattle. There, they would team as co-coaches and lead the Conquerers to a state girls championship in 2009, and then, in a move they had planned all along, they would quit basketball to concentrate on raising a family.

High above Hennig's chair, hanging from a heating duct, is a net slung open to display a commemorative basketball from the 2011 WNBA draft, signed by Courtney Vandersloot.

She wasn't much to look at the first time Hennig laid eyes on her, in her early years at a feeder middle school for Kentwood. He would occasionally take the Conquerers there to watch games in the spring and encourage involvement by the youngsters. One of those was a girl Hennig remembers as having braces on her teeth and weighing perhaps 70 pounds.

But she could play. Vandersloot had grown up a tomboy, ready to roughhouse with the boys in her neighborhood in basketball, baseball and yes, football. In that milieu, only one thing mattered –

whether she could hang with them. And she could. She flourished, and invariably was a quick pick when they chose up sides.

"I didn't want them to treat me like a girl," Vandersloot says. "Especially a little girl, because I was probably the youngest."

Hennig says Vandersloot probably would have started for Kentwood as a freshman, except it was then a three-year school. A year later, she made an immediate impact.

"Courtney, from the second she stepped into the program as a sophomore, we didn't install any press breaks," says Hennig.

Vandersloot was a human press break. Opponents tried 2-2-1 zone presses, half-court traps, full-court man-to-man and she dismantled all of it. But she was hardly a finished product. Hennig wanted his players to attack the rim, and she should have had the tools for it, thanks in part to an explosive first step and quick feet developed playing years of soccer.

Thing was, getting her to finish those forays to the hoop, or to shoot from the perimeter, was a major production. "Courtney," Hennig would lecture, "you could have 35 points if you'd just finish."

"Why," Vandersloot would parry, "when I can pass it to this person?"

Her reluctance to score from outside began to weigh on her team. "She wouldn't even look at the basket, wouldn't even pump-fake," says Hennig, who kept preaching that the offense would open up if she became a deep threat.

"I remember telling her at one practice, 'If you don't shoot a three when you're open in the game, then I'm going to pull you out and you can sit the bench and think about it,'" Hennig says.

She came back a more aggressive player as a junior, and Hennig, recognizing a special talent, decided she needed to be pushed. And that he would do the pushing. He and his wife regularly practiced with the team, and he usually played the heavy, joining the second team and playing opposite his star pupil. Hennig muscled

Vandersloot, bodied her and generally did anything he could to knock her off her game.

"I was not nice to her at practice – in a good way," he says. "I would shove her, push her, put my hand in her face. She was always, 'You fouled me.' I would say, 'There's no refs out here. I'm the ref.'"

The two sides would play to seven baskets – except his side started out ahead, 6-0. The setup would rile Vandersloot, but it was merely firing a naturally competitive streak.

That year, Kentwood lost in the state girls 4A quarterfinals to University High of Spokane, before the Conquerers were eliminated with a loss to Woodinville in which Vandersloot scored 21 points. But it was the day before the tournament that marked something of a milepost in Vandersloot's life.

Gonzaga was the first school to take a hard look at Vandersloot. It happened when she attended the Zags' elite camp, one of a group of high schoolers who were paired against existing teams. Despite the individual talent, the deck is stacked in favor of the team entries.

"She dominated," says Jodie Kaczor Berry, the former Zag assistant who coached Vandersloot's unit.

Fast forward, to early March 2006. Berry was bonkers for Vandersloot, but she wanted to stay in the shadows and get an unfiltered appraisal from Graves. With Graves due to attend the state tournament, Berry asked him to attend a Kentwood pre-tournament practice, without designating the player to watch.

"Holy cow, Jode, who is this kid?" Graves blurted over the phone after seeing the practice. "We need her. She's gotta be a Zag."

The recruiting of Vandersloot was an amalgam of mirth and mystery. Graves loves to tell the story of an unofficial visit the Vandersloot family took to GU before he knew much about her.

"I'm one of those coaches that, I don't gush over a player – 'Boy, you're so good at this and this and this,'" says Graves, sitting in his office at the University of Oregon. "I say, 'You really need to work on this at the next level,' to balance it out."

So here's Graves, still somewhat in the dark about Vandersloot, going into wing-it mode, "kind of making stuff up."

"I really think," Graves told the young prodigy, "you can be a better passer."

He might as well have told Bryce Harper he should bat right-handed.

"I literally laughed out loud," says Berry.

The family left. If there had been a potted plant handy, Berry might have been inclined to chuck it at her boss. She looked at Graves incredulously and asked, "What are you talking about? She's the best passer in the state."

"The rest is history," says a chastened Graves, "but I almost blew it, because I'm an idiot."

Fortunately, the unassuming Vandersloot took the comment in stride, though today she says whimsically, referring to Graves' misstep, "Wish I would have known that then."

Her recruitment was a head-scratcher for at least two reasons: She was playing at a large, fairly high-profile school in Kentwood, and a teammate two years younger, Lindsey Moore, was already drawing interest, which potentially could have attracted suitors to Vandersloot.

All of it left Hennig bemused. He reached out to schools to spread the Vandersloot gospel and got lukewarm responses. One night, then-University of Washington assistant Mike Daugherty watched Kentwood play, and Hennig remembers Vandersloot having a big game.

The next day, Hennig had a message to call Daugherty's wife June, head coach at the UW, and he relayed the information to Courtney, who was his fourth-period teaching assistant. Surely this was the start of interest by the big school.

Not so much. Hennig says June Daugherty inquired about Moore and not a word was said about Vandersloot until he brought up the name. Too small, he was told.

Says Vandersloot, "I knew right then and there that was an excuse, because they had been recruiting Sarah Morton." The Monroe High School standout, listed at 5-8 as an upperclass Husky, "was literally the exact same size."

Washington State didn't give Vandersloot a sniff. Nor, even, did Montana, though her grandparents live in Missoula, and she attended Griz camps and as a child yearned to play there someday. She says they knew of her interest, but nothing came of it.

Vandersloot was smitten by the Zags from that first camp she attended. Her mom took a business trip to Los Angeles and urged her to come along to look at Pepperdine and Loyola Marymount. Vandersloot took unofficial visits, and could hardly wait to ask, "OK, can I commit to Gonzaga?"

If Vandersloot was flying under the radar, it might have also owed to the fact she didn't play on a high-profile AAU team. Often, she was competing in outer gyms on the AAU circuit, not the place a recruiter would typically make a chance discovery.

So she finally made a call to Graves to commit, and he couldn't resist torturing his assistant, Berry, one more time. Graves called Berry, affecting a downcast tone, and told her Vandersloot had decided on another school.

"I was mad," Berry says. "You've got to be kidding me."

About then, Vandersloot's line was ringing Berry's phone. "I'm a Zag," she said happily, to Berry's relief.

The Vandersloot that showed up for her senior year at Kentwood was all grown up. "Me guarding her in practice was nothing for her," says Hennig. "She could, at will, get by me. She could, at will, do anything she wanted. She had to guard me, too."

Meanwhile, once Graves realized Vandersloot could pass the ball, he applied a figurative full-court press.

"I had already committed and he was at every single one of my games," Vandersloot says. "He was still making the effort. I just knew there was no way I was changing my mind. When I went to

Gonzaga for camp, I knew then, like I knew right away, that was the school."

Vandersloot's senior year was a tour de force. She averaged more than 25 points and better than six assists. Kentwood ran the table in the regular season and entered the state 4A tournament top-ranked.

In the semifinals, the Conquerers (27-0) faced fourth-ranked, 23-3 Lewis and Clark of Spokane, the defending champion, led by a future teammate of Vandersloot at Gonzaga, Katelan Redmon. It was a struggle from the get-go for Kentwood, which trailed by 11 points early in the fourth quarter.

Then Vandersloot got hot. She scored 15 points in the fourth quarter, giving her 34 for the night, and she pulled her team into a 57-all tie in the last minute. Hennig sent his team into a clear-out for Vandersloot, who sized up the moment from the perimeter, drove and scored through contact. Then, the whistle.

"The official underneath the basket was giving her an and-one," says Hennig, "and an official ran in from half-court and called her for a charge. I have no doubt in my mind, she hits her free throw, we would have won the championship. It was crushing for Courtney. She had worked so hard, done everything she needed to do."

With the game still tied, Lewis and Clark looked to Redmon but she was covered tightly. She passed to teammate Lyndi Seidensticker, who hit a deep three to win it. Four seconds later, it was done, and Vandersloot covered her eyes deep in her singlet. Later, through the disappointment, she told reporters, "That's the way it goes."

"I've got to go and take my blood medication," said Jim Redmon, the Lewis and Clark coach. "Courtney Vandersloot is incredible."

She had one final calling card. The next night, Kentwood was going to play Prairie in the dreaded third-place game, the one right after the highest hopes have been dashed and the emotional tanks are exhausted.

Vandersloot went one of eight from the field in the first half. Then she rallied her teammates, scoring 22 of her 24 points after intermission, and Kentwood prevailed, 63-51.

In a few months, she was on to something new and different and revelatory: Gonzaga.

Vandersloot wouldn't waste a lot of time with her introductory to Zag basketball. On the night of Nov. 12, 2007 at the McCarthey Athletic Center, Gonzaga played Washington for the first time in 10 years, and beat the Huskies for the first time in history, 91-72 – "just ran 'em out of the gym," says Graves. In the 17 previous games between the teams, starting in 1984, the Huskies had won by an average of 23.7 points.

Playing 26 minutes off the bench in the season opener, Vandersloot had 10 assists and no turnovers. Says Berry, "I remember thinking, 'OK, this is good. This'll be fun.'"

The Zags, though, found the first month a struggle. They were 4-3, and at point guard, Graves was going with Rachel Kane, deferring to a senior even as Kane suffered through a shooting slump. But Vandersloot was getting big minutes off the bench.

Finally, in early December, says Graves, it was, "Why are we doing this?"

With that, he flipped the keys to the rig over to Vandersloot, who says, "Kane was really good about it. I remember her like pushing me, like helping. It was like she understood, she knew."

The Zags muddled through three more non-league losses, and those proved to cost them, even as they left the rest of the WCC in their tracks with a 13-1 record, winning the regular-season title by five games. In the conference-tournament final on San Diego's home floor, Gonzaga fell behind by 17 points early before it fought back and lost a 70-66 decision. A nervous week ensued, capped by the disappointment of being jilted by the NCAA women's selection committee. The season ended badly, with a 14-point loss at Colorado in the second round of the Women's National Invitation Tournament.

Even as Vandersloot made two of 13 field-goal tries in that game, it was apparent good things were in store for the Zags. Not only would she be back for three more years, Gonzaga had Heather Bowman for two more; the two are among only four WCC players in history to be all-league four times. Among others returning was a future all-leaguer, forward Vivian Frieson.

But Gonzaga's drink was now being stirred by Vandersloot. Graves had always been a possession-by-possession grinder but the intuitive lead guard from the west side of the state was pointing him in a new direction. Now the Zags were pushing the ball at every turn, and he and his staff found themselves seeking a different type of frontcourt player, ones who could outrun their counterparts and make a perimeter jumper, not just take up residence on the low block.

"What she did for us, that's a whole book right there," says Graves of Vandersloot. "We became a lot more free-flowing, a lot more transition-oriented. Kayla Standish, Katelan Redmon, they were thoroughbreds. We didn't want a big, slow beast who couldn't keep up."

Gonzaga went from 77th in the nation in scoring the year before Vandersloot's arrival to fifth at 77.2 points a game in 2007-08. Three years later, the Zags' 85.3 led the country.

Even though she wasn't especially vocal, Vandersloot found other avenues to lead. If the game-day shootaround was at 11 a.m., she'd be there by 10. If it was a 6 p.m. tip and teammates got there at 4:30, she'd arrive at 4.

Sophomore year, Vandersloot evolved into a truly superlative player, winning the first of an unprecedented three straight West Coast Conference player-of-the-year awards. She averaged 16.4 points, shot the three better than any of her other Gonzaga years, and when the Zags took down San Diego in the maiden year of the league tournament's move to Las Vegas, she had a triumphant hug for the coaches. Silently, they had all remembered the disappointment of missing the NCAA tournament in 2008.

Now began a cozy tradition for the Zag women, of favorable placements in the big tournament. They were sent to Seattle's Hec Edmundson Pavilion at the University of Washington, a mere 12th seed, but they made their first NCAA victory a signal occasion by throttling fifth-seeded Xavier, 74-59. Bowman scored 23 points and Vandersloot added 15 and 11 assists.

Two nights later, the Zags extended fourth-seeded Pittsburgh – and could have beaten the Panthers – but succumbed 65-60 when they committed key turnovers down the stretch, a couple by Vandersloot, who told reporters through teary eyes afterward, "I have to move past it, but it's killing me."

Her line that night wasn't exactly shame-inducing: 18 points, seven assists, five steals, four turnovers. It did, however, hint at the occasional Achilles in Vandersloot's game – turnovers. Among those in the national top 40 that year in assist-turnover ratio, her miscues (120) were highest. Still, she was 16th in assist-turnover ratio, and to those around her, it was obvious the turnovers were a small price to pay for all the other benefits. And forcing the pace meant more possessions.

"One thing we had to work on with her was making good decisions," says Lisa Fortier, who was an assistant coaching the guards then. "But you've gotta let 'em go a little bit. Sometimes it was on her, sometimes on her teammates. They had to be ready for the ball in a way they'd never been ready before."

It's a topic Vandersloot is comfortable talking about. In her world, it's an equation of risk/reward. She harks back to an NCAA victory over UCLA in 2011 when she amassed a remarkable 17 assists.

"Everybody talks about the 17 assists, but I also had eight turnovers," she says. "That's something I remember because that's something I care about. But I probably don't have seven of those assists if I'm not willing to take chances, and coach Graves understood that. Not that I'm trying to justify turnovers; something you have to be very good at as a point guard is taking care of the ball. But I think even some of the best point guards turn the ball over because they have the ball in their hands."

By now, another unspoken imperative had taken hold. Vandersloot was such a premier talent that the Gonzaga coaches felt a responsibility to be better for her, to reciprocate her contribution with the very best they could give her. That has been couched in jaunty phrases like, "We just didn't want to screw her up." But it was more than that, it was a need to know that they were giving as much as they had.

"I wanted to coach her the best I could," says Fortier. "I was willing to do whatever I could to help her get better."

A similar urgency extended to teammates, perhaps for different reasons. Fortier says she has heard Gonzaga's men talk about a certain pressure to maximize themselves on the occasions they're on a practice floor with Zag legend John Stockton, and she could see that with Vandersloot.

It was about halfway through her Gonzaga career that Vandersloot availed herself of an opportunity to pick the brain of Stockton in informal workouts. It hardly came easy for her. Graves gave her Stockton's phone number, and no high school boy calling a girl for a date to the prom ever was more apprehensive.

"It was the hardest thing," she says. "I was nervous. He wasn't like overly welcome; that made it difficult for me to call him back again and again. It was never like a 'Yeah, anytime!' kind of thing. It was like, 'Yeah, I'm working out with David (his son), you can join.'"

In those few sessions, she was taking an advanced class in the fine art of point guard prestidigitation. Stockton showed her how to do things like shoot a layup or floater off the wrong foot, when a routine layup in traffic would be rejected. He showed her how to apply passes with spin.

"Up until then," she says, "I had only learned the fundamental things about basketball, the things everybody worldwide teaches. It was like, this is a whole new world to me. Now I can see why he's special." A couple of summers ago, she happened to catch a televised classic game involving the Utah Jazz, and "he had like 18 assists in the game, and not one of them was normal."

Vandersloot was an Associated Press honorable mention All-American her junior year, which probably slighted her in that she led the nation in assists (9.3 a game) and was fourth in steals. The Zags blew through the WCC schedule undefeated and got another favorable nod from the NCAA selection committee in getting sent to Seattle. There, seventh-seeded GU ousted North Carolina behind Vandersloot's 15 assists, and then beat No. 2 seed Texas A&M, 72-71, as Vandersloot's 11-turnover struggle was forgotten in the glow of the game of her life from Frieson – 23 points, nine rebounds, five assists and four blocks.

That was a school-record 29th win (bettered by two the next season) but it ended sourly in the Sweet 16 in Sacramento with a blowout loss to Xavier. This was the last college game for Frieson and the school's career scoring leader, Bowman, and Vandersloot had a nagging feeling the Zags left wins on the table.

"I felt that team should have been the best team," she says. "I remember feeling that what we had in this locker room was the best. Bowman, as much as she got recognized, I think she deserved so much more. She was one of the best to me. Vivian was playing out of her mind. Kayla (Standish) was still young but playing well. We had all these pieces."

The years were speeding by. Vandersloot had long since gravitated to the coaches' offices, particularly Fortier's, to analyze game film, to talk about life, to simply hang out. By the time she was a senior, she had a diminished course load, making her a fixture in Fortier's office. Of all Vandersloot's double-doubles and impossible assists and baskets in transition, that's Fortier's favorite memory of her. In mid-discussion, Fortier blurts something echoed among Vandersloot's old GU colleagues: "I love her so much."

If Vandersloot's take is accurate about her team's finishing shortfall in her junior year, it only flatters what she accomplished as a senior. She averaged 19.4 points, shot a career-high both from the field and foul line and led the nation in assist-turnover ratio at 3.08. All of it earned her consensus All-America honors and the women's Frances Pomeroy Naismith Award, given to the top player nationally 5-feet-8 or shorter.

As it happened, while Vandersloot's game was coming to full bloom in 2011, the Gonzaga men were experiencing a mini-crisis with Demetri Goodson at point guard. Goodson provided elite athleticism, but the offense had a way of stopping when the ball was in his hands in the half-court.

Referring to Mark Few, his counterpart with the men's team, Graves says, "I remember in '11, he goes, 'Kelly, we'd be five games better if Courtney was running our point.' A bit of that was obviously tongue-in-cheek, but at times, I think he was serious."

Her final NCAA tournament – all played out in Spokane – was sensational. It began with a career-high 34 points in a victory over Iowa, following by 29 points, seven rebounds, 17 assists with the aforementioned eight turnovers to help upend UCLA. Then another ridiculous stat-stuffer to oust Louisville – 29 points on 8-of-10 shooting, along with seven assists, seven steals, seven turnovers.

That brought the Zags to their first Elite Eight. It would have taken divine intervention for it to go further, because No. 2-ranked Stanford stood in the way of a trip to the Final Four. Indeed, the Cardinal dominated inside, controlling the boards, 49-25, and after Vandersloot scored 21 points in the first half, it limited her to four after intermission on the way to an 83-60 victory.

Vandersloot left to a thunderous ovation with 74 seconds showing, having contributed 25 points and nine assists against a single turnover.

She wouldn't, couldn't, take off the jersey – "which I never do," she says, "because I'm a sweater."

It had all hit her, the finality of it. There would be no more unprecedented heights to push her team toward, no more sizzling nights in the Kennel, no more pressing need for film study with Fortier.

"It obviously was way more than us losing the game," she says. Her eyes glisten. "The fans, the environment, everything there. It was like, I was never going to do this again, you know?"

These were the numbers in Vandersloot's last NCAA tournament: 117 points, on exactly 50-percent shooting from the field, and 44 of 48 from the foul line, with 40 assists, 22 rebounds and 21 turnovers.

Vandersloot went No. 3 in the 2011 WNBA draft, to the Chicago Sky, a team that had finished 14-20 – last in the Eastern Conference – in 2010. Notwithstanding her sensational senior season, Vandersloot had never regarded the WNBA as a given, more as an opportunity that presented itself.

She had had setbacks, certainly, in her high school and college days, but those tended to be fleeting – the occasional heartbreaking loss, the shooting slump everybody must endure. But now she was embarking on the biggest challenge of her life.

The competition was fierce. The West Coast Conference was a distant second to the big collegiate leagues, so she was essentially taking two giant steps up. Injuries bit the Sky's veteran guards, so she was thrust prematurely into a key role.

She had found Gonzaga a comfortable cocoon after high school, a place where people around her helped the transition. Suddenly, she felt out on her own, flailing in a world that seemed jammed with games and airline flights but insufficient time to get her game up to speed.

"Overwhelmed is the perfect word to describe it," Vandersloot says. "I was so out of my comfort zone in terms of like life, more than just basketball, that basketball wasn't coming very easy to me. I struggled. I really, really struggled."

She was named to the league's all-rookie team, averaging 6.5 points and 3.7 assists. But the ratio of 127 assists to 92 turnovers wasn't good. In player efficiency rating, an advanced analytic measuring production, she totaled only 8.0 when the league average is supposed to be 15.

Then she did what most other women pros do – go overseas to play for a few months. She ventured to Turkey, then returned to the Sky for a sophomore season. Her numbers were better – 8.9 points a game, 4.6 assists – but turnovers were still an issue, and for the third straight year, Chicago went 14-20. The time to develop her game seemed to be missing. She was on a treadmill that wasn't going anywhere.

At the worst, she questioned whether she was good enough to be in the league.

One day on the way to practice during that second year, she dialed her mom Jan's phone number and said, "I can't do this anymore. This isn't for me. I just want to be home."

What Jan told her wasn't exactly tough love. She said Courtney needed to do this for herself, nobody else. But she encouraged her to work her way out of the doldrums, and it struck a chord with her daughter.

"Not that that talk just turned it around," Vandersloot says. "But it's something I always remember because I know I had to work really hard to get to where I am. It's just a reminder that what I'm doing is really special. Playing basketball for a living is pretty cool, but it doesn't come without a lot of hard work and a lot of sacrifice."

Things began to change. Vandersloot, feeling overburdened by the unstinting WNBA-to-overseas schedule, decided to play only a month after the 2012 Sky season and return home to train for three months before continuing in Europe. It gave her a break.

A trainer with the Sky picked up on the strain showing on Vandersloot and recommended a psychologist at nearby Loyola University who had worked with Olympic athletes. Vandersloot would see her once a week. Sometimes they'd merely talk about things outside of basketball and Vandersloot found it to be of considerable benefit, "to help me realize I'm here for a reason and to kind of put everything in perspective so that I can just enjoy what I'm doing and know that I can't control everything."

Never a player who could easily put on solid weight, she set about to gain 15 good pounds to maintain strength and stamina. The weight would usually come off, but at least her baseline weight wasn't being compromised.

Things began to get better around her as well. In 2013, the Sky took as the No. 2 pick in the draft Elena Delle Donne, and the 6-5 Delaware product immediately infused the Sky offense with 18 points a game.

Chicago went 24-10 that season, winning the Eastern Conference regular season before being swept out of the conference semifinals. It was a turnaround year for Vandersloot, who bumped her assist-turnover ratio well beyond 2-to-1.

Save for a knee injury that roughly halved her 2014 season, the trajectory has since been mostly upward for Vandersloot (discounting the disappointment of a failed bid to make the 2016 Olympic team, as the guard selections favored the most seasoned veterans). The Sky came from a sub-.500 record to reach the league final in '14, and she then seemed to come to full flower a year later. She led the league in assists in 2015, her effective field-goal percentage of .514 was highest on the team, she downed 90 percent of her free throws and she had a robust 2.8-1 assist-turnover ratio. That player efficiency rating, so modest her rookie year, boomed to 19.6.

Mid-Sky career, she worked a lot with the team player-development assistant, Jonah Herscu, who drilled her on every facet of the game – pick-and-roll offense and defense, shooting, dribble combinations.

"I love her as a person and as a player," says Herscu. "We've done questionnaires with our team, just to get more of a gauge as coaches – who you'd want to take the last shot, who has the most respect. Without a doubt, she has the most respect from her teammates."

Herscu prizes Vandersloot's footwork, saying, "We always talk about 'getting skinny' through screens. Men, women, NBA, WNBA, she's the best at not getting contacted by the screen. It seems like a small thing, but if she's guarding 20 to 30 screens a game, if you get skinny on 90 percent of those, it helps your defense a lot."

Now those travails of her early WNBA days seem so far in the past. Says Herscu, "We say a lot of things to our players. One of them is, it's not supposed to be easy."

It never is. She incurred a couple of ankle injuries early in the 2016 season, a factor in her numbers dipping slightly, to 9.5 points and 4.7 assists a game. But she was formidable at the finish; with Delle Donne – the league MVP in 2015 – gone with a thumb injury, Vandersloot turned in a 21-point, 13-assist gem in a single-elimination playoff victory against Atlanta. And in the semifinals, her 17 points in the third game helped stave off elimination against Los Angeles

Here's another thing Herscu has said to Vandersloot: "She could be one of the best point guards ever to play."

You won't catch Vandersloot saying that, but Lauren Niemiera, the Sky's media-relations director, appreciates her growing ease with interviews.

"Even though she's not outgoing, not overly talkative on her own," Niemiera says, "when you do sit her down for an interview, she's in my top three as far as responses to questions, always very thorough."

The schedule remains crazy, but she has figured it out. She has played in Turkey two different years, Croatia, Hungary, Italy and Poland – enough to appreciate what she's seen but enough to know that when she's done with all this, she doesn't want to travel again. She loves the kebabs in Turkey, but she also yearns for her dad's tri-tip beef.

Away from hoops, 'Sloot has a big liking for Justin Bieber. And she has room for contemporary country music – Rascal Flatts or Lady Antebellum – but quirkily, only in the summer. For her, it's an outdoor, breezy kind of sound.

In his office at Lindbergh High in suburban Seattle, her old high school coach, Hennig, can only laugh in telling a story on himself. Back when Vandersloot was 15, not that far removed from the kid he first laid eyes on, the team was helping prepare a standing game program with players' photographs and a brief bio.

Under goals, Vandersloot wrote: "I want to go to the WNBA."

Hennig blanched a little, thinking that was perhaps a bit bold for a callow sophomore. He didn't want her to come across as big-headed.

"Why don't we say something about, 'I want to make basketball my life?'" he counseled Vandersloot.

So they toned it down. Turned out her instincts were as good then as they are with the ball.

– 7 –
THE LONG SEASON

IT'S NOVEMBER 6, 2015, only a few days before the start of another Gonzaga basketball season. Only a matter of hours before the Zags launch another campaign they trust will have life deep into March.

Up on the second floor of the Martin Centre, in the modest Gonzaga weight room, the view is a much longer one, of necessity and circumstance. Nigel Williams-Goss, Johnathan Williams and Jeremy Jones have transferred into the program, and while their new teammates will board a plane to Okinawa, Japan later in the week, their own seasons are a year away – or just short of forever in the mind of an eager, young athlete.

"You got 15 minutes on the dumbbells!" Travis Knight barks out to the three. "Ain't no time for rest with all the work we've got to do!"

Today, they're working on upper-body strength, and Knight, the Zags' 40-year-old strength and conditioning coach for basketball, is the choreographer as the threesome hoists dumbbells in several different lifts.

"You got 10 minutes! I need one more set after this! Burn those shoulders out!"

The rapper Juvenile is playing over the sound system. A good measure of playful jiving takes place, but the lifting is all business, the exertion unmistakable.

"Fight for it!" Knight exhorts. "There should be nothing left when we're done! Fight for it! Burn it up, burn it up for the next five minutes! Two-minute drill, two-minute drill!"

The three pace through the dumbbell repetitions and then push through some of Knight's specialized resistance challenges. In one, the player lies beneath a squat/bench press rack, torso on the floor, knees bent with feet on a bench. Holding the handles at the ends of a rope draped over the rack supports, the player raises his upper body, torching arms, hips, core.

Knight slaps hands in triumph with the three at the end of the hour. "Legs tomorrow," he tells Williams.

For Williams-Goss, Williams and Jones, this is their year-in-waiting. Just don't call it a year off.

John Calipari became renowned for milking one-and-done talent at Kentucky. Villanova evolved into a factory for guards. Michigan State has long built a reputation on toughness.

If, in a long run of consistency, Gonzaga has co-opted any identity, it's this: The Zags have become known for players maximizing a redshirt season and earning elite status in college basketball.

Dan Dickau left a culture at Washington that he didn't feel was conducive to fulfilling potential, and after sitting out the 1999-2000 season, he became a first-team All-American at Gonzaga in 2002. Kelly Olynyk became a first-round NBA draft pick upon leaving Gonzaga with this distinction: Only player in the history of the game to become an All-American after redshirting, without injury, following at least two seasons. Kyle Wiltjer departed with mixed reviews at Kentucky, and after a redshirt year spent in the weight room, turned himself into a 2015-16 preseason player-of-the-year candidate.

Let's face it, this might not be a selling point in the living rooms of high school recruits who never dream they might redshirt. But in the overall scheme, it's a reflection that if you go to Gonzaga, the machinery and the institutional commitment are in place to develop. Embedded in the program's core is a willingness to take players who have run their course somewhere else – often seduced by a better conference, a bigger weight room or a glitzier players lounge – and give them the tools to realize potential.

Understand, it's only the tools. The rest is on you. But by nature, transfers usually arrive chastened, having found something lacking at their first stop, and now they're ready to make sure it's not a failure of their work ethic.

Zag transfers, Knight says, come to know that they're part of special forces having conquered something that isn't always easy. "It's kind of a badge of honor," he says. "If you survive that, you kind of have this respect from the other people who have redshirted, of just how difficult it is."

While Mark Few has accepted transfers throughout his head-coaching tenure, the refinement of the working parts in their off-year development – the school's emphasis on strength and conditioning, the mesh between Few and Knight philosophically, and the mandate for Knight to work his wonders – blossomed mostly in the back half of the Zags' NCAA-tournament streak.

Olynyk was the gold standard for that progress. He had had a major growth spurt in high school, and in his early years at Gonzaga, his legs didn't seem to obey what his brain wanted. Among the celebrated features of Knight's regimen for him was directing tennis balls, fired at close range, to his right or left hand by the markings "R" or "L." Or Olynyk being commanded to move right or left if the number on a second ball was three greater than the first.

For Knight, this isn't paint-by-numbers stuff. He brainstorms his own routines. Olynyk told me in 2013, "He put me through stuff that, I swear, no one has ever done before."

So now, Williams-Goss, Williams and Jones are embarking on a journey to the corners of Travis Knight's imagination. As a general rule, when they graduate from his redshirt lab, Knight wants them to be at a level of first-team all-West Coast Conference. No doubt there are higher aspirations among them, and Knight won't discourage them.

"There's just no substitute for getting in there every day for 12 to 18 months," he says. "That 12 to 18 months can accomplish more than the normal kid can accomplish in four years, just because they're building on top of yesterday without any interruption."

December 9, 2015

"What's up, Three?" greets Knight, slapping hands with Williams, who is Johnathan Williams III.

Shortly, Williams is hard at it with Williams-Goss on a day dedicated to core strength and lower-body explosiveness. Rapper Rick Ross is on the sound system (I had to ask; "I got you, don't worry about it," Williams-Goss says, smiling) and before the hour is done, they will invest sweat toward their season of re-emergence.

Williams uses his legs to stretch an elastic band tethered to a weight machine. The new teammates raise a medicine ball over their heads, rotate it and slam it down. Lying on the floor, they hoist an empty barbell for stability and swing their bent legs side to side.

Williams-Goss asks Knight if they can turn up Rick Ross. They do. They begin a series of squats. Then Knight places a series of orange apparatuses – think the shape of bicycle handlebars – with about four or five feet between each, at the end of which is a two-foot-high box. Feet together, the players do a jump over each apparatus, finishing with a climactic leap atop the box. Then they do it sideways.

With repetition, the tempo becomes smoother. "That's a high level," says Knight. "To do that continuously is a high level. Make that your goal."

The sweat beads are flying now. Then comes another diabolical exercise: Knight pulls out BOSU balls, half-spheroids with a hard, flat side that when turned up, undermine stability. The players put one foot on a bench and the other on the unsteady half-ball, while fully extending one arm to the air and, with a kettlebell in the other hand, lower and raise themselves. It looks beastly.

"It's burnin' my legs," confesses Williams-Goss, "especially after those squats."

It turns out the paths of Williams-Goss and Williams crossed well before a weight room at Gonzaga. Years ago, as grade-schoolers, their AAU teams met in the 11-and-under nationals at Cocoa Beach, Fla. Williams' Memphis team got the better of Williams-Goss' Portland Hoop Kings.

Williams-Goss grew up in Clackamas, Oregon outside Portland, son of an insurance man and a therapist. His father Virgil was an Air Force staff sergeant, his mother Valerie a counselor who recently earned her doctorate in human services. When, at 14, Nigel was offered a scholarship to play at Findlay Prep in Henderson, Nevada, the family went with him. He calls his time there "the best experience of my life."

The University of Washington-based website Gohuskies.com, in a profile his freshman year at the UW, wrote that Williams-Goss had never received anything less than an A grade in any class, and that he learned Mandarin by the fifth grade.

Discussing the emphasis on academics in his family, Williams-Goss says, "It was never 'I had to get straight As.' But it was to put in maximum effort in the classroom to get the best grades I could possibly receive. If that was a C and I studied and did everything I could, that was going to be tolerated. My capability always was to get As, so that kind of became the standard."

Williams-Goss committed as a sophomore to Nevada-Las Vegas and its coach then, Lon Kruger. The call to Washington coach Lorenzo Romar, who had known Williams-Goss since his middle-school days, "was like the hardest phone call I've ever made."

Kruger made it easier, departing UNLV for Oklahoma just after Williams-Goss' sophomore season at Findlay. That reopened the door for Romar and Washington, although Williams-Goss was also sorely tempted by Harvard. It had a rising program under Tommy Amaker and an assistant coach, Yann Hufnagel (now at Nevada), to whom Williams-Goss was close.

But he couldn't say no again to Romar, and Williams-Goss chose Washington. He brought glowing credentials: He had led Findlay to a 35-1 record and made the McDonald's All-American and Jordan Brand Classic teams. In a Martin Luther King Day tournament dotted with future college players at one of basketball's citadels, Springfield, Massachusetts, Williams-Goss led a Findlay comeback with a three at the buzzer to beat Montverde Academy.

His freshman season at Washington was mostly a success individually, save for the 92 turnovers. A lot was asked of him; he started, played the second-most minutes on the team and averaged 13.4 points, shooting .464, including .356 on three-pointers and .723 as a foul shooter. He set a UW freshman assist record with 140, and on January 25 in Seattle against Oregon State, he showed what was possible: He scored 32 points on 10-of-15 shooting, nine of 10 at the foul line, with five rebounds, three assists and no turnovers. More than athletic explosiveness, his game was a sort of probing, intuitive attack from the point guard position, highlighted offensively by a reliable floater.

The team was unremarkable, and when it bowed out of the Pac-12 tournament in its first game against Utah, it finished at 17-15, 9-9 in the conference.

Washington's 2014-15 team would likely intrigue sociologists. It blew to an 11-0 start, undefeated all the way past Christmas. Then it lost at home to Stony Brook, the first of four straight defeats. Late in January, Romar booted star center Robert Upshaw for rules violations – amid reports of failed drug tests there and at his previous school, Fresno State – and the Huskies plummeted to a 16-15 ending, 11th in the conference at 5-13.

Williams-Goss led the team in scoring at 15.6, while his shooting slipped to .442 and only .256 from the arc. He was second in the league in assists at 5.9 a game and third in assist-turnover ratio at 2.08. His superlative game came February 1 against Cal, as he hit 11 of 17 shots on a 31-point afternoon, with six rebounds, five assists and no turnovers.

When, on senior day at the UW, he had 28 points in 39 minutes to lead an upset of 13th-ranked Utah, no Husky fan, not even Romar, could have guessed what was coming next.

The team was fragmenting. Darin Johnson and Jernard Jarreau were outbound, and deep-reserve center Gilles Dierickx was dropping down to Seattle Pacific. A couple of seniors were done, and there was some continuing buzz that Williams-Goss might enter the NBA draft; he had contemplated it after his freshman year.

Williams-Goss points out that another element of the turmoil was assistant coach T.J. Otzelberger, who was leaving to return to Iowa State. Says Williams-Goss, "It was just a lot of change in the program. I was kind of at that halfway point. I kind of said, do I want to rebuild midway through my career or go elsewhere?"

It wouldn't have floored Romar to know that Williams-Goss was going to explore the NBA. Transferring was something else entirely. Williams-Goss recalls him saying, "You know, it's one thing to think you were going to leave to try to enter the draft. It's another thing knowing you're going to play for someone else."

Indeed, Williams-Goss was, and he obtained his release from Washington. He upped the ante considerably three weeks later when he announced his destination: Gonzaga, the school across the state, the place that had been a burr in the Huskies' backside competitively as well as in the public discourse after Washington curtailed the series in 2007.

"I mean, it was tough," Williams-Goss says. "One, telling coach Romar I was leaving the program in general was hard. And again, when I said I was going to Gonzaga. I didn't look too much into the rivalry or anything like that. I was making a decision into where I thought was best. It just so happened it was Gonzaga. At the end of the day, coach Romar has his career and his family he has to take care of, and my career is still young and I'm still developing mine."

Williams-Goss made it clear to me he didn't want to make his transfer from Washington to Gonzaga a noisy, contentious episode. Still, it was apparent that his departure was about more than just the attrition around him.

"I felt after my freshman year, a lot of the things we had talked about (that) were going to change going into my sophomore year, I didn't see a lot of that change happening," he says. "It's one thing, I feel like, to lose, but it's another thing when you're not doing everything in your power, or your capability, as far as preparation in trying to win. I just felt there were a lot of stones left unturned before games, and stuff like that. I had talked to past players, where they kind of had similar experiences . . . I just felt it was best for me to move on."

Was he saying that people weren't working hard enough? "I'm not saying guys didn't work hard," Williams-Goss says. "I just felt there are a lot of things that go into preparing and stuff at this level – the margin is so small at this level – and I just felt there were just a lot of things that weren't being done that could have been done. That [they] said were going to be done that weren't."

Naturally, he became one of the premier transfers on the market after the 2014-15 season. He spent a weekend sifting through feelers and phone calls – UNLV, Providence, Ohio State, Michigan State,

Texas, Notre Dame, Georgetown, LSU, St. John's, Vanderbilt, Gonzaga.

"A big list," Williams-Goss says. "I remember being on the phone with like Tom Izzo, and Thad Matta would be calling, and John Thompson from Georgetown. It was kind of overwhelming."

What wasn't overwhelming, initially, was Gonzaga. Zags assistant Brian Michaelson was close to one of Williams-Goss' former AAU coaches, and Michaelson called during that hectic weekend. But Williams-Goss hadn't heard from Few, while he was taking calls from head coaches around the country.

But Few got to Williams-Goss on Monday, and they set up a home visit. Accompanied by Michaelson, he made an impression.

"They completely elevated in my mind," says Williams-Goss. "Again, it was going back to the preparation, the workouts . . . like the amount of film they watch, just the preparation that goes into being successful. Again, like some of the issues I had leaving the UW, they were kind of on top of everything I was kind of looking for. Their whole thing was about developing and winning, those two things exclusively. It wasn't about the facilities or the location or the conference. It was strictly making me the best player I could possibly be, and having a chance to win at the highest level."

As Few puts it, "Literally, there isn't a stone that goes unturned here."

Going way back, even as far back as middle school, Williams-Goss had a saying: "I just want the platform." He just wanted the surroundings, the ingredients, to help facilitate his own initiative and ability.

It helped, no doubt, that Gonzaga was coming off an Elite Eight appearance, and could point to 17 successive years in the NCAA tournament. That's a platform. It had appeal, especially in contrast to Washington's growing tournament drought. After an extended run of success under Romar, the Huskies had failed to make the tournament four straight years, a number that grew to five in 2015-16.

Williams-Goss visited Gonzaga with his parents, did the campus tour and had a meeting with Few in his office. On the last night of his visit, he and Gonzaga players were gathered at Few's rustic home southwest of Spokane, and the Zags were glued to the television showing the long-awaited Manny Pacquiao-Floyd Mayweather fight.

Williams-Goss slipped away to the kitchen, where it was just him and Few. There, he told the coach he wanted to transfer to Gonzaga.

It was strictly a chance meeting that united Gonzaga with Jeremy Jones. He was in Houston in late March 2015, attending Rice University when the Zags played two games at cavernous NRG Stadium, reaching the NCAA Elite Eight.

"I just loved what I saw from the outside looking in, that perspective," Jones says. "I did a little research, picked up the phone and called coach [Tommy] Lloyd. He was telling me how big they were on player development. That was like the one thing, when I left Rice, was player development. That's what really drew me to this school."

For Jones, the path to athletic fulfillment has hinged on two dynamics: Choosing a sport and staying healthy. At 6-feet-5, he was a quarterback at East Central High in San Antonio, as well as a four-year basketball letterman.

Through most of high school, Jones' mindset was football. He got an early offer from Rutgers, then Rice got involved, and Jones was so pointed toward football that he gave up AAU basketball in the summer of 2013 between his junior and senior seasons.

But something kept drawing him to basketball, and as his senior season wore on, he realized he didn't want to give it up – even as he signed a football letter in early 2014 with Rice. There was a football injury; he tore his right labrum that fall, forcing a decision: He could have surgery immediately and be sidelined four to six months, which would kill his basketball season. Or he could rest for a month, finish the last couple of games in the football season, play basketball and schedule the surgery after that season was done.

He chose the latter option. But the shoulder didn't cooperate, and when it should have been healed late in the calendar year 2014, he was still feeling discomfort. Another MRI revealed the shoulder was torn again, so he redshirted Rice's football season and worked to rehab the shoulder. By now, he was feeling a stronger preference for basketball. He would try to do both.

Jones sat out of the first eight games of his freshman basketball season and made a slow return to a game at which he was now rusty in the first-year tenure of Mike Rhoades, a scion of Shaka Smart's regime at Virginia Commonwealth. Complicating his return was the fact that while he saw himself as a swing player between guard and small forward, Jones, relatively willowy at 205 pounds, frequently was stationed inside because of a lack of big bodies.

He played in 24 games, his minutes cresting with two starts in the Conference USA tournament. He shot an even 50 percent (but only .424 from the foul line). It was his rebound numbers that catch your eye; in 102 minutes his last five games – 20 a game – he had 29 rebounds.

By season's end, he was thoroughly committed to basketball over football. But his coaches – both Rhoades and football coach David Bailiff – wanted him to go through spring football. He did that, and showed promise as a wide receiver. Because of the shoulder problems, he wasn't going to be playing quarterback.

"Basically, the basketball coach and football coach got together and somehow came up with the theory that I hadn't played a season of football so I didn't know if that's what I wanted or not," says Jones. "So they wanted me to play a season of football and if I didn't want to do it, they agreed I didn't have to play football after that, and I could go straight to basketball. That's not what I wanted. It was basically a situation where nobody was going to get their way, so I just asked for my release."

Because of his youth, the injury and the indecision over a sport, Jones has farther to come physically than either of the other two transfers. But he's confident he can make it happen at Gonzaga.

"This is a place where you're not the only one that's working hard," he says. "Basically, the whole team's like in the gym, extra. You can always ask a teammate or a manager if you want to work out. Or a coach. The answer is always yes."

Perhaps it's debatable whether Williams-Goss left behind some frayed feelings at Washington. That isn't the case with Williams, who clearly had a fractious departure from Missouri.

He was from Memphis, a 6-feet-9 four-star recruit from Southwind High who played a little of every position on the floor. His college finalists were Michigan State, Georgetown, Missouri and Tennessee. Williams opted for Mizzou and coach Frank Haith, not knowing that his first season in the program was going to be Haith's last.

Haith had been a controversial, head-scratching choice for Missouri when Mike Anderson left for Arkansas after the 2011 season. The widespread derision around the hire mounted when Haith was suspended by the NCAA for five games of Williams' freshman season in 2013 for failing to promote an atmosphere of compliance at Miami, his previous stop.

Williams is complimentary of Haith, saying, "He did a great job. He brought out aspects of my game, like my rebounding, which I never knew I had."

That 2013-14 season ended at 23-12 in the National Invitation Tournament, followed by a surprise. On April 18, Haith accepted a job at Tulsa, in what USA Today called "perhaps the most surprising development in college basketball's off-season so far." Soon, it would turn out that four days earlier, Missouri had received a letter of inquiry from the NCAA – the official first step of an investigation – but Haith maintained he knew nothing of it until well after.

By early 2016, Missouri was announcing self-sanctions for major violations in the program, mostly for the actions of a couple of rogue boosters. Haith wasn't named in the report.

Williams had had a promising debut under Haith, as the fourth-leading scorer (at 5.8 points a game) and leading rebounder, at 6.5. His 57 blocked shots were No. 5 on the Mizzou season list.

With Haith gone, the Tigers turned to a former standout from their 1970s teams, Kim Anderson. Williams led the 2014-15 team in scoring (11.9) and rebounding (7.1, with more than twice as many boards as anybody else on the squad), but his shooting fell off to .412, including .344 from three-point distance. He scored 27 points against Mississippi State and 22 against Oklahoma State, but all of it came in a 9-23 mess of a season, marking Missouri's fewest victories since 1967.

Williams decided the fit wasn't for him. He isn't specific, saying, "Just the coach going down the wrong path, and I didn't want to be a part of it. I didn't think the program was going to get any better anytime soon. I didn't want to waste two valuable years if I knew the program wasn't going to head in the right direction."

That's when it began to get interesting. "The University of Missouri made it really complicated for me to transfer," Williams says. "I did everything the correct way."

He says he went to the coaches and then to the compliance office. As part of his release from his scholarship, Williams wasn't allowed to attend a school in the Southeastern Conference, Big 12, or Illinois or Arizona. Mizzou is in the SEC, the league contests the Big 12 annually in a "challenge" of conferences, the school plays Illinois annually, and it had just set up a contract with Arizona.

There was more. One of the managers told him he was instructed not to work with Williams anymore. Williams says he was also forbidden from using any of the facilities – the arena, locker room or weight room. He had a couple of months left on campus to finish spring semester, but he was persona non grata athletically. (I reached out to Missouri for comment, but the school didn't respond.)

"It made it difficult, but I knew there was going to be a brighter side one day," Williams says. "I had to just keep praying about it, that everything was going to work out OK." He admits to wondering: "Dang, why are you treating me so bad when I did so much for the school?"

In the end, perhaps Missouri's release terms helped Gonzaga. At any rate, Williams was excited when he got a call from Michaelson; Williams had grown up seeing Memphis and the Zags tangle in an annual series.

On the rebound, he considered Georgetown again, and Southern Methodist came into the picture when coach Larry Brown called. But Williams was wary about possible sanctions at SMU – for good reason, it turned out – and Georgetown seemed to have lots of candidates his size. He concluded Gonzaga was the best fit.

He plans to begin proving that in 2016-17. Says Williams, "I want to be my opponent's worst nightmare every time he sees me on the court. I want to be a beast that averages a double-double."

When Travis Knight speaks of his mission with the redshirting players, his words take on an almost reverential tenor, as if failing them in some manner would be breaking a sacred trust.

"You don't have to drag them and insist and convince them," he says. "If anything, it probably is more challenging to me to be around these athletes. It ensures that I'm meeting their desire and level of commitment in what I'm doing for them. There's a kind of reciprocal sharpening that happens; in making them better, I have to constantly evaluate: Am I really giving them all they need right now?"

If he isn't, it's not for lack of dedication. "I told them from the beginning," Knight says. "If you want to come in and do extra work, the answer will always be yes. I will always be here for you to do extra work."

If it's remarkable that Gonzaga pieced together an 18-year run of NCAA-tournament appearances, the feat seems more astonishing when you consider the place didn't have a full-time equivalency for strength and conditioning until 2003.

When I wrote "BraveHearts" in 2002, Mike Chrysler, then 29, was the strength coach. He told me he spent six to seven hours a week at Gonzaga, making a "minimal" wage at what was a part-time job. Citing an athletic budget that was "a little tight," he said strength and conditioning was something largely left up to the coach of each sport.

Since then, Gonzaga's devotion to individual physical development has grown substantially. Much of the impetus is from former defensive standout Mike Nilson, in historically alternating roles as head of strength and conditioning, or in contracted services stemming from his partnership in nearby U-District Physical Therapy and Institute of Sport Performance.

In some sports, Gonzaga still contracts for those services. Since 2006, though, men's basketball has relied on Knight, first as a U-District emissary and since 2013, as a full-time GU coach. Nilson and Knight had been Gonzaga chums back in the late 1990s, when, says Knight, "He had been the guy who cut my hair through college."

Knight was a baseball player at Gonzaga. He hailed from Kent-Meridian High School, and before that, his junior high baseball coach was Dave Jamison, who later would coach Gary Bell Jr. in basketball at Kentridge.

Knight walked on at Gonzaga, initially playing second base before falling in love with third. At 5-feet-9, he had a blocky build that suited the position, and he learned to use his hands to throw more quickly. With a background in physical education, he figured he'd go into teaching and coaching. He and his wife settled near her Midwest roots and he went to grad school at Wichita State, while developing a strength and conditioning program for a small, private high school.

They came back to Spokane in 2004 and two years later, he was working full-time with Gonzaga athletes.

It would be a while before there was an airtight alliance between strength coach and basketball program. The strength and conditioning component at Gonzaga was still a developing organism. As Knight puts it, "I think there was an assumption that it was kind of the wheel that went around and around and around and you don't have to grease it too much."

If the path of strength and conditioning was still finding its way at Gonzaga, so too was Knight. His isn't a loud and commanding personality, and he came off as vulnerable to some of the players.

"There was a culture at that time," he says, mentioning players Josh Heytvelt, Jeremy Pargo and Micah Downs. "Pretty strong-willed kids and pretty high opinions of themselves. That team (in the 2006-08 time frame) had so much talent, it was crazy. For me, I'm kind of trying to figure things out. It was my first strength and conditioning job at the college level, a lot of trial and error going on, probably a lot of mistakes on my part, probably trying to get guys to do what everybody else is doing – or probably going too easy on them and I don't know what they're capable of.

"They could smell me a mile away, that I didn't have the confidence. I hadn't garnered enough respect to be able to assert myself with those guys."

Gradually, Knight found his voice. He put in extra time and gained respect. The personalities changed, to booming Robert Sacre and the determined Olynyk and tireless Kevin Pangos. Knight, who says he didn't work very closely with Few in those early years, found himself spending more and more time with the coach, who not only expressed what he wanted in player development but offered advice: Take the job and run with it.

"One of the things he's always been repeating is, if he hadn't been assertive in making things happen, he would still be a low assistant coach somewhere and not the head coach," says Knight. "He had to step up and assert himself and make it happen. That's kind of how it is for all of us."

But there was another aspect to Knight's evolution. He didn't want to be merely one more strident voice in players' ears, he wanted them to look forward to workouts, wondering what might be coming next. Weight training and agility drills can be grinding and monotonous – especially if you're redshirting and the day when you're on the floor again seems light years away. After something as mundane as a squat workout, he wanted players telling teammates, "Wait 'til you hear about this."

So Knight's redshirts might be found out on the baseball field one day, playing home run derby. Or playing ultimate Frisbee with a medicine ball. Or pushing his car around the parking lot if they lost a competition. Knight wants an element of fun.

It's not all work and no play – although you might have fooled Williams-Goss, Jones and Williams.

February 10, 2016

While the Zags practice at one end of McCarthey Athletic Center, their scout-team point guard is confined to activity much more sedentary. Williams-Goss is sitting on a chair beneath a side basket, his left foot encased in a boot, and from two feet away from the hoop in the key, he's flipping a basketball through the net and catching it before it hits the floor. Near him is a medical knee walker, one of those mobility-aiding contraptions with short handlebars, a small cushion and four wheels.

"Lot better than crutches," says Williams-Goss, whose redshirt season has been marred by an ankle problem resulting from cumulative wear. He has just undergone clean-up surgery for it and will be mostly inactive until April.

Each injury, whether to somebody in the playing rotation or among the scouts, affects just about everyone. For instance, when

Przemek Karnowski went down early in December with a back injury – eventually to be out for the season – seven-footer Ryan Edwards had to move from the "five" spot on the scout team to being in the rotation. That moved Williams to center on the scout team and nudged Jones' scout duties to – you guessed it – the big-forward position he disdained at Rice.

Even in the best of times, these would be the dog days for the redshirts. They've been at it for several months without reward. Their teammates go on the road for critical games and leave them behind. March, the only month that truly matters to a college basketball player, is coming soon, but their time really doesn't arrive until next fall.

It's fair to suggest that the redshirt-year assignment of Williams might be the most challenging of the three sitting out at GU. Like Williams-Goss and Jones, he has a steady diet of Travis Knight. But daily, he has to go against rugged, indefatigable Domantas Sabonis ("He'll try to bully you," Williams says) and uber-scorer Kyle Wiltjer ("the toughest job ever").

Beyond that, there's a more subtle part of his routine. Coaches prize the scout-team player who can most closely mirror what the opposition presents, not just the one who competes hardest. It's like an actor getting in character. And typically, it isn't easy for Williams, because there aren't a lot of players like him in the West Coast Conference, a league dominated by guards. Combine that with the fact he's lefthanded, and staging an Oscar-worthy performance becomes difficult.

Jones learned about this early in January, as the Zags prepared for a game against Portland. He was impersonating a center for the Pilots when he found himself with the ball in the right corner. His instincts told him to attack the basket, which he did. That drew an admonition from Few, who called out, "Their five man isn't going to take two dribbles and dunk it, that's not their game. You guys [imitate] Portland, not the red-squad all-stars."

"Sometimes," Jones laments, "the (other) team's 'four' and 'five' men are non-scorers. So it's like, we'll catch the ball open at the three-point line, and we can't do anything, and no one's guarding us."

If next fall seems a long way off, so, even, is spring. It's been only a moderately harsh winter in Spokane, not the worst it can dish out, but that doesn't matter to Jones and Williams. To Southerners, it seems severe.

The teams they left, Rice and Missouri, are still struggling. Washington, though, has perked up and is threatening to end a four-year NCAA-tournament drought. Williams-Goss says he talks frequently to senior Andrew Andrews and texts often with freshman star Dejounte Murray.

They soldier on, redshirts whose world is class, practice and Travis Knight. Some days it's weights, others agility or cardio. Near the end, Knight will often tell them the game is going into overtime and they need to dig deeper.

"Sometimes it's kind of ridiculous," Jones says. "We find a way to get it done."

April 14, 2016

Not that the redshirts need to be reminded how long and eventful a couple of months can be in a college athlete's life, but they've just seen their team experience a complete reversal of fortune.

Gonzaga's doomsday season suddenly burst into sunshine. Downbeat morphed into beatdowns. The sour Senior Night loss to Saint Mary's gave way to a breakthrough at Brigham Young, and then wins over BYU and Saint Mary's in the WCC tournament, followed by hardly-a-doubt victories over Seton Hall and Utah in the NCAA tournament. To be sure, the finish of the Syracuse game stung, but it was truly a redemptive season.

"It was awesome," says Williams-Goss. He's striding toward a weight workout, having just been cleared to start running. "Everyone knows the adversity we had to overcome. I saw it first-hand every day in practice, the meetings and everything. It was good for us to really have to earn our way, like nothing was given to us. We didn't have an easy road to the Sweet 16."

On this day, Williams has headed off to a community-service commitment. Jones is over at the Hemmingson Center, chilling with some teammates, saying he knew all along they had a run in them.

"For the longest time, I kept saying, 'They'll peak at the right time,'" he says. "Everyone comes back to the gym late at night, to work on something individually almost every single day. At some point, they had to be rewarded. The story wouldn't make sense if everyone was doing all this extra stuff, and no reward."

Jones has been focusing on balance drills, aimed to give his right leg the same capability as his dominant left. Too often, when a defender rides him, he gets knocked off his feet when attacking the basket.

Williams-Goss has gained about 10 pounds, to 195, and says a steady body fat reading tells him it's good weight. He's stronger in the core and his bench press has improved.

The two will see a lot more of each other in the summer. Jones planned to join Williams-Goss for two weeks to train in Las Vegas, and if that went well, he'd meet him again there later. Coming up on a year at Gonzaga, they'll know the culture, the expectations, how they might best funnel their attributes into the program.

"It's amazing; such a special place to be," says Williams-Goss. "I just feel really, really fortunate I'm here, because of the amount of support we get from our fans and the true investment the coaches have in each and every one of us – not just by their words, but they show it every day in what they try to do to help us become better players. It's just a really special place. I'm really glad I'm here."

Now the next game is theirs as well as their teammates'. They're on equal footing. They're pledges no more, rather part of the brotherhood of redshirts at Gonzaga. History says it's pretty good company.

– 8 –
THE FIFTH BEATLE

ADAM MORRISON IS WEARING A TANK TOP with shorts, his long, dark hair wrapped in a ponytail. Later in the day, he'll be staging a clinic for Hoopfest, Spokane's annual 3-on-3 street basketball bacchanal, and then it's off to his summer place on Lake Coeur d'Alene.

The temperature will touch triple digits, and that's one of the reasons he doesn't participate in Hoopfest. There's also the hassle of being a Type 1 diabetic and managing his blood sugar for several games.

And finally: "You get the guy that wants to fight. I'm not into that. I just don't want to play. It's a pain in the ass."

Morrison has long since tired of the guy who wants to fight – or merely to provoke. What he'd like is a little peace, and a little peace of mind, and neither has come easy. He's back in Spokane now, where the supernova ignited on its crackling journey. He's doing something at once mundane and profound – figuring out what he wants to do with the rest of his life.

His saga inevitably loses something in the retelling. You almost had to be there, to see the autograph-seekers and the fans crowding the team buses, and the bloodless gunnery that Morrison perpetrated on opponents, and the rage that propelled him, and the mouth that infuriated defenders, and the time he pointed maniacally at the Loyola Marymount student section as he was dropping 37 points in the second half on their team.

You had to see a show-stopping 19-day stretch in late 2005. You had to catch him on the cover of USA Today sports, retreating downcourt, arms upraised, sweaty hair flopping near his eyes. You had to see him in a full-page shot in Sports Illustrated, rising, off-balance and willing in an unintended bank shot to deny Oklahoma State. You had to see him on a regional cover of SI, driving to the basket. You probably even needed to see him at practice, where by the force of his rare offensive powers, he changed some of the rules at Gonzaga.

You had to witness his long-distance duel with Duke's J.J. Redick for national player of the year in 2006, an unforgettable game of one-upmanship, spiced by the contrast in style and program bloodlines, the likes of which we haven't seen before or since.

The wild child.

There was even talk he was going to be the No. 1 pick in the 2006 NBA draft. Instead, he went third, and he embarked on a jagged, unfulfilled pro career that served as a dour counterpoint to his collegiate brilliance. And, this being the age of instant, crude commentary, Morrison was laughed off as a charlatan.

Safe to say that few athletes have ever been visited by such bipolar reaction, from the frenzy of his best days at Gonzaga to the disillusionment of those who expected more of him as a pro.

Morrison captivated, inflamed, mesmerized and polarized.

And scored. And scored.

"Nobody was going to stop him," says his former teammate Blake Stepp. "Hell or high water, he was going to do it his way. Most of the time, he did."

Nursing strawberry-and-cream frappucinos at a coffee shop near the Gonzaga campus, John and Wanda Morrison retrace the whole improbable path, beginning with their roots. They came from tiny hamlets in northeastern Montana, Peerless and Scobey, hard by the Saskatchewan border.

John became a junior college basketball coach in Wyoming, Wanda a secretary, a couple of modest means. They never attended a West Coast Conference tournament during their son Adam's time at Gonzaga, saving their money for the NCAA tournament.

"A very middle-class family," says Wanda, "just trying to do right by our kids."

They settled in Spokane, where early, Adam showed the proclivity for basketball one might expect of a kid whose father still gives shooting lessons. But he was hardly a prospect who screamed "NBA player," especially when he was diagnosed with diabetes in eighth grade.

He began to blow up about midway through his years at Mead High. And the story became legend about how Gonzaga coach Mark Few soldiered out skeptically one night to watch him play and was immediately alarmed by Morrison's odd gait, by the mincing, old-man strides and the hunched shoulders. Few couldn't help but notice Morrison played no defense and literally would come to take the ball from his point guard.

Over the phone at halftime, Zags assistant Leon Rice asked Few how many points Morrison had.

"Thirty," Few confessed sheepishly. "I think I better stay for the second half."

Morrison was about 6-feet-5 as a junior when Gonzaga decided his offense was too explosive to pass up, and he quickly accepted a scholarship offer. He continued ascendant as a senior, growing toward 6-8, and in the 2003 Washington state 4A championship game, scoring 37 of Mead's 55 points in a loss to Franklin, whose future NBA guard Aaron Brooks had 38.

Morrison did it while troubled by the flu, possibly exacerbated by the diabetes.

So unsuspecting was the Gonzaga coaching staff about what it had on its hands that Rice advanced the idea that Morrison should "grayshirt" – defer enrollment until January 2004 and begin playing the next season, so as to aid Gonzaga in managing NCAA scholarship restrictions.

"I had no idea what a grayshirt was," says Wanda Morrison.

Not that it mattered. In pickup games, Morrison was killing it against his future teammates. Stepp would come upstairs to the coaches' offices and tell them nobody could guard him. The notion of grayshirting, even redshirting, was being rendered moot.

The Zags were beat up entering their 2003-04 opener against St. Joseph's. On November 13, the eve of the game at Madison Square Garden, John Morrison was working in the yard when the phone rang.

"Your son wants to tell you something," Wanda called out.

"Dad, I'm gonna start," Adam told John. Never mind that he didn't know all the plays.

Says Wanda, "We're just excited he's even on the team."

Much like Few's first scouting appearance to see Morrison, a sequence in that game – a loss to a St. Joe's team that would crack the 2004 Elite Eight – would be told and retold around Gonzaga. Morrison took the ball, dribbled from right to left – righthanded – looked at Stepp and cast up a perimeter jumper that went down.

"I looked right at coach Few and started laughing," says Stepp, the point guard. "Looked off by a true freshman – that kind of sums him up."

He was different then. He had a buzz cut, and on a very good 28-3 team that earned a No. 2 seed for the NCAA tournament, he settled into a reserve role. He got eight shots a game, hit 53 percent and was the Zags' fourth-leading scorer at 11.4 points, showing more mid-range game than three-point dependability.

Morrison says he liked it that year, "kind of being an X-factor guy, coming off the bench and no real chance of you losing a game. If you're not playing well, no big deal. Just kind of being a guy that lets it fly."

His hair had grown out by his sophomore year, along with his game. In Indianapolis against Illinois – which would go to the NCAA final that season – Morrison scored 26, but it was a hollow 26 as the Illini romped.

The real launch would come in the next game, the first one of import in the new McCarthey Athletic Center. Washington was 14th-ranked and unbeaten and the Zags were reeling, in search of themselves.

"We got housed by a top-five team (Illinois), and we got a bunch of pros coming in," Morrison recalls. "It was time to get going. I just remember the game being fast-paced and really fun to play in. The atmosphere in the Kennel was amazing."

Morrison unloaded another 26 on Washington, Ronny Turiaf scored 23, Derek Raivio played a sensational game, and Gonzaga won, 99-87. Morrison experienced a slump in midseason, but by now, even in Turiaf's senior year, Morrison had become the go-to guy, taking 145 more shots than Turiaf, leading the team in scoring at 19 a game. In the final half-dozen games of the season, save for a Senior Night breather against Northern Colorado, Morrison averaged 26 points.

His profile was expanding. He was as intriguing off the court as he was explosive on it. He riffed with Sports Illustrated about Che Guevara. He didn't seem like merely a jock. He chattered with defenders and baited their fans. He was fresh, raw, unfiltered, somebody for fans to embrace – or despise – with a passion.

There was nobody like him.

For a time, he roomed with Erroll Knight, the transfer from Washington. Initially, it seemed like oil and water, the African-American product of Seattle and the white kid from Spokane. Knight, an orderly, tidy sort to Morrison's Oscar Madison, one day had to draw a line down the middle of the apartment. Knight would keep his socks in his hamper, and Morrison's might be anywhere.

Knight liked rapper Brotha Lynch Hung and one day, popped a CD into a player.

"No way this guy from Mead, Washington would know who this guy is," says Knight. "I turned the music up, and I see him kind of bobbing his head. I'm like, 'What does he know about this song?' He goes, 'Erroll, you listen to Brotha Lynch? That's one of my favorite artists.'"

Morrison had been discussed as an early-entry candidate for the NBA, but he was coming back for his junior year. Zags assistant Tommy Lloyd advised the Morrisons to consider the NCAA disability insurance plan Turiaf had purchased for his senior year. They filled out the application and faxed it in, and before John Morrison got home, Lloyd was calling to tell him a projection of Morrison's financial ceiling was twice that of Turiaf.

"These are NBA people saying this," John Morrison said. "That's when it hit me: It was gonna be real."

Then came the 2005-06 season. Then came Maui. Then came the most electrifying 19-day stretch of college basketball you could imagine.

Previewing the Maui Invitational and eighth-ranked Gonzaga's opening-round game against No. 23 Maryland, ESPN's Dick Vitale said skeptically, "The Zags better bring their 'A' game." As it happened, they did. They shot 56 percent, Morrison went for 25 points and Gonzaga won 88-76.

What followed was a game for the ages, or as Morrison puts it, "absolutely one of the funnest things I've ever been a part of."

It was hoops at its purest, Gonzaga meeting 12th-ranked Michigan State in a sweaty, 2,400-seat gym in Lahaina, with no real stakes, no win-or-go-home hammer, just college basketball for the joy of it. Picture a triple-overtime game in which, from the eight-minute mark of regulation to the finish – 23 minutes – neither team led by more than three points. Picture one team (Gonzaga) making 27 of 28 free throws, and the other hitting 26 of 29.

During one dead-ball stoppage late in the game, Morrison, bent over, clutched his knees, spied three Northwest sportswriters and winked. He played 52 minutes that day.

"I can think of Final Fours that weren't this good," said Tom Izzo, the Michigan State coach.

Morrison scored a Maui Invitational-record 43 points, hitting half of his 28 shots. Spartans guard Maurice Ager went for 36.

An agent from California had been pestering the Morrisons, and now the heat had been turned up. "We were there with friends," says Wanda Morrison, "and he literally came through the crowd and tried to introduce himself to us anyway. I didn't care for that. And he didn't become Adam's agent."

It was almost anticlimactic when, in the finale, third-ranked Connecticut won by two on Denham Brown's late basket. The tournament MVP award went to Morrison, who scored 18 points on 8-of-19 shooting.

Eleven days later came a long-awaited matchup at 18th-ranked Washington, which had lost seven straight times to the Zags. Earlier that week, students had gotten hold of his cell-phone number and sent a barrage of calls his way.

Here's how the Associated Press began its recap of the night: "Gonzaga star Adam Morrison walked into Hec Edmundson Pavilion with his dark hair in a long, throwback Pete Maravich-style cut, a Pistol Pete mustache and thick red-and-blue 1970s stripes on his white tube socks. Washington students and some alumni greeted Morrison with bars of soap, chanting, 'Take a shower!'"

It was another sizzling game, more of what Gonzaga had generated in Maui. Morrison was merely marvelous, hitting 18 of 29 shots for another 43 points, on a night when Raivio departed with an early back injury and Gonzaga fell, 99-95.

John Morrison was there that night with one of Adam's sisters and a cousin. They waited for Adam to emerge from the Gonzaga locker room.

"There's pro scouts there and I don't know them and they don't know me," says the senior Morrison. "I overheard one gentleman on the phone. I don't know who he was talking to. He says, 'I don't care, coach, but the SOB can score.'"

Six days hence, the Zags were in KeyArena for a Battle in Seattle game with rugged Oklahoma State, trailing most of the way. The Cowboys led 62-61, missed a free throw and Morrison probed the middle of the floor. With a few seconds remaining, he wove right. There was no opening. He cast it off from 20 feet.

"Here comes the All-America," Gus Johnson narrated for CBS, his voice rising. "Morrison . . . fires . . . aaaaoooohhh! What a game! . . . Larry Bird . . . maybe!"

"Gus, oh, major . . . onions!" exclaimed Johnson's sidekick, Bill Raftery. "Oh, what a smooch! Wow, this kid is extraordinary."

No matter that Morrison's bank shot was a stab in the dark; it added to his growing legend. By now it was a full-on inferno. The Zags went to Memphis shortly after Christmas, and the place was pulsating with anticipation. John Calipari's Tigers were fourth-ranked and Gonzaga eighth.

"Calipari told his team, 'At no point does anybody get into it with this guy,'" recalls Few. " 'Don't get him going. Don't talk crap to him.'"

But shortly into the game, freshman Shawne Williams did, and Morrison was off and running.

"Timeout," Few recalls. "Calipari just loses it, loses it on his guys."

Morrison went for 34 points, hitting 9 of 20 shots, but when the Tigers held him scoreless over the last nine minutes, Memphis won, 83-72.

"So we ended up creating things for Adam that year," Few says. They'd tell him this coach had disrespected him. That player didn't think he was any good. Whatever it took to get the fire blazing.

As the calendar turned to 2006, the Zags had played five ranked teams and three others from power conferences. Now they withdrew to the regimen of mostly nondescript West Coast Conference games, which could have been a two-month bore, except life was never very boring around Adam Morrison.

The coaches had long ago learned that Morrison would put it on autopilot in practice if every segment wasn't designed to be competitive. So each drill needed to have a winner and a loser, and Morrison would be engaged.

"Early in his career, if you were doing a defensive drill, that was a time when he had to go check his [diabetic] numbers," remembers Rice. So instead of merely going without him during those periods, the Zags began using them to shoot free throws, and Rice says Morrison sensed they'd outfoxed him: "Damn it, they're onto me."

Rice wishes they'd saved videos of the short scrimmages, when they kept making it more challenging for the first unit, but Morrison would somehow rescue it with an off-balance, 35-footer ahead of the buzzer, and his teammate Knight would chase him ecstatically around the gym.

"Guys are jumping on each other," Knight recalls. "It's pandemonium."

Other times, they wanted Knight, the WCC defensive player of the year in 2005, on Morrison, creating some ferocious confrontations.

"Adam was one of those guys, he'd always use elbows," says Knight. "I'd say, 'Adam, if I get hit with another elbow, you're going down. Don't touch me with the elbows and everything will be fine.'"

If Morrison wasn't bigger than life, he became bigger than some of the program's standards. Says his teammate David Pendergraft,

"There'd be times in practice, we'd want to run a certain play, kind of a competition. Last possession, you're down two, he won't run the play. He'll just go down and hit a three. Few will say, 'We said, run this play.' It's like, 'No, I'm here to win, this is what's gonna win.' That's that hard-headedness. That's also what made him great."

In short, he could be a rube, immature and sometimes irrational. But also brilliant.

"He was so competitive, I didn't care," says Few. Referring to his longtime by-the-book staffmate, Few adds, "He was tough on a guy like Billy Grier, who's like A-B-C-D-E. I'm just like, 'Nobody has anybody else like him. He can score on anybody. We've got the best player in college basketball. I know he wasn't good in the drills at two o'clock on a Monday, but I'm fine with that when he's that good.'"

He could wear on teammates, too. He might get into it with somebody in an open gym, as he did once with J.P. Batista, one of the most cheerful souls the program has produced. But jealousy didn't seem to be an issue, even as players who had themselves come to Gonzaga as valued recruits set screens for a guy who took 617 shots in 2005-06.

"I was thankful for that," Morrison says a decade later. "I still am."

Says teammate Sean Mallon, "I've seen certain guys start to think a little much of themselves. That wasn't Adam's deal. We were roommates on the road, and it was the same old Mo. I really appreciated it. I never got the sense he was bigger than the team."

College basketball's transcendent players have come in all forms – postmen, playmakers, point forwards. All of them, dating to the first players of the year in the late 1950s, were supreme in some facet of the game. But how many checked a multitude of other boxes as well, for magnetism, improbability and personality?

Morrison was a lightly recruited player with rare offensive skills who had a wider view of the world, who played with diabetes, who became a pop-culture figure, whose allure attracted a new set of curiosity-seekers to the game, who had a long-distance joust with the other player-of-the-year candidate.

Jimmer Fredette had a little of that. Christian Laettner had the polarizing part down. Larry Bird had a lot of the same style as Morrison, with a more expansive game. In a different time, a less connected time, Pete Maravich set the standard for star power.

Few remembers traveling with Morrison like being around the "fifth Beatle." The Gonzaga athletic director, Mike Roth, recalling how students on the road scrambled to grab the gauze Morrison had stuffed into a bloody nose, termed it like "freakin' Mick Jagger."

"Let's say you're going out to play Pepperdine, out in the middle of Malibu," says Pendergraft. "People would start following the bus, and they'd mob the bus all the way to the walk-through. He'd just stick his head down, trying to get into game mode. Then you'd look on the court and the Lakers' starting five is there – there's Kobe and Jerry West."

Autograph-seekers, many middle-aged, besieged Morrison. In Portland once, a man jockeyed to get a photograph with Morrison, even trying to get on the team bus. Steve Hertz, the former baseball coach now an associate athletic director, herded Morrison toward it.

The man was persistent.

"Steve Hertz is the nicest guy; he wouldn't hurt a fly," says Knight. "I just remember Steve Hertz going, 'Get the hell away from this program!'"

"It happened all the time," says Pendergraft.

In hotels, Morrison checked in as Dirk Diggler – the porn star from the film "Boogie Nights."

"Just some of the girls, I mean, golly," Knight says. "Some people were just in awe. The guy couldn't go anywhere in Spokane without doing something for somebody. I think Adam got a bad reputation just because of how much he's been approached. Sometimes he just wanted to eat his sub sandwich and go home. There were times he couldn't eat. He'd get interrupted two or three times. Some people would do things just to piss him off."

His family was gathered one night at a Spokane tavern after a golf benefit for the American Diabetes Association when a woman came up from behind and planted a kiss on Morrison's cheek. Minutes later, her husband was there, alleging they'd been rude to his wife before Morrison's sister defused the situation.

"You didn't want to mess with us," says Wanda Morrison.

Then, as if there weren't enough juice to the Morrison story, along came a foil.

In truth, Jonathan Clay (J.J.) Redick didn't sneak up on anybody. He had averaged 21.8 points in his junior season at Duke in 2004-05, and unlike Morrison, his basketball genealogy was pure. He was a McDonald's All-American (and the MVP of that all-star game), a five-star recruit from Roanoke, Virginia.

Known primarily for his catch-and-shoot offense, Redick averaged 15 points as a true freshman at Duke, and bumped that number slightly the next year.

He was also a target of serious enmity in the Atlantic Coast Conference, but in a different way from Morrison. He seemed to take heat for his All-American-boy looks, for a perceived overheated love affair between the media and Redick, and the fact that it simply had become *de rigueur* to pounce on somebody from the Duke roster.

One rogue website, listing "Ten Reasons Why You Hate J.J. Redick," attributed one to: "Everybody loves Adam Morrison because of his butt stache and floppy hair. J.J. is clean-cut and handsome."

As Redick began his senior year bearing down on both the ACC record for career points and three-point shots made by a collegian, anybody could have predicted he'd be a prime candidate for national player of the year. In fact, he had already won the Adolph Rupp Award in 2005, in a year in which Andrew Bogut took most of the national player honors.

What few saw coming was Morrison's incendiary emergence, or the crazy, can-you-top-this, long-distance shootout that lit up the season.

Redick lobbed the first grenade when his top-ranked Blue Devils routed No. 2 Texas on Dec. 10 and he scored 41 points, hitting nine threes. A few hours later, Morrison cut into Redick's media splash when he coaxed in the bank shot to beat Oklahoma State.

Redick called and raised with 41 points at Georgetown Jan. 21 in Duke's first defeat. Morrison matched him with 41 at San Francisco two days later. The next week, Redick scored 40 at Virginia and later that day, Morrison threw in 42 against Portland.

In mid-February, Redick became the NCAA's premier career three-point maker. Four days later, Morrison, stunted to seven points at halftime by Loyola Marymount's sagging zone defense, strafed the helpless Lions for 37 second-half points.

Sports Illustrated's cover, with Morrison and Redick posed full-length, back-to-back, asked, "Who's the best?" It was compelling theater, a question with seemingly no wrong answer.

Word got out that they had hooked up, three time zones apart, to play Xbox Halo 2. A decade later, they agree that the rivalry – at least that part of it – was overstated.

"It really was," Morrison says. "You know how it is with the media. Once it gets a head of steam, it's hard to put the brakes on."

In early 2016, Redick hosted Morrison on Yahoo Sports' weekly "Vertical Podcast." He pooh-poohed the notion of regular Halo 2 confrontations with Morrison, saying, "We made the mistake of agreeing to let ESPN film us. Stupidest thing ever. There was the idea, you and I were up late at night, you'd finish your game on the

West Coast at midnight (on the East Coast) and I'd text you: 'Hey, Bud, I'll be on in 20.' Never happened."

For Morrison, the story lines had long been plumbed, and the questions grown repetitive – the diabetes, the shot-making, the eye on Redick. There were no new ways to say it. He told Redick on the podcast, "It was like after a while, man, 'Just cut and paste.' It was like, 'I'm done with this crap, it's getting old.'"

Late in the season, his coach sensed it was wearing on Morrison as well. He told the Gonzaga publicist, Oliver Pierce, that Morrison was done with interviews aside from postgames – much to Pierce's chagrin, because a television crew had already been scheduled in from Los Angeles to talk to Morrison shortly.

Pierce went to Grier, Few's assistant, and pleaded his case. "We'll take care of it," Grier promised.

"It was like this covert operation," Pierce remembers. "They set up right across from my office. Practice ends, and it's 'OK, where's Mark?' We sneak Adam in and do the interview. If Mark finds out, he's going to freakin' kill me."

The Zags blew through the WCC schedule undefeated, but the 25-3 record entering the league tournament was a bit deceiving, mostly because they couldn't stop anybody. The team seemingly evolved in the vein of Morrison's jocular T-shirt with the advisory: IF IT WASN'T FOR OFFENSE, I'D PLAY DEFENSE. After the post-Christmas loss at Memphis, they won 16 straight heading into March, but 10 were by 10 points or fewer.

"We couldn't play any defense, just by who we had," says Morrison. "We just outscored people."

For the first time in history, Gonzaga was going to host the league tournament. It looked like a slam-dunk for Gonzaga – right up until GU had to go to overtime to beat San Diego, and then had to scramble from behind to beat Loyola Marymount by a point. And then only when an unfortunate big man named Chris Ayer fluffed a layup for Loyola off a set play in the final seconds.

A few years later, after Morrison's NBA career brought him to the Lakers, he found himself in pickup games that included Ayer. "I would always laugh in my head, like, 'Thank you for missing that layup,'" Morrison says. "We'd have been the team that finally gets it [the tournament] here and we lose."

A couple of weeks before Morrison's college career would be extinguished, a fiery subplot also died. His association with Redick was an abstract thing, two prolific collegians doing their scoring deal on opposite coasts, leaving much to argument and imagination. Their respective teams would never meet.

On the other hand, his battles with Corey Belser were brusque, physical and in-your-face.

Belser was the son of a career Army man, and he wanted to go to Gonzaga. When the Zags burst onto the national scene in 1999 with their Elite Eight run, Belser was sitting in his dad's Chevy truck, listening on the radio. Belser had kept tabs on Gonzaga's forward of the late 1990s, Mike Leasure, who had preceded Belser in high school at Spanaway, Washington, outside Tacoma.

Belser and Knight had been teammates on Seattle's Friends of Hoop AAU team and developed a solid friendship. Rangy, long and 6-7, Belser attended a team camp at Gonzaga and played some open gym there. But the fit wasn't ideal, and Few helped get the word out that Belser could help a program. He eventually picked San Diego over Nevada.

Before the 2003-04 season, when he would be a junior, Belser tore an ACL. So he could only seethe on the bench, watching Morrison "talking trash and me being so motivated to get back and compete."

The next year, they did, bringing about one of college basketball's fiercest individual confrontations, a classic collision of offense and defense. "I think Brian Michaelson says it best," Morrison observes wryly, referring to the GU assistant coach. " 'If they had the review, like the elbow review, you guys would have been ejected.' Luckily, we didn't at the time."

Six times, Morrison and Belser went at each other, Morrison chattering incessantly, Belser cloaking him like Southern humidity. The first two games, Belser held Morrison to single digits. Each drew a technical foul in the second one. In the third game, in the 2005 WCC tournament at Santa Clara, Gonzaga won handily, Morrison scored 25 points on 10-of-17 shooting and left an impression on Belser, as if he hadn't already formed one.

"I remember him coming down and hitting a three in my face," says Belser, now an assistant coach for the Miami Heat's Developmental League team in Sioux Falls, South Dakota. "He hit his knuckles to his head."

Whatever for? "It was Adam Morrison, him being crazy."

With Morrison and Belser, at times it was basketball, at times mud-wrestling. Once, Corey had to warn his brother Chris, who had played wide receiver for the Idaho football team, to keep his cool in his baseline seat at a game when he saw him "acting like he wanted to run on the court."

It all boiled over in the semis of the 2006 WCC tournament at the McCarthey Athletic Center. With Belser's family in the crowd, Morrison kicked off the evening's conversation by telling Belser, "It's cool that your family could be here for your last game."

They tangled, they jousted, they warred. Belser got a technical foul for flicking the ball at Morrison during a stoppage, later saying he was merely retaliating. When it was done – Gonzaga's tenuous, 96-92 overtime victory – Belser and his coach, Brad Holland, were bitter about the officiating. The Zags shot 45 free throws, 26 more than San Diego. Morrison's 24 points came on 11 of 14 at the line and only five of 16 from the field.

"He's always saying to me, 'Welcome to Spokane; we get the calls,'" Belser said that night, adding, "He says some personal things.

The last game when we lost to them, he told me if I got hit by a train and died, he wouldn't care."

Morrison denied the train comment after the game, saying he'd heard some unprintable names from Belser. And he added, "Like I always say to him: 'Scoreboard.' I've never lost to him, and losers never get a chance to talk trash."

The next night, before the tournament final, Grier confronted me, upset that the bruising repartee had ever made its way into the newspaper. His point was that the gamesmanship in the heat of battle shouldn't be transferred to real life.

In their six games on the same floor, Morrison averaged 15.2 points against Belser, shooting 40.5 percent. A decade later, they have a competitor's respect for each other.

"I respect him as a player," Belser says. "I don't really know him as a person."

Then he added something telling: "At the end of the day, I've always wanted Adam Morrison to be successful. Kind of like a piece of me was in Adam."

Anyone with a perverse yearning for Morrison to experience comeuppance got it on the night of March 23, 2006. It happened at the Oakland Arena, where Gonzaga mishandled a nine-point lead with 3:27 left and lost a 73-71 game to UCLA after leading the entire game. It came in the Sweet 16, and given that the regional-final opponent would have been Memphis – which Gonzaga had hung with on the road three months before – the misstep is widely viewed as the Zags' most devastating loss in history, their best chance at an elusive Final Four gone up in flames.

With 2.6 seconds left, when the Bruins had finally taken the lead following a strip of Batista and the Zags had turned the ball over, Morrison collapsed near midcourt and broke down in tears.

When Gonzaga met UCLA at the same juncture of the tournament in 2015, it was natural for Morrison to field questions about the 2006 finish. Three months after that, he brought up the issue himself.

"It is what it is," he says. "People always ask, especially this year: Does it still bother you? The loss does. But the whole other stuff doesn't. I put that stuff to bed a long time ago. Like one of my buddies told me, if that's the worst thing you've done in sports . . . you didn't punch your girlfriend in an elevator, you didn't get a DUI . . ."

Was it unusual? No doubt. Perhaps it could even be called unseemly. But it happened. It was spontaneous, something that simply broke out. So be it.

Imagine that Gonzaga locker room. In a side room, Morrison and Mallon struggled to tame the emotions. They were two Spokane kids who had been brought together by proximity, rivalry and records – Mallon had set a Greater Spokane League record for scoring, and Morrison had broken it – and now their alliance as players was done.

Morrison had decided about halfway through that season that he would pass on his senior year, but nothing had been announced. As obvious a choice as it was, his junior season began to make him feel as if he were a senior, and it seemed weird.

The silence was deafening. Morrison walked out of an arena for the last time as an amateur, numb. He couldn't know it then, but it was the end of innocence.

Given the lock-step nature of Redick's and Morrison's seasons, it was probably fitting that their college careers ended on the same night, a few hours apart, in the NCAA tournament. A week later, they were to connect at the Final Four in Indianapolis.

Pierce suggested to his sports-information colleague, Jon Jackson of Duke, that they tag-team the two players for radio and TV interviews, with the idea they would be more at ease together. They were walking back to their hotel from renowned St. Elmo Steak House when a driver slammed on his brakes and a man emerged with a stack of parquet-floor tiles for Morrison to autograph. He signed several.

"No more, we're done," Pierce said firmly.

The next morning, they met at nine o'clock in the hotel lobby for the next round of media and awards. And the same pushy fellow was there, looking for more autographs.

"Redick blended in," Pierce says. "J.J. didn't get hounded a tenth of what Adam did."

In the end, Redick pulled down most of the awards. His head start entering the season was probably important. So, no doubt, was a suspicion that Morrison's competition in the West Coast Conference was dubious – even if he had left a lasting mark on every high-level team Gonzaga played in its front-loaded schedule.

Redick was named player of the year by Naismith, Wooden, Associated Press, Rupp and The Sporting News. Chevrolet chose Morrison, and the U.S. Basketball Writers Association and National Association of Basketball Coaches split the award.

At the USBWA breakfast feting the players as Oscar Robertson Trophy winners that Friday morning, Morrison looked a little ill at ease in an off-green suit. "They only had the one [trophy]," recalls John Morrison. "Adam says, 'You're the oldest, you take it.' Well, it took a year and a half before we got a replica of that same trophy."

A couple of weeks later, Morrison declared for the NBA draft amid speculation that he might become the No. 1 pick, held by Toronto. Morrison flew back to the draft site, Madison Square Garden, the place where he had launched his college career with that unorthodox basket against St. Joseph's back in 2003. With him were his parents and his two sisters; a few extended-family members; and his high school coach, Glenn Williams, and his wife.

The Raptors chose Italian forward Andrea Bargnani with the first pick, and Texas forward LaMarcus Aldridge went second, traded immediately by Chicago to Portland.

That brought up Charlotte. After 14 mostly competitive seasons known as the Hornets following an NBA expansion in 1988-89, the team had bailed for New Orleans in 2002 due to an arena squabble. After a two-year absence from the NBA, Charlotte came back as an expansion team, with the usual expansion growing pains; the Bobcats won 44 games those first two seasons, and local and NBA icon Michael Jordan joined the team's ownership in 2006.

The Bobcats picked Morrison, amid much pomp and exuberance. Morrison did the usual round of post-pick interviews. His parents were greeted by Dell Curry, the Charlotte career scoring leader, who had been designated to chaperone them.

"The Bobcats would like to have you and your family at the press conference in Charlotte," Curry told them.

"We were treated like king and queen," says Wanda Morrison. "We could never have afforded that. For someone from small-town northeastern Montana, it was fabulous just to feel all the energy. It was great, great, great fun."

The Morrisons flew out commercial the next day, trailing Adam. The press conference in the Bobcats' practice gym was waiting on them. At their hotel, you could look outside the window, and playing on a large video screen were highlights of their son at Gonzaga.

There was a buzz about Morrison. It was impossible to separate the actual goods he brought to Charlotte from some of his mythic achievements at Gonzaga, especially at a place hungering to win. Somewhere along the way, John Morrison recalled the words of the former Oklahoma coach, Billy Tubbs, in reference to ex-Sooners All-American Wayman Tisdale.

"If you're a high draft pick," says John Morrison, "that means you're going to a crappy team. And the pressure's on to get 'em out of that crap. And that's exactly what Adam's situation was."

Nobody denies that. Bernie Bickerstaff, his coach that first season in Charlotte, told me, "He was under a lot of pressure with the hype, and what he had done at Gonzaga. So the expectations were really high. There still had to be a process to go through to develop."

As early as mid-November of his rookie year, Morrison was talking about having felt being under the gun. That was when he scored 27 points in a road win at San Antonio. He had another 27 in a loss to the Heat 10 days later, and in the last game of the 2006 calendar year, he dropped a career-high 30 in a win at Indiana.

"It was good for the first half," Morrison says. "Then I kind of hit a lull and didn't play well the last half of the season."

"It's a natural progression when young guys come into the league," says Bickerstaff. "They hit that wall. You're talking about playing three collegiate seasons in one NBA season."

In games through December 31, Morrison averaged 33 minutes and launched 14 shots a night. From February on, his minutes dropped to an average of 26 with 10 shots. The Bobcats finished 33-49.

Morrison couldn't have known he was on a professional downward spiral he would never fully reverse.

Sam Vincent had replaced Bickerstaff as coach for Morrison's second season, and Morrison was ticketed for a new role, playing 20-25 minutes off the bench. But, in a closeout against Luke Walton of the Lakers late in the exhibition season, Morrison crumpled, tearing his left ACL. He missed the entire season.

"I hurt that quad when I was a sophomore in college, and never told anybody, or it just wasn't like a major [injury]," Morrison says. "It never healed properly."

Morrison says an examining doctor asked him, "You ever hurt your quad?"

"Three years ago."

"Well, that's what did it."

Misfortune morphed into gloomy happenstance. Vincent went 32-50 and Larry Brown was imported to shake up the franchise.

"Yeah, he's a legend," Morrison concedes. "But he was just . . . he's very critical of guys – which is fine, it's professional sports. But he's a guy that can just wear people out."

Adjusting to the rebuilt knee and to Brown, Morrison averaged only 15 minutes and five shot attempts in 2008-09 for the Bobcats. The controlled rage he played with at Gonzaga was a thing of the past. Later, *Charlotte Observer* writer Rick Bonnell would post on a blog:

> It was that half-season playing for Larry Brown, when he seemed so scared to shoot. He was so hyper-conscious of the town's expectations that he played dramatically worse at home than on the road (not that he was playing well on the road). One night Brown put him in a game, and every time the ball hit Morrison's hands, he'd immediately pass it, like it was made of plutonium.
>
> After that game, Brown posed this question: How could he play Morrison – a guy whose only real skill was as a scorer – if he refused to shoot? Sometime around then, Brown asked Morrison how he couldn't have grasped the attention that being the No. 3 overall pick entails . . .

One day, Morrison's parents got a call from his agent, Mark Bartelstein.

"I can't get hold of Adam," Bartelstein told them. "He just got traded to the Lakers."

John and Wanda Morrison high-fived, so badly did they want him away from Brown.

If Morrison was miscast in a pressure-cooker in Charlotte, now he was headed to completely different environs, playing for the Zenmaster, Phil Jackson, on an established team that won two league championships in Morrison's season and a half there. It had Kobe Bryant, Pau Gasol, Andrew Bynum, Lamar Odom, Derek Fisher and more.

Morrison found playing for Jackson "awesome," even as his game role diminished. "I've always told people he was fair," Morrison says. "He was open and honest. The mood was – you say laid-back, and people think it's not serious, or it's grab-ass. He just didn't add another layer of pressure."

As rich – and ring-producing – as the experience was, it might have been counterproductive to Morrison's career. Surely a team somewhere between dreck and colossus, someplace that might have needed 20 good offensive minutes a game, could have used him.

"I couldn't get a job," he says of his post-Lakers days. "So I did training camp with the Wizards [in 2010] and got cut. By that time, I was kind of over basketball, to be honest with you."

It was the darkest time in his basketball career. In the information age, he was cut no slack. He was the No. 3 pick that had flamed out. He appeared on "bust" lists. Jimmy Kimmel ridiculed him.

He says he took a year off, coming back to Spokane. Asked what he did during that time, he answers quickly: "Nothing. Literally."

His family worried about him. Says his mother, "I didn't like that. That's a form of depression, it really is. As a parent, I knew his heart was sad. I knew he was mourning something he was really passionate about. Who wouldn't?"

At one point that year, John Morrison says, referring to the memorabilia amassed during his son's golden time with the game, "If I had gone to the dump and dumped everything, it was fine with him."

Gradually, he pulled out of it. He began working out at Gonzaga, getting back into shape for one last surge at The League. Eventually, he landed in Serbia, regaining the old fire. But after a couple of summer-league stints, and then a training camp with the Blazers in 2012, Morrison sensed his time had run out.

He says he was at peace with it. With the Blazers, he played the style he used to – running off screens, moving, scoring from mid-range, shooting well. It wasn't enough. At 28, he was done.

What didn't work? Why wasn't Adam Morrison's NBA story a happier one?

I'm convinced even Morrison himself might struggle for the correct answer.

A hint might be reflected in one of basketball's simplest metrics: Free throw shooting. At Gonzaga, Morrison was a .761 foul shooter. His career percentage in the NBA was .710. It wouldn't be preposterous to suggest he found elusive the level of confidence that propelled him as a collegian.

Don MacLean, the Pac-12's career scoring leader while at UCLA a generation ago, and who helped train Morrison after Gonzaga, told SportsIllustrated.com in 2011 Morrison "lost a lot of his confidence, and that was what his game was built on at Gonzaga – superior, supreme confidence . . . once you took that confidence away . . . it kind of took away his game."

Confidence lost: It's a catch-all diagnosis that leads you down many different paths. If it's true, what caused it?

Surely the knee injury didn't help. Morrison says it didn't feel right until his second year with the Lakers.

"There's been sort of a narrative out there that Adam Morrison was a bust," says Bartelstein, his former agent. "If he didn't have that knee injury, I think he would have been a dynamic scorer in the NBA."

There's the imponderable of the diabetes. A scout for an NBA team in the lottery in 2006 told me a trainer from that club voiced reservations about potential recovery time, so the scout took particular note of how Morrison did his rookie year on the trail end of back-to-back games.

But those numbers are less revealing than the fact he struggled overall the last couple of months of 2007 – which could have been rookie fatigue or diabetes-related. He made only 34 percent of his shots on the second half of back-to-backs after Feb. 1, but earlier in that situation, he had several stellar games, including the career-high 30.

Perhaps there was an element of the collegiate buzz around Morrison exceeding his capacity to deliver. To some degree, did Charlotte buy into the hype?

"I think they bought into the results," says Bickerstaff. "And the results, in terms of his [college] career, they were pretty good."

Bickerstaff insists the Charlotte roster Morrison's rookie year "had really good chemistry and work ethic," but that's not a universal opinion. In his podcast with Redick, Morrison described "kind of like, a friction amongst everybody there, because every guy the year before was supposed to be 'The Guy.'"

His college teammate, Pendergraft, recalls how the Zags of 2006-07 pitched in to buy the NBA League Pass so they could watch Charlotte games on television.

"You had guys that were really selfish," Pendergraft says. "You could see guys like Raymond Felton, where he'd just screw him over. He'd [Morrison] be at the end of the shot clock and have to throw something up. It wasn't just Adam. It was kind of a poisonous environment – Gerald Wallace taking shots he shouldn't have been taking, ever."

The view of Francis Williams is not as generous. Williams, former Rainier Beach High and AAU coach in Seattle and TV analyst, became a scout with the Bobcats in the post-Morrison years.

"I thought he was going to be like John Havlicek," says Williams. "He couldn't guard anybody, he wasn't going to get any rebounds, but he could score. He couldn't necessarily get his own shot. I think there were two things with Adam Morrison. Unfortunately, he got hurt, and that was too bad. [But] he just didn't take care of his body."

So Adam Morrison is doing what every NBA player must do – figure out a life after basketball. He's just doing it earlier than he would have expected.

He was a student assistant at Gonzaga while he returned to get his degree. His father thinks he'd make a good NBA or Development League workout coach; the two of them helped prepare former Gonzaga All-American Kelly Olynyk for the 2013 draft.

Coaching, in some fashion, appears to be his calling. But that idea comes with a caveat. He doesn't want an itinerant life that would take him away from two young daughters who live with their mother in Spokane.

He plays a lot of golf and has the summer place on the lake. He has a collection of classic cars – a 1961 Chevy, a 1969 Camaro, and a 1969 Chevelle, among others. His own ride is a Maserati.

"I don't know if there's another one in Spokane," his father says.

The other day, John Morrison says, his sister was in a hotel near Staples Center in Los Angeles. On a wall was a large photograph of the Lakers' championship parade in 2010. John and Wanda Morrison were on that float, and so was Adam, holding his older daughter, a toddler then. So was Kobe Bryant.

Morrison ascended spectacularly and fell hard. Just as he was always pricking skin to regulate blood-sugar level, he seeks a comfortable equilibrium between those extremes.

What could have been. And oh, what was.

– 9 –
JOSH HEYTVELT:
THE ABYSS AND THE ATONEMENT

In the final minutes of February 9, 2007, everything about the Gonzaga narrative changed. Suddenly, Gonzaga wasn't the feel-good, out-of-nowhere story about a college basketball program succeeding in the face of great odds. It was the place that spawned this advisory crawling across the bottom of your television:

Josh Heytvelt of Gonzaga was arrested Friday night and charged with felony possession of hallucinogenic drugs . . .

Josh Heytvelt? Gonzaga? With psychedelic mushrooms? Seventeen hours before the Zags were hosting Saint Mary's in a West Coast Conference game?

None of it made a lot of sense, and even if the same could be said about a lot of things that happen on a college campus, that didn't lessen the impact of an incident that jarred college basketball and made Gonzaga – the school, not just the basketball program – shudder to its core, prompting a self-examination of its purpose and its mission.

"Josh, unfortunately, took stupid to a new level," GU athletic director Mike Roth would say years later, an observation as stark as the crisis that confronted Heytvelt and the school.

Time, it is said, heals all wounds. In this case, time had its work cut out.

Rolin Heytvelt opens a door to the garage at the fire station in Clarkston, Washington, and alongside a gleaming red truck is a basketball hoop with a tattered net. This is where his son Josh shot some of his first baskets.

The elder Heytvelt's grandparents were Dutch immigrants who came through Ellis Island. His grandfather found work in the Seattle shipyards in the 1920s, and half a century later, Rolin and Michelle Heytvelt would settle in Clarkston, he a firefighter, she an elementary schoolteacher.

Rolin, a large, affable man, remembers a Clarkston youth coach telling the Heytvelts that he didn't have room for the pre-teen Josh on his basketball team – he already had a serviceable post player – so for about three years, he went across the river and played in Lewiston, Idaho.

By the time he was a sophomore at Clarkston, he was a gangly 6-feet-8, but springy and a shooter, enough of a prospect that AAU programs around the Northwest were calling the Heytvelts. Josh decided to cast his lot with Rotary in Seattle and a team that included future pros like Marvin Williams and Aaron Brooks. In the very first practice, Josh took an elbow flush to the mouth. He had braces on his teeth and when Rolin looked inside, he saw a stream of blood.

"What do you think?" he asked his son on the drive back across the state.

"I'm going to stick it out," Josh said.

Early, he was a substitute as a sophomore – until a senior, Ryan Gillie, went to coach Brendan Johnson and suggested that Heytvelt ought to have his starting spot.

Soon, the hubbub around Heytvelt would grow. As Rolin says casually, "That's about when Cameron Dollar got involved."

Dollar, who as a player had stepped in for injured Tyus Edney and helped spark UCLA to the national title at the Kingdome in 1995, was looking to make another mark in Seattle. As a member of newly hired Lorenzo Romar's staff at Washington, Dollar went aggressively – and improperly, it turned out – after Heytvelt and Williams, the Bremerton phenom. Dollar had impermissible phone and personal contact with the two, and the Huskies copped to 23 incidents of NCAA violations traced to him.

The indiscretions were all news to the Heytvelts, plain people who were in uncharted territory because of Josh's emerging talent. "I had no clue," Rolin says. "I played church-league basketball. I didn't understand the pressure these coaches are under."

They were delightfully naïve on other fronts as well. Josh was a baseball pitcher – indeed, Rolin contends that might have been his No. 1 sport – and the elder Heytvelt persuaded Josh's baseball coach to let him attend an AAU basketball tournament in Houston. There, they came to learn about a prospect of some renown named LeBron James.

"Josh and I are from Clarkston, Washington," says Rolin. "We like to go fish. We don't really like to watch professional basketball on TV. We don't know [at that time] who the heck LeBron James is."

Now Rolin Heytvelt produces a keepsake recruiting letter, written by New Mexico assistant coach Scott Didrickson to Josh's high school coach, Johnson.

"I had a chance to see Josh play down in Houston," Didrickson wrote. "He was great. He probably told you he played against LeBron James' team, and Josh singlehandedly kept the Rotary team in the game by hitting three or four threes in the first half. He probably had 20 points and 10 rebounds in the game . . ."

"It's one of those things I saved," Rolin says. "It's the first thing where a dad says, 'Wow. Somebody else sees potential in your kid.'"

There were all sorts of Heytvelt family ties to the University of Washington. Rolin's parents were graduates, and he had cousins who went there. But Gonzaga was winning, assistant Leon Rice had established a bond with the family, and at his heart, Josh Heytvelt was a small-town guy. In June after his junior year, he picked the Zags.

He redshirted as a freshman in 2004-05, owing to Gonzaga's wealth of front-court veterans in Ronny Turiaf and J.P. Batista. A season later, in a loose-ball pileup against third-ranked Connecticut in the championship game of the Maui Invitational that No. 8 Gonzaga lost narrowly, Heytvelt sustained a broken bone in his ankle requiring surgery and would be sidelined until February.

Then came 2006-07, when nobody could have foreseen the heights and depths Heytvelt would visit. Gonzaga, too.

Heytvelt, now starting for the first time at GU, hit up Eastern Washington for 22 points and Rice for 25 early in the season. But it was a game in the National Invitation Tournament Season Tipoff that turned heads. On a night when the 23rd-ranked Zags brought down second-ranked North Carolina, 82-74, in the event's semis in New York, Heytvelt had 19 points and nine rebounds, while Carolina mega-name Tyler Hansbrough scored just nine points. Sixteen months later, Hansbrough would win the Wooden Award.

In the ensuing weeks, Heytvelt would have a double-double as the Zags upended a Kevin Durant-led Texas team. But, bridging the end of the calendar year and the start of 2007, he and his teammates would lurch through a four-game losing streak – the only one of the Mark Few era and the first at Gonzaga since the final games of the Dan Fitzgerald regime in 1996-97.

The last of those four losses was one of the most dreadful in the Few tenure, a 108-87 debacle at Virginia that the Zags trailed 60-26 at half. Guard Sean Singletary scored 37 points for the Cavaliers, and, asked afterward why he was shaking his head upon retreating down the floor following one of his threes, he said, "I was just wondering why they didn't play more D."

Few didn't argue, telling reporters, "That's as badly as we've been beaten, certainly, in the eight years since I've been the head coach."

A personnel move made it obvious that, even as Heytvelt averaged a robust 15.5 points that season, GU coaches felt he had more to give. After an 0-for-6 night at Virginia when he went scoreless in 15 minutes, he came off the bench for the next three games, all Gonzaga victories. He returned to the starting lineup when the Zags fell at Saint Mary's, 80-75, scoring 20 points, but he was offset by a freshman named Omar Samhan with a career-high 20, and Few said afterward, "In the second half, our defense just totally broke down, especially our post defense."

He stayed in the starting lineup and, playing against the Lopez twins at Stanford in a midseason non-league game, had some key points down the stretch in a 12-point, 12-rebound night (albeit on 4-of-13 shooting).

The Zags stayed on the road for a Feb. 3 game at an outmanned, 6-17 Pepperdine team, and this turned out to be the day envisioned by all those recruiters who had made their way to little Clarkston. Heytvelt was a beast in a blowout win, posting career highs in points and rebounds – 27 and 22 – as well as blocking six shots. But right in step with the inconsistencies of this team, the Zags dropped a 67-61 decision to Loyola Marymount two nights later despite 18 points from Heytvelt.

At that point, Gonzaga was 17-8 and tied at 7-2 for the WCC lead with Santa Clara. It was already an uncertain, jagged sort of season, and it was about to take a sharp and shocking turn.

Nobody remembers who made the phone calls, how they heard first, what time it was. Those became footnotes in the fog of an early Saturday morning in February, details lost in the blur of the moment.

Even the first one, from Josh Heytvelt to his home in Clarkston, was fuzzy. "I think initially I hung up on it," says Rolin Heytvelt.

"Middle of the night, you know, what's this? Then it rings again. It was like the whole bottom dropped out."

The message from his son was cryptic: "That he was in trouble and needed help. I had no clue what was going on."

At 18 minutes before midnight in nearby Cheney, 15 miles from Spokane, Heytvelt, accompanied by freshman forward Theo Davis, was stopped in a gold 2006 Chevy Trailblazer that he identified as his father's.

Late the next afternoon, the Zags were to host Saint Mary's. Coincidentally, Josh's older sister Heather, whose husband worked for the Defense Department in South Korea, had flown in for the weekend to see him play, as had another sister, Amy, from San Diego.

It would be a somber reunion.

Cheney patrolman David Bailey stopped Heytvelt's vehicle because the headlights weren't turned on. Another cruiser operated by Eastern Washington University officers arrived on the scene, and one of them, Todd Kusler, saw through the rear window a clear plastic bag of dried mushrooms protruding from a black backpack. Inside it were three muffins with embedded mushrooms.

Heytvelt and Davis weren't exactly professional in their cover-up. One of the two Eastern Washington patrolmen, Christopher McMurtrey, wrote in a report that he smelled a strong odor of burnt marijuana coming from Davis, who produced a blunt from a jacket pocket.

They were booked at the Cheney Police Department at 1:20 a.m., and after 2 o'clock, while their teammates slept in preparation for a rematch with Saint Mary's, the two were transported to Spokane County Jail.

Well, some of them slept, anyway. David Pendergraft, rooming then with Derek Raivio, recalls the phone ringing at about 2 a.m. It was teammate Micah Downs, who roomed with Davis. Downs called Pendergraft again at 4 a.m., and in his sleepy haze, Pendergraft wondered why Downs was awake. What was he doing?

Very soon, Internet sites would be crackling with the news:

Josh Heytvelt, the guy who not so long ago one-upped Tyler Hansbrough . . .

Gonzaga, the little school that could, but now couldn't . . .

"I remember reading it on-line," says former teammate Erroll Knight. "I get goose bumps just thinking about it."

About four hours before the arrest of Heytvelt and Davis, Roth addressed a group of high-end boosters. It was a dinner then; now it's called the "AD's luncheon." It recognizes some of those most devoted supporters of athletics at the school.

As usual, Roth appended his talk with a reminder. Yes, we have great kids, he said, adding, "They're 18 to 22 years old. They're going to do stupid stuff. Think about some of the stupid things you did, and you're glad you didn't get caught."

Now, before daybreak, Roth would be at the nexus of a crisscross of benumbed phone calls – coaches to coaches, players to players, administrators to vice presidents, Roth to GU president Robert Spitzer.

It wasn't by phone that Gonzaga's deputy athletic director, Chris Standiford, found out. He got the word from his eight-year-old son.

"That magnified it for me," Standiford recalls. "You're professionally incredibly proud of what Gonzaga basketball has meant in this community. All of a sudden, to have that ideal . . . to have my son in tears . . ."

Before the Heytvelts would make a hasty departure from Clarkston to bail Josh out of jail, Rolin took a call from Few.

"I remember being extremely angry," Rolin says. "I think the words I said to coach Few were, 'There's not enough words with F's and K's in them to let you know how I really feel.'"

Sitting in a jail cell, awaiting his release on the most miserable night of his life, Josh Heytvelt was cloaked by a dogged sensation: "You know, this isn't real. There's no way this is real."

The coaches gathered in the office of assistant coach Bill Grier, trying to wrap their arms around the situation, when, out of the whole depressing mess, a slice of levity emerged. But only with the passage of time.

"So I'm trying to be King Solomon and saying, 'What are we gonna do here, guys?'" Few recalls.

He heard two distinctly different schools of thought from Grier, a hard-liner, and Rice, who saw the possibility of some wiggle room.

"Billy was like, 'Get him out, kick him out of the program,'" Few says.

Rice protested. He wanted to go easier on Heytvelt. "It's a victimless crime," he argued.

To this day, when the subject of discipline comes up randomly, Few needles Rice with his own words: It's a victimless crime.

Among the layers of incredulity, there was this one: *Mushrooms?* Not marijuana, not cocaine, but mushrooms? Few grew up 10 miles from a liberal college town in Eugene and spent the early '80s there as a student at the University of Oregon, but says, "I hadn't heard it by the time I got into college. They were almost like, 'Aw, that's a '70s deal.' So I was just flabbergasted."

At mid-morning, Roth found himself in the office of Spitzer, along with a couple of school vice presidents and the chairman of the board of trustees. It's safe to say the gravity of the incident, and the attendant adverse publicity, was new to most of them. As Spitzer told me years later, "My heart sank when I got the call from Mike Roth. We put a lot of eggs in our character basket – the character of our players and the character of the school."

They arrived at a decision: Heytvelt could remain in school, but essentially he was a free agent. He'd be suspended indefinitely from the basketball team, booted from the athletic facilities for the duration. He'd have to manage on his own.

"If you miss a class in the foreseeable future," Roth said, "you're done."

Overshadowing the institutional issues, of course, was the criminal case. Lab tests would show Heytvelt to have been in possession of 33.2 grams of mushrooms and 261.9 grams of muffins, and the hallucinogenics psilocyn and psilocybin. The offense was a Class C felony, punishable by up to five years in prison and a $10,000 fine.

Amid all the turmoil, the Zags took the floor and gathered themselves for a 60-49 win over the Gaels. They would be guard-dominated now, and it was the backcourt of Raivio, Matt Bouldin (12 points each) and Jeremy Pargo (11) that made the difference. Truth be told, those Gaels were not the ones of later years; the loss dropped them to 13-13, and their 17-15 record that year was their last one shy of 20 victories under Randy Bennett. Still, under the circumstances, it was a win from the heart for Gonzaga.

About 10 p.m., hours after the horn had sounded and the McCarthey Athletic Center crowd had long dispersed, Few shuffled into a near-deserted press room to say hello. He looked completely shot.

His face mirrored the way Standiford remembers February 10, 2007: "It was a brutal day, an awful day."

While his court proceedings played out and February bled into March, it was hard to find anybody who didn't have an opinion about Heytvelt, or about the way Gonzaga dealt with him. In an earlier time, the spotlight would have been glaring enough. But this was the age of social media, of heartless – and anonymous – commentary. Dennis Thompson, Heytvelt's attorney, warned the family to stay off the Internet, away from television, that reporters might come to their door – they did – but don't talk to them.

Heytvelt's first baby steps toward rehabilitation came with a simple commitment to going to class, to being normal again. That was the prerequisite to any action the basketball program might take.

The first one was taught by Dr. Karen Rickel, in the department of sport and physical education. "The school was very accepting," Heytvelt says. "One of the best days after getting arrested was my first day at class. I figured all these people are going to make a big deal about it. Nobody mentioned anything in class. That class had a big role [in his rehabilitation]."

Around him, however, the questions swirled. Had the university lost its moral compass in the name of big-time basketball? How had a high-profile athlete who had never been in trouble suddenly gone off the rails?

The Gonzaga board of trustees had its regular February meeting in Scottsdale, Arizona and Roth was summoned to answer tough questions. "How did we let this happen?" he says, recalling the grilling. "Literally, why did I as an athletic director let this happen?"

Says Spitzer, referring to Heytvelt, "There were a lot of people who wanted to cut him loose, quite frankly."

Secondary to the bigger issues, but certainly no less public, were the Zags on the basketball floor. Two nights after the Saint Mary's victory, but now emotionally out of gas, they fell behind 13-0, trailed by 13 at halftime and lost by double digits to Santa Clara – their first defeat in four seasons at the MAC.

They were shorthanded, then and for the rest of the season, which underscored the violation of the athletic code Heytvelt had committed. Being out late the night before a game, endangering his availability, was a slap to the ideals for which his teammates were striving.

"There were players whose names are unmentionable," Spitzer says. "I can't even use the words. 'That blankety-blank. He besmirched us all. You ought to kick his blank out of the program.'"

"Oh yeah," says Few. "They were done with him."

Even among those who might have taken a softer stance, there was no lack of head-scratching. Says Raivio, "I never really had any ill feelings. I just kind of didn't get why he'd jeopardize so much just for a fun night."

Heytvelt was getting it from all angles. A satirical video surfaced, produced by benmakesmovies.com.

Two apartment roommates, one on the phone: *"Yeah, can I order a large Heytvelt?"*

A nerdy-looking guy on the street, on his phone: *"I'll get the Heytvelt special with extra Heytvelt, please."*

Later, one of the roommates is sampling the delivery order: *"Dude, this pizza's making me hungry. Let's get some more!"*

As the attorney had warned the Heytvelts, stay off the Internet.

If the episode was jarring to Gonzaga and to Spokane, it was no less so in Clarkston, a town of a little more than 7,000 population. A longtime resident of Clarkston who knows Heytvelt saw the reaction cleave into two camps: For those who had watched him grow up; had known him as the son of solid parents and as part of schools and community; and perhaps had been touched by him in some way, there was genuine concern and a desire to see him recoup his good name.

Then there was the other side: In a hardscrabble place where the percentage of residents under the poverty level was at an alarming 20.6 percent in 2013, compared to 12 percent just across the river in Lewiston, there was a certain fatalism about what Heytvelt did: *This is what happens to people from here.*

"We have such a high percentage of generational poverty," says the longtime Clarkston resident. "Mom and dad didn't work and grandma and grandpa didn't work, so redeeming themselves isn't anything that matters to them." To those, says this person, the conclusion is, " 'Well, he blew it, like everybody else that comes from this town.' They don't really want to improve themselves because they've never seen anybody else do it."

Notwithstanding a love for basketball – as a kid, Heytvelt always had a ball under his arm – he was a bit of a loner. Says Rolin Heytvelt, "He didn't hang out with jocks. He'd just as soon be fishing. He'd just as soon be playing video games with the little kid next door."

In retrospect, Few says he saw an element of the small-town kid for whom things happened quickly. "He got so good so early and had all this attention thrown at him," Few says. "He was really recruited hard there for a while. A lot of people were after him early. Then the whole UW thing blew up, so I think that put a lot of pressure on a kid that wasn't ready for that kind of pressure."

Few goes on: "He kind of socially struggled coming to college, with interacting and all that. He wouldn't always catch onto the wit of all of our guys early on. It's a pretty quick-witted bunch. He was probably lacking a little bit of self-esteem because of that."

Pendergraft, then and now a good friend of Heytvelt, put it a different way, saying, "He was kind of – he would admit to this – he was kind of a follower."

Heytvelt developed friendships outside of basketball. But even as his father says, "He was going down the wrong path with the wrong crowd," Heytvelt demurs, saying, "I wouldn't ever say it's the wrong people. In college, everybody wants to try things and do different stuff. A lot of the people I hung out with are very successful right now. It was all personal choices, of wanting to do recreational drugs and that type of stuff. I still have a lot of these friends today."

Still, he doesn't try to defend his behavior then, saying, "I was doing bad things I shouldn't have been doing."

In the weeks after his arrest, his attorney and the Spokane County prosecutor's office agreed to recommend a diversion program. Heytvelt had to stipulate to a finding that he didn't have a significant drug problem, submit to urinalysis/drug/alcohol tests as directed, and to fulfill 240 hours of community service.

Meanwhile, Spokane County Superior Court judge Michael P. Price received a score of letters from extended-family members of

Heytvelt, former coaches and friends, people willing to vouch for the good in him. They wrote about how he was respectful, how he interacted positively with children, how he volunteered to help with fire-department fund-raising activities. A marketing instructor at Clarkston High, Lynn Carey, wrote that "I have been teaching high school for the past 19 years and feel Josh is in the top 10 percent of the students I have taught."

Among the letters was one that came from the desk of the men's basketball coach at Gonzaga.

"Our program was stunned by the recent incident," Few wrote. "We have concluded that Josh Heytvelt made a huge error in judgment, exhibiting behavior not in keeping with our standards or with the general direction of his life. He is very sorry, extremely embarrassed and working very hard to show both teammates and coaches that he is remorseful and willing to earn back their trust . . .

"Josh is a good person with a good heart and our program is willing to give him another chance to realize all his personal, academic and athletic goals . . ."

The decision to give Heytvelt a pathway back – either to school or to basketball at Gonzaga – was hardly a universally popular one. This was Gonzaga, after all, not the University of Cincinnati under Bob Huggins, and it had standards.

"By definition, fanaticism is probably not the most stable thing," says Standiford. A significant portion of the GU fan base was "very judgmental, very angry."

They wanted him gone? "I think executed would have been good for some of them."

Had they a vote, his teammates no doubt would have voted Heytvelt off the island. Pendergraft uses the word "betrayal." But he also came to appreciate the stance of Few and the university in taking the longer view.

Says Pendergraft, "Fewie had the foresight and character to say, 'OK, guys, I know you're frustrated, you want certain things to happen. But we believe in grace. This guy deserves a second chance. We've all messed up.'

"To have that kind of grace and humility through a lot of pressure, through crazy-difficult scenarios – looking back now, that's how I would want that situation to be treated."

But it was a raging controversy. Roth got a call from the CEO of a sponsor, one that represented appreciable cash to the program.

"We need to meet," he told Roth.

They went to lunch. The CEO said his company had zero tolerance for drug-related offenses.

"We're in the business of educating," Roth told him. "There's times when we have zero tolerance, too, but we felt this was not one of those."

They agreed to disagree and shook hands amicably. The sponsor hasn't been back.

Just south of Interstate 90, astride a steep hill and a stone's throw from the hospitals that overlook downtown Spokane, is the Ronald McDonald House. Here, families come to stay and try to manage the cruel hand dealt a child.

It's a cheerful place framed by heartache. It has 22 resident rooms, none of which have televisions. TV is available in a large, welcoming foyer. The hope is that families won't feel inclined to sequester themselves in their rooms, but meet and mix and perhaps find some encouragement in their kindred struggles.

About 40 percent of families are here because of pediatric cancer. Premature births account for half the residents; it isn't uncommon that a mother of a premature child will be housed for three months.

Sometimes the family of a cancer patient might be here only a week for a brief treatment. Sometimes they'll be there nine or 10 months.

This RMD House covers a wide geographic sweep. The next one east is in Billings, Montana; south in Boise, and west in Seattle and Portland. To qualify, would-be residents must be at least 40 minutes or 40 miles from here. Routinely, there's a waiting list, sometimes of 20 families, and there's talk about expansion – so, explains the affable executive director, Mike Forness, "Those 20 families don't have to pay for a hotel, or sleep in their child's room, or even sleep in their car."

Forness leads a short tour of the place, to the kitchen, laid out in such a way as to facilitate interaction; to the SpongeBob game room downstairs; and outside, to the yard toys and a professional-grade basketball stanchion, backboard and hoop.

It was in his office that Forness took a call not long after Heytvelt's episode in Cheney. Jerid Keefer, long the organizer of Mark and Marcy Few's annual effort with Coaches Versus Cancer, asked if Heytvelt might fulfill some of his community-service requirement at the Ronald McDonald House.

This would be an exception. The RMD House normally accepts no court-mandated assignments for community service. But the house has a close relationship to Gonzaga – its charity game between the Zags and Memphis came a mere week after Heytvelt's arrest – so Forness consented to meet with Heytvelt.

They talked for 90 minutes. "He was visibly remorseful," Forness says. Heytvelt's unease was palpable, Forness says, "But I did judge he was sincere and he wasn't going to just walk through the motions. If that had been the case, I may not have had him volunteer here, or I may not have placed the emphasis on getting to know the families and the children. He seemed sincerely sorry for letting down his teammates and for the bad decisions he had made."

There were work-a-day chores to do at the RMD House – laundry, kitchen cleanup, shelf-stocking. But Forness wanted more than that. He wanted Heytvelt to know families in pain, to feel the crisis they were enduring. He directed his house manager to steer Heytvelt that way.

Back in early spring 2003, about the time Heytvelt was blowing up as an elite college prospect at Clarkston, a woman in Missoula, Montana named Angie Barron was concerned about her little boy Skyyler. A couple of times a week, he was feeling extreme pain in his midsection, and doctors were puzzled.

Twice, Angie took him to an orthopedic specialist. Then came a long day of tests, hour upon hour. Angie surmised it might be childhood arthritis. Never in her darkest vision did she suspect cancer.

Then a doctor emerged and was talking about a mass.

"What do you mean, a mass?"

Indeed, it was cancer, neuroblastoma. Angie's daughters, Sarah and Terry, 18 and 16, were there, tears pouring down their cheeks at the news.

It was a nightmare, striking a family that had already known too much hardship. A couple of years earlier, Angie's adult son had taken his own life. Angie herself is a recovering addict and alcoholic.

Her little boy was three years old.

The morning after the diagnosis, friends took Angie and her son to Spokane to see a pediatric oncologist, the first of a seemingly endless itinerary of trips west to hospitals there and in Seattle.

Angie recites a litany of treatments that would dominate Skyyler's next years: Chemotherapy; a 6 ½-hour surgery to remove the tumor that had wrapped itself around vital organs; more chemo; a bone-marrow transplant; retinoic acid, which caused his skin to peel.

For two years and four months, Skyyler was in remission. Then, when he was seven, Angie took him in for a checkup and they found a spot on his hip. More cancer. More treatment.

It wasn't long after that that the worlds of Skyyler and Josh Heytvelt converged. By now, Angie had found Ronald McDonald houses, both in Spokane and Seattle, a godsend.

"If he'd get a fever of 100, you go," she says. "Throw what you've got into a suitcase and you go. It's very dangerous. And we'd be there for weeks, because if there was an infection, they'd have to take care of that. Then they'd have to start chemo."

There were times when she was told that those 22 residential rooms in Spokane were booked.

"By the time we got there," she says, "there would be a room for us."

Only peripherally did Angie know Heytvelt's story. He was here, and he was helping, and that's all that mattered.

"I thought it was wonderful that it was community service at Ronald McDonald House and not picking up garbage along the highway or something," she said. "Josh was such a sweet kid, just a quiet, polite young man."

Angie remembers how Heytvelt towered over her son. Recalling how Skyyler had a bit of a potty-mouth – she says he got it from her – she imagines what he might have told the big guy on their first meeting: " 'Holy shit, you're tall.' Hopefully, only that mild."

They would shoot baskets outside, and afterward, the wisecracking "old soul" Angie remembers in Skyyler would tell people, "Yeah, I took Josh to the hoop."

It was at Ronald McDonald House that Heytvelt seemed to find himself. A couple of years later, only days before the end of his Gonzaga career, he told me the service there was "an eye-opening experience, just seeing all the families that had no choice in what would happen to their kids. That's how I processed it: Seeing what they had to go through affected what I went through.

"A lot of it was my choice, how things happened. They have no choice on what happens to them."

Clearly, it was a time of self-awakening for Heytvelt. Down in

Clarkston, I asked Rolin Heytvelt if he ever understood where his son's head was when he was busted, why it all happened.

"I don't think there was ever any of that kind of talk," he says. "But it was . . ." – he takes an extended pause – ". . . we had some long talks we never had before. My wife would probably tell you, I can drive for hours without saying much. It's kind of, I guess, a family tradition. Josh and I could go on a road trip to Seattle for the AAU tournaments and not have a bunch of conversations on the way. But there were a few times after that, a lot of times after that, we had some good conversations."

Meanwhile, Skyyler would continue throwing out one-liners, enjoying the people he met along the way, mastering the art of moving on heelies, those wheels on tennis shoes. His mom says he found fun in 90 percent of it.

It was that other 10 percent that was hell.

"There towards the end, we just carried the puke bucket around," Angie says. "A pink hospital puke bucket. He'd throw up, then get right back to what he was doing."

Bloody noses were a constant, and so was intense pain, sidetracking him from getting on his bike or climbing the huge tree in the front yard.

Now it was February 2011, and he was in hospice care in Spokane, and Angie worried that he might not last long enough to come home to Missoula.

"What should I tell your sisters if we don't get home?" she asked Skyyler.

"Tell them to take good care of you."

Five days later, he died.

He, and others, had long since left a mark on Josh Heytvelt. Annually, the Gonzaga team spends time at a nearby children's hospital and stops by the RMD House. And this one time, they had their tour guide in the normally reticent Heytvelt, who stepped forward without being asked.

That day, Forness says, "He was a leader. "I think he was very proud of what he had done here."

Rice, then a Gonzaga assistant, had long felt a connection with Heytvelt. He had been the primary recruiter on the big kid, and, Clarkston being little more than 100 miles from Spokane, he had been around him a lot. Rice also coached the big men during a run with the Zags that ended when he was named head coach at Boise State in 2010.

So he was invested. And he remembers the depth of Heytvelt's despair upon seeing him for the first time the day of his arrest.

"I just remember how down he was," Rice says. "He knew he'd really, really screwed up. That's also when I knew we could save him."

It was anything but easy. Heytvelt admitted to me back in 2009 that for a few months after the arrest, "I wanted to go into a shell and hide. I had to be out proving things, to the school and to the fans. I had to go to the coaches and tell them it was getting really, really hard. Every time I was looking for support, I found it."

Rice, in particular, propped him up. He stayed home from a routine trip to the Final Four. He says he stopped drinking alcohol about that time, explaining, "I wanted to be in the boat with him."

Spring melted into summer, and by the fall, Heytvelt had fulfilled his community-service commitment and was ready to be welcomed back into the basketball program. There was one small hitch.

According to Roth, Heytvelt's attorney told him he advised his client he shouldn't talk to the media. Recalls Roth, "I said, 'OK, that's fine, your client's not going to be part of the program then. If he wants to be part of the program, he needs to talk to the media. This is the last step for him. He needs to look the media in the eye and tell his story.'" (Heytvelt's attorney, Dennis Thompson, didn't respond to two attempts for comment.)

On October 12, 2007, seven months to the day after court papers were signed stipulating terms of his diversion agreement, Heytvelt appeared with Theo Davis at a news conference. Roth and Few were with them as the players' teammates watched.

"He did a great job," says Roth, referring to Heytvelt. "He never once tried to deny that he didn't screw up."

(As for Davis, he fulfilled a brief community-service commitment, and it was probably fitting that, in an uncertain period in Heytvelt's life at the time of their arrests, he would have been Heytvelt's companion. After a circuitous path to Gonzaga involving multiple high schools, Davis left the GU program just two months after his reinstatement, the school citing a stroke suffered by his father. A season later, he was closer to his Ontario, Canada home at Binghamton University in New York, but he departed that program during the 2008-09 season, only months before a scandal that included another player convicted of dealing cocaine and an audit of the school showing changed grades for basketball players and preferential academic treatment. According to the Welland, Ontario, Tribune, Davis then attended Rogers State in Oklahoma before landing back home at Brock University in St. Catharines, Ontario. His coach at Brock, Brad Rootes, told me Davis lasted about half a season before leaving. Said Rootes, "As a person, he was fine with us. I don't think being at a university, playing basketball, going to school was really where his mindset was at that point in his life. It wasn't of benefit for us to get part of him." Davis went on to play for Brampton in the National Basketball League of Canada.)

So what's the proper way to remember *l'affaire Heytvelt*? Is it merely one more example of a university bending its principles to accommodate a star athlete?

It doesn't seem so. The easy way would have been for Gonzaga simply to have offed him. The incident would have been a temporary blight on the program, but there would have been no regular reminders, no discomfiture on campus, no fences to mend with teammates, no "jeering and spittin'," as Rolin Heytvelt recalls it, in packed WCC gyms looking for a piece of Gonzaga.

This wasn't a premier player, just a good one.

But as much as Gonzaga avoided the path of least resistance, Heytvelt went above and beyond. The easy way would have been to transfer, to get out of Dodge and build a new life someplace else, where, yes, the story would have been retold, but it wouldn't have resonated as loudly.

"Did he make a mistake? Absolutely," says Erroll Knight, whose final two years in the program were Heytvelt's first two. "Is he a bad guy? Not at all. For Josh to take that ridicule . . . and still walk around the community with his head up, I commend him for that. Josh took that black eye and still lived his life, a really good life."

In his return in 2007-08, Heytvelt struggled. His father said he played on a damaged ankle. And who knows what sort of mental demons there were to overcome, to say nothing of the off-season work he missed? His scoring average dropped to 10.3 points and his rebounds fell by almost three a game.

"In some ways," Roth says, "the results justify that we weren't doing it just for wins."

Always, there was the push-pull over Heytvelt's game. Few wanted him to bang; Heytvelt's style was to drift to the perimeter and shoot threes. The first time I laid eyes on him, after walking into the Tacoma Dome for a state 3A tournament game between Clarkston and Meadowdale, there he was behind the arc in warmups, launching treys.

"I think coach Few and Josh kind of butted heads because Josh's game was so different from what coach Few wanted," says Knight. "He still had a decent career, but it probably should have been better, had he listened to coach Few, honestly."

His final season, Heytvelt averaged 14.9 points and the Zags made it to the Sweet 16 before they were blown out by North Carolina's abundantly talented national champions.

After he was passed over in the NBA draft, Heytvelt was in the Washington Wizards training camp before launching a career overseas that took him to Turkey twice, Italy, Croatia and ultimately, Japan. In late 2015, he signed a two-year deal to return to the Hitachi Sun Rockers, where he became a teammate of former Zag reserve swingman Ira Brown.

Recently, though, it hasn't been all seashells and sunsets for Heytvelt. When he turned 30 late in June, he was rehabilitating from a knee injury that led him to some soul-searching as to whether to hang it up or try to continue playing.

The homebody whose simple passion was fishing is now an experienced world traveler (whose passion is still fishing). "It's opened up my eyes to a lot of things," he says. "I've never been the guy to want to go to all these countries and see all this culture. It's kind of a neat thing to experience."

Heytvelt married former GU basketball player Claire Raap and they have a home on a ridge above Spokane. He has a daughter who was an infant during his time at Gonzaga. His dad says by the time he's finished playing in Japan, he'll be essentially debt-free.

The simple act of settling in Spokane, where once he was so vilified, seems to suggest that Heytvelt is at peace with the community.

"Josh is not a bad guy," insists Pendergraft. "He has a wonderful heart. He made some bad choices. But when you talk about coming through, Josh has come through."

Life, in other words, is good. With the passage of years, Heytvelt can look back on his time of crisis and shade it appropriately.

Without it, he says, "My life wouldn't be where it is right now, and I wouldn't be the same person. It completely turned my life around."

Unwittingly, he helped Gonzaga shine, too, but not before the two parties soldiered through shame and embarrassment and ridicule. Together.

"I would say we were at our best," observes Chris Standiford, "when he was at his worst."

– 10 –
THE GREAT DIVIDE

ON A COOL EVENING in early February 2016, all is abuzz around Seward Park Avenue and Henderson Street in south Seattle. The top-two-rated Class 3A boys basketball teams in the state, Garfield and Rainier Beach, are meeting – for rankings, for Metro League supremacy, and maybe most important, for bragging rights in the city.

"GAME SOLD OUT," blinks an electronic marquee outside Rainier Beach High School.

Pockets of people are converging on the school, but at the main entrance, the doors have closed. A ticket-taker waves some hopefuls to a pass gate at a rear door.

There, a huge, menacing security guard is monitoring identities skeptically, shaking his head at one, slipping another in. Quietly, a knot of tall young people appears – a few members of the University of Washington basketball team. There's Marquese Chriss, Noah Dickerson, David Crisp, a Rainier Beach alum. Shortly, they're in the gym.

Inside, the temperature and the anticipation are rising. Several future Division I players are warming up, including Sam Cunliffe (Arizona State) and Keith Smith (Oregon) of Rainier Beach.

Some local hoops glitterati are on hand. Eldridge Recasner, former Washington and NBA guard, has a seat, as does Donald Watts, another ex-UW guard. Bobby Hurley, the Arizona State coach, is there, because his Sun Devils will play at Washington the next evening. Nate Robinson, the Beach grad, explosive Washington guard and a decade-long NBA player before his release early in the season, is in the house.

The current Washington players have seats saved for them, courtesy of UW assistant coach Will Conroy, a few rows behind the Rainier Beach bench.

Then, 15 minutes before tipoff, Washington coach Lorenzo Romar, wearing a black leather jacket, strides in. He greets Beach coach Mike Bethea with a handshake and a man-hug. He repeats the pleasantries with Bethea's assistants. Then Romar walks down to the other bench, to Garfield coach Ed Haskins and his assistants, and goes through the same ritual.

It would be very hard, in other words, to find somebody in the gym – around Jamal Crawford Court – who hasn't figured out Romar is in attendance.

The scene oozes city ambience, easy familiarity and an unmistakable sense of home turf. Lorenzo Romar is in his element.

In Gonzaga's improbable 18-year run of NCAA tournaments, a trend has taken hold, defying conventional expectation.

Think of it like this: If you were a moderately versed college hoops fan, in, say, Indiana or South Carolina, you might know some basics about the state of the game in Washington. Surely you would know of Gonzaga's prominence, and you would likely know about the reputation of Seattle as a wellspring of premier high school talent.

You would probably conclude, then, that a key component to Gonzaga's success is having tapped into that pool of prospects in Seattle.

You would be dead wrong.

Consider: In the past decade, the Zags have made more tangible inroads into Chicago (Jeremy Pargo and incoming 2016 freshman Zach Norvell) than they have in the Emerald City 300 miles west. (Guard Gary Bell Jr., a four-year starter from 2011-15, was from Kent, 15 miles south of Seattle. If you want to contest the point, you could argue a committed Gonzaga recruit for 2017, Corey Kispert, is from Seattle, but his King's High School is in Shoreline, north of the city.)

When I asked Gonzaga coach Mark Few whether his program's elevation to nationally recognized force had helped it resonate in recruiting Seattle prospects, his reaction was equal parts scoff, scorn and offense taken.

"I really didn't get that," he said.

And here's why. While Seattle city basketball reflects a tight little insular subculture in which the University of Washington dominates for recruits, Gonzaga's impact on the city is negligible, at least on signing date. The Zags have come to be highly selective, based on two elements: One, a high percentage of Seattle recruits don't project as a "fit" for Gonzaga's style, and two, many such prospects don't hold Gonzaga in a regard that would prompt the Zags to reciprocate interest.

The topic is tiresome to Few, who concludes, "We get the guys who should be here."

More than a decade ago, Few expressed frustration at the phenomenon, saying, "Some people in Seattle think Spokane is in North Dakota or something." Now, he seems to have made peace with it – albeit, perhaps, an uneasy peace – and, when you're annually getting to the NCAA tournament and TV networks are calling to arrange high-level games and power-five-conference programs are willing to play home-and-home, it's hard to argue.

A little wearily, he says in reference to the homebodies in Seattle, "Those kids over there are really kind of dialed into staying into the

206 [area code]. I don't know . . . they don't often leave." As for the challenge in getting Gonzaga's message out, he adds, "It seems to get lost. You just kind of scratch your head and after a while, hey, if you don't get it, we'll just go get somebody else. That's where we're at now."

Remember Bell talking about how cronies on his AAU team in Seattle questioned his college choice? (Bell told me on the March day Gonzaga was newly ranked No. 1 in 2013 he didn't think those teammates would be quite as critical.)

The longtime former secretary of state in Washington, Ralph Munro, used to refer to the "two Washingtons." The west side of the Cascades was so different from the east – different politically, different socioeconomically, different in geography, different in population density, different in climate. Over time, there have been isolated calls to split Washington into two states, one blue, one red.

Nobody has yet included the basketball programs at Washington and Gonzaga as illustrative of that contrast, but indeed, they're also of largely different worlds, underscored by the disposition of basketball talent in the city of Seattle.

In 2011, I interviewed a handful of University of Washington players for a piece based on a full, four-year class now having passed through both the UW and Gonzaga without the schools meeting in men's basketball. Washington opted out of the series after the 2006-07 game.

Isaiah Thomas said he had seen the electrifying 2005 game between Gonzaga and Washington – Adam Morrison versus Brandon Roy – and said he had always wanted to play Gonzaga. At the same time, he heard nothing about the Zags on the UW campus, and added, "I know of Steven Gray – I watched him in high school – but I don't know anybody over there. It's crazy, I've never been to that side of the state. I don't know what it looks like."

Jason Kerr, longtime high school coach in Seattle – at Franklin and now at O'Dea – tells the story of taking one of his teams to

Gonzaga's camp. As their bus was rolling over the Cascades, a player in the back of the bus piped up, "Coach, are we going north or south?"

As geographically challenged as that traveler was, Kerr says it shouldn't be taken to reflect that the typical Seattle inner-city kid might look at Spokane as so different – in so many ways – that it's not on his radar.

"I think you're giving kids too much credit," he says. Rather, Kerr says, those kids might know Spokane as site of the wildly popular Hoopfest, or having seen a reference to Gonzaga on social media or something on television. Only if such a recruit takes a deeper dive into Gonzaga, might a family member point out a demographic difference.

For similar reasons, says Jason Hamilton, a guard from Husky teams of the mid-'90s and now analyst on UW radio broadcasts, it's ill-advised to conclude that if Spokane is seen as a remote outpost by Seattle kids, that would remove it from their consideration. He points out that many, if not most, college-basketball hotbeds are in non-urban locales, places like Lawrence, Kansas; Ames, Iowa; Durham, North Carolina, and a host of campuses in the Big Ten.

So, if there's an indifference about Gonzaga in the Seattle inner city, what drives it? Or is it that Washington, the school that's only a couple or three or four miles away, is that difficult to beat?

It's accepted that Romar has won over the inner city, and that talent acquisition is what he does best.

"Lorenzo is the best, whether he's winning or losing," says Francis Williams, former Rainier Beach High and AAU summer coach. "The person he projects himself to be is the person he is."

In Seattle, the basketball subculture is uncommonly thick, much of it entwined in players that have attended Washington. The older ones are said to look out for the younger ones. The youthful want to emulate their elders. And in the summer, they unite in the local gyms.

"You can't help when the season is over, being in the same gym," says Watts, who helped Washington to the Sweet 16 in 1998. "The city is so beautiful in the summertime, everybody is home ballin'. It's not like you want to get out of there. It's the best place in the world to be."

Casey Calvary, the standout former forward at Gonzaga, came from Tacoma and says the loyalties to hometown run deep there and in Seattle. While he says he understands it and accepts it, he has a chilling observation about it, saying, "Dragging a Seattle kid away from the UW . . . they'll go to the UW even though they know it's a bad basketball decision. Like, 'This is my town, all my buddies are around here, I'm a Seattle guy.'"

There are the defectors. Terrence Williams of Rainier Beach escaped for Louisville, as did guard Peyton Siva of Franklin. Some others who came from outlying areas – but did considerable time on local AAU teams – included Marvin Williams of Bremerton, who attended North Carolina; and Zach LaVine of Bothell, who went to UCLA for one season.

Ironically, it's another such outlier who might be called the godfather of Seattle city kids, and happens to be the No. 1 promoter of the 206. Ironic, because Jamal Crawford went to the University of Michigan in 1999-2000 before he was suspended by the NCAA for an improper living arrangement in high school with a benefactor.

"Jamal has a very, very strong influence," says Bethea, longtime coach at Rainier Beach. "One thing about Jamal, even though he didn't go to the University of Washington, he's just a Seattle kid, period. Whatever success Seattle can have, whether it's the University of Washington or the Seahawks, he just wants success for his city."

On KJR AM in the winter of 2016, former UW standout Brandon Roy, co-hosting an afternoon show, featured Crawford as a guest. He called him an "honorary Husky," and Crawford acknowledged the label. Roy said that after the ballyhooed 2005 meeting with Gonzaga won by the Huskies, 99-95, he was down. Adam Morrison had one of his all-time games with 43 points, while Roy, battling foul problems, had 10 points and five turnovers. Calling Crawford a "mentor," Roy said he spent that night riding around the city with Crawford, whose New York Knicks were in town to play the Sonics.

Of course, it isn't just the Huskies that Gonzaga is contesting, as the paths of players like LaVine and Marvin Williams suggest.

"You've got to beat the storied programs," says Francis Williams. "If a kid is on a national level, you're competing with Louisville or North Carolina. I know in their little cocoon they live in over there, they feel they're on that level, but they're not on that level."

Tommy Lloyd, the veteran Gonzaga assistant coach, invokes an economic term: *Opportunity cost.* The Zags have long since learned to cut losses in Seattle rather than bang their head against a wall that is too often unyielding.

"Washington is entrenched there," he says. "We're not going to try to beat them on a kid that may not be a perfect fit for us. If not, we'll go find somebody that is. You have to understand opportunity costs. I can sit there and bust my ass on an inner-city Seattle kid, and he goes to Washington or Arizona or Louisville, or I can recruit a kid who's a solid performer for us for four years. What's better?"

Truth be told, the fit that would mesh Gonzaga with the Seattle inner-city prospect is seldom perfect. Take, for instance, Dejounte Murray, the Rainier Beach product who considered Gonzaga. At first blush, the addition of such a budding NBA first-round talent would seem a no-brainer for any program. But consider how the Zags' guards struggled with their new roles through much of the 2015-16 season – and a couple of them were fifth-year seniors, no doubt anticipating heavy playing time – and the inclusion of the free-wheeling Murray could have turned transition into turmoil.

As Kerr puts it, "I don't think Mark and his staff are necessarily dying to have every single four- and five-star, top-notch recruit that comes through the city of Seattle. I mean, they're pretty particular in who they look for, what type of player and person they are to buy into their environment, their work ethic, their standard of how they do things."

The combination of Gonzaga's selectivity and a tendency for some prospects to have reservations, either about the Zags or Spokane, hasn't exactly made the connection the stuff of Match.com.

"I tell my kids, they win every year and they go to the Big Dance every year," Bethea says. "There's a great chance of going to the Sweet 16 and beyond. Unfairly, a lot of kids look at Spokane as being a small, country town."

Conference matters. The Pac-12 is the big dog in the region, and while that league enjoyed its most competitive season in history in 2015-16, it's a matter of debate whether the WCC has been improving over the long haul outside of the Gonzaga-Saint Mary's-Brigham Young triumvirate.

Knowledgeable observers also posit that comparatively less structure in the Washington system favors the Huskies. Says Hamilton, "If you're a kid with aspirations of playing on the next level, the style of play in the NBA kind of rewards being able to score one-on-one, and that's not how Gonzaga plays. Washington produces more NBA players, but the winning record favors Gonzaga."

"It's probably more an illusion than anything," Watts says, "but Gonzaga is not as much up and down, not as much free-form. One of the great things they do over there, and they've done for a long time, is get the best kid they can get and develop them, both to fit their system and develop their system to fit their personnel at the same time.

"But I don't know if that's anything a recruit is really looking at, or attracted to."

For recruits looking deeper, there's the potential issue of going to a campus and city that is less diverse, part of the everything-about-Spokane-is-just-different theory. Francis Williams points out that the Washington State campus, in rural Pullman, would be more diverse than Gonzaga, simply because WSU has a football team.

But it's debatable whether that's of significant impact to recruits. Says Gonzaga assistant Donny Daniels, who has recruited for UCLA and Utah, among others, "At the end of the day, a high school kid doesn't care about diversity. Somebody else cares about diversity. It's a parent, an AAU coach. When a kid goes to school, he wants to play ball, get an education, be around his teammates, stuff like that. He's not thinking, 'How many African-Americans are there, are there any Hispanics?' Kids don't even think that way."

For some prospects, bigger will always be better, and don't muddy up my thought process by pointing out that I'm going to play in the NCAA tournament every year or that my game is going to take a quantum leap in your program.

"At the end of the day," says Recasner, "the big fish in the pond here is the University of Washington. There's 40,000 students, a great tradition for football . . . all that plays a role."

Two decades ago, before Gonzaga was Gonzaga, Mike Nilson was coming out of Shorecrest High just outside Seattle, hoping to continue his basketball career.

"UW was No. 1 and it wasn't close," says Nilson, whose Spokane company contracts with Gonzaga for strength-and-conditioning services in some sports. "If they'd offered me a walk-on (chance) and Gonzaga a scholarship, I probably would have stayed there, mostly because of family reasons. I'd be away at school, but I'd have that safety net of being able to be with my brothers and my sister and my grandparents and my aunts and uncles."

Then he had a terrific showing in a workout with Gonzaga players, was invited to walk on and became a key piece on Gonzaga's program-turning teams. A generation later, his mindset has changed and so has Gonzaga's. The school balances the pedestrian WCC schedule by playing one of the toughest non-league agendas in the nation, and in just about every other facet of the basketball operation, is first class.

"We have quality coaches, we have quality gear, we don't waste time on things that look pretty," says Nilson. "If I was going to guess, when you're 17, you might be influenced a little more by the bigger school, the nicer buildings." Nilson would tell you those things don't matter. "But," he admits, "I'm pretty biased."

The fact Seattle and Gonzaga rarely line up only serves to accentuate what the Zags have accomplished. A school on the all-time top-10 list of consecutive NCAA tournaments has a recruiting base of . . . what? Spokane? California?

"We've tried to make sure we're a factor in every pool of recruiting," Lloyd says. "International kids, transfers, high school kids, junior college kids. We try to make sure we're not putting our eggs in one basket."

Ah, Seattle, an enchanting city of international trade, soaring vistas, beguiling neighborhoods and world-class restaurants.

And oh yes, a place where it rained 33 inches from November 1, 2015 to the end of February 2016 – exactly four months.

A place where, by April 2016, the median price for a single-family home had reached $637,250, up 15 percent in a year. Where the housing market was so overheated that it became commonplace for offers to exceed asking prices. In April 2015, the Puget Sound Business Journal wrote about an 1,120-square-foot, three-bedroom home in Ballard that was listed for $559,000. By the time bidders had finished overreaching for the property, it sold for $717,000.

And traffic? Hideous, by any statistical or anecdotal measure.

Fair to say, the various consciences of Seattle include these two, and they're not necessarily exclusive of one another: One, we're the greatest. Two, we're beset with so many challenges, it's time we got over ourselves.

Danny Westneat, a Seattle Times columnist who frequently assesses Seattle's livability, wrote in February 2016: "This deep-down belief – that our city is special – comes as close as we can get to an official religion."

But it comes with a mea culpa, as noted by irreverent Times columnist Ron Judd in May 2015: "Locals can take heart in knowing [Seattle] remains firmly ensconced as No. 1 on the nation's Most Soul-Suckingly Congested, Self-Absorbed and Criminally Overpriced list."

Count the Gonzaga basketball coach as one who doesn't get the whole Seattle fixation-with-itself thing. That wouldn't be particularly notable, except I think it's symbolic of the Zags' evolution in their emergence as a player in college basketball. Few's view is consistent with a hardening of position – in scheduling, in discussion of conference future, in relations with the West Coast Conference office – that reflects Gonzaga's evolution from doughty underdog to major force.

Few says he has long felt something like an inferiority complex on the part of people in his region vis-a-vis Seattle.

"I was always like, 'What's wrong with you people?'" he says. "They were always just comparing themselves and wanting to be acknowledged. I've always thought, 'You guys are all wrong. You got it better off, especially now that this place has grown.'"

So the battle lines are drawn. Increasingly, the Zags look out for No. 1. Both Washington and Washington State used to be on the schedule; now that future is cloudy with each opponent.

In 2014, seven years after Washington opted out of the Gonzaga series, a resumption was announced for the 2016-17 season, but in the spring of 2015, the Huskies' Nigel Williams-Goss revealed his transfer plans to Gonzaga. That imperiled the resumption, and only after the Gonzaga staff consulted Williams-Goss and his family did it move forward.

Then there's Washington State, which Gonzaga is keeping at arm's length, first forcing a game at Spokane Arena outside the home-and-home framework, and now suspending the series.

Yes, they're longtime neighborhood adversaries, kindred spirits in their distrust of Washington. And the series has been played since 1907, 150 games of easy travel that has made sense.

But it's increasingly difficult for the Zags to justify the Cougars. True, WSU indulged the Zags for decades, but it was a different time. Until 1975, nobody besides conference champions could get to the NCAA tournament anyway, so Gonzaga was no drag on the Cougars. And when that changed, there was always sufficient punch in Washington State's Pac-8/10 schedule to ensure that Gonzaga was doing it no real harm. (On a side note, the element of computer rankings – the Ratings Percentage Index – wasn't used by the NCAA basketball committee until 1980-81).

WSU bailed on the series from 1988-95, but precedent isn't what should drive Gonzaga. What is, is that GU's streak of 18 straight trips to the NCAA tournament now represents about 30 percent of its existence as a Division I entity. Meanwhile, WSU's basketball history can be described, charitably, as mostly lamentable. The Cougars have tended to have brief spasms of success, suffocated by much longer periods of ineptitude, some of it massive. While the Zags have a string of winning NCAA-tournament games eight years in a row, WSU has won six NCAA-tournament games in its history.

On both sides, that's a pretty significant body of work. So it's hard to accuse Gonzaga of making a snap judgment when it looks upon having to play Washington State much as it would if it were making an everything-to-lose-nothing-to-gain trip to Loyola Marymount or San Diego. Where's the upside? In this millennium, if you take away Tony Bennett's golden run in 2007 and 2008 – when WSU and Gonzaga staged electric games, both won by the Cougars – WSU's annual average RPI has been 166, and five times it has been in excess of 200.

Referring to my analogy of WSU as akin too frequently to another low-level WCC team, Few says, "But it's harder, because it's 10,000 to 12,000 people. Then everybody says, 'Well, it's a great atmosphere.' Well, anywhere we go is a great atmosphere. If we go play at Purdue, it's going to be a hell of an atmosphere. Of course they're going to come out. But what good does that do us?"

Turns out the GU president, Thayne McCulloh, was hearing from influential people concerned about a halt to the series. McCulloh was shown WSU's computer numbers from recent years, which dimmed the prospect of any upper-level mandate from GU to sustain the series.

"This isn't how Joe Wheat Farmer with a bunch of money feels," says Few, emphasizing the need to get high-end RPI victories in an era of an expanded, 18-game WCC schedule. "Or a politician that thinks it'd be good for the region."

Few is similarly wary of Washington because of its recent struggles, although the potential RPI risk would seem to be relatively low. Meanwhile, it's obvious Gonzaga's achievements have outstripped the Huskies in recent years. So the series restarts in 2016 with a backdrop of what Few told me in the spring of 2015: "The way it stands right now, I think it'd be really foolish to start up anything with either one of these two schools. That's how I honestly feel about it."

He's dug in on the matter. When I suggested that causes detractors to conclude he's become too big for his britches, Few laughed. "I hear you," he said. "But again, it's not about britches. It's solely about top-50 and top-25 wins."

So there's a strain of isolationism to Gonzaga's approach these days, at least with regards to their rivals in the state. The Zags would tell you it's nothing more than looking out for their best interests.

Partly as a result of that, Gonzaga gets largely ignored, occasionally mocked, by most west-side media outlets. Few doesn't appear on Seattle-area sports-talk radio shows, mostly owing to some experiences neither side found satisfying in the past. (He does them only infrequently in Spokane).

In Seahawk-obsessed Seattle ("How we gonna replace that deep-snapper?"), a Gonzaga tournament victory in March is likely to be greeted by crickets. Meanwhile, the Zags seem to get everything from snarky to perplexing from some Puget Sound-area journalists.

Writing on Sportspressnw.com before the 2014 tournament, longtime, respected columnist Art Thiel broached the possibility of "another loss in the first round" by Gonzaga – it had three of those in the previous 15 years – and added, "March Sadness gets old after 15 tourneys in a row."

Seattle Times columnist Matt Calkins, writing in March 2016 about the Pac-12 Conference's recent failures on the national stage in the big-ticket sports of football and men's basketball and noting the early exits of five of its seven entries from the '16 tournament, issued "a plea for Oregon or Utah to march all the way through this madness."

Right. And for Utah, that would have meant a march commencing with its next game against a team from the state of Washington – Gonzaga – one with 5,914 alumni in King County.

ESPN anchor Neil Everett, who attended Lewis and Clark High in Spokane, often makes tongue-in-cheek reference to Gonzaga as "America's Team." Somehow, the Zags have succeeded in winning favor nationwide, while around Puget Sound, the reaction is "Meh."

Father Robert Spitzer wasn't a basketball sage, but he knew when he had a vehicle that could help grow the Gonzaga University brand (*Gonzaga photo by Jeff Green*)

The brothers McCarthey, Tom (left) and Phil, gave generously to make a new arena a reality at Gonzaga

Mike Roth, with WCC commissioner Lynn Holzman, is considered one of the unsung heroes in Gonzaga's protracted basketball prominence (*Gonzaga photo by Torrey Vail*)

Mark Few's streak of making the NCAA tournament is
longest by a head coach to start a career in NCAA history
(*Photo courtesy of the West Coast Conference*)

Before launching his head-coaching career at Boise State in 2010, Leon Rice put in a productive 12 years at Gonzaga (*Gonzaga photography*)

During a 16-year run as an assistant, Bill Grier helped lay the foundation for GU's rise to prominence (*Gonzaga photography*)

Tommy Lloyd's burgeoning contacts overseas helped keep Gonzaga rosters robust and made him one of the nation's most effective recruiters beyond U.S. borders (*Gonzaga photography*)

Tom Lloyd

Senior

Tommy is the most experienced player that we bring to the Hilander front this season. Tom's offensive and defensive skills have continued to elevate, and as a result he will be one of the top players in the Greater St. Helens League this year.

This *Longview Daily News* clip evokes a time when Tommy Lloyd helped Kelso High to its first state tournament in 33 years

Basketball's strength and conditioning is under the imaginative tutelage of Travis Knight, who played baseball at GU

Dan Monson coached the Zags in their breakthrough Elite Eight run in 1999, then left that summer for Minnesota (*Photo by Garth Patil/POV Image Service*)

Both times when Gonzaga upended a No. 2 seed in the 1999 and 2000 NCAA tournaments, Matt Santangelo came up huge (*Photo by Garth Patil/POV Image Service*)

A key part of seven NCAA-tournament victories, Casey
Calvary gave Gonzaga an athletic, energetic force inside
(*Gonzaga photo by Dale Goodwin*)

Dan Dickau became well-traveled, both in his path to first-team All-American at GU and in an itinerant career in the NBA (*Brock Scott Photography*)

Ronny Turiaf was a dynamic scorer and rebounder but so much more: He was at the forefront of Gonzaga's foreign recruiting and became a hugely popular figure (*Photo by Zero Gravity*)

With a mid-range game that was almost unstoppable and a panache that attracted casual fans, Adam Morrison won a couple of player-of-the-year awards in 2006 (*Gonzaga photo by Jeff Green*)

As much as anybody, Derek Raivio helped sustain the Zags' streak of NCAA tournaments, winning WCC-tournament MVP honors in 2007 (*Gonzaga photo by Jeff Green*)

A product of inner-city Chicago, Jeremy Pargo brought a big personality and a physical game to his point guard position (*Photo courtesy of the West Coast Conference*)

Josh Heytvelt turned his darkest moment into a success story, overcoming an arrest to graduate and forge a long career overseas (*Photo courtesy of the West Coast Conference*)

A booming personality and a bullish inside presence were Robert Sacre's calling cards (*Photo courtesy of the West Coast Conference*)

A productive redshirt season made all the difference for
Kelly Olynyk on the way to 2013 first-team All-America
honors (*Photo courtesy of the West Coast Conference*)

Much of Elias Harris' work was done above, not below, the rim; he's Gonzaga's No. 2 career rebounder and No. 4 scorer (*Photo courtesy of the West Coast Conference*)

Stocktons a pair: David (left) carved out a nice GU career, three decades after his famous father John (*Photo courtesy of the West Coast Conference*)

In a storybook run from uninvited walk-on to starter on a No. 1-ranked team, Mike Hart did a little bit of everything for the Zags (*Gonzaga photo courtesy of Torrey Vail*)

Shooting, not driving, was Kevin Pangos' chief offensive asset; his 322 made three-pointers tops the Gonzaga career list (*Photo courtesy of the West Coast Conference*)

Gary Bell Jr. soldiered through multiple injuries and teamed with Kevin Pangos to become one of GU's best backcourts (*Photo courtesy of the West Coast Conference*)

Kyle Wiltjer became a multidimensional scorer for the Zags following his transfer from Kentucky and a productive year as a redshirt (*Photo courtesy of the West Coast Conference*)

The Zags prized Domas Sabonis almost as much for his fiery, competitive style as his rebounding and scoring inside (*Photo courtesy of the West Coast Conference*)

Gonzaga's women made the NCAA tournament in half of Kelly Graves' 14 seasons, and interest in the program grew by leaps and bounds (*Gonzaga photo by Torrey Vail*)

Lisa Fortier's first two years as GU women's coach yielded
a Sweet 16 appearance, then an injury-riddled 2015-16
NIT season (*Photo courtesy of the West Coast Conference*)

Heather Bowman's 2,165 points put her at the top of the GU career list; she's also No. 3 in rebounds (*Photo courtesy of the West Coast Conference*)

Somehow, Courtney Vandersloot wasn't highly recruited, but she became the best player in the history of Gonzaga women's hoops (*Photo courtesy of the West Coast Conference*)

High times became routine for the Gonzaga women, who made three Sweet 16s and an Elite Eight in this decade (*Photo courtesy of the West Coast Conference*)

Mark Few tested his location on an invitation to throw out the ceremonial first pitch at Seattle's Safeco Field (*Few family photo*)

The 1981 Creswell (Ore.) High starters, including Few (far right) had to share billing with a bovine friend in this *Eugene Register-Guard* photo

His mom, Barbara Few, recalls Mark picking up reading skills at age four (*Few family photo*)

Well before he kept his car equipped with all sorts of athletic equipment, Few got acquainted with a baseball bat (*Few family photo*)

Clearly, a gift of a scooter was a hit with a young Mark Few (*Few family photo*)

The first Gonzaga hoops alumni game attracted a few dozen players in 2016 (*Photo by Randy Cahalan for Spokane Hoopfest*)

– 11 –
POSTCARDS FROM
FARAWAY COURTS

IN FOUR AND A HALF DECADES of hacking my way through three Northwest newspaper sports departments, I thought I recognized a blind spot. Most papers tend to lose track of the college athletes they covered religiously for four years. Ah, but that shouldn't imply their stories have become any less captivating.

To wit:

Dan Dickau

It's probably safe to say no ex-Zag has had as disjointed a life after college as Dickau, the 2002 first-team All-American who transferred in after an unsatisfying start at Washington. If there weren't a sort of happy chaos around the family of Dan and Heather Dickau, it wouldn't have been life itself.

In 2015, Heather noted to her husband that they'd moved only twice in the past four years. Before that, their existence was as unstable as the Greek economy, marked by 20 moves in 13 years.

This is a guy who, in the span of five months, was on four NBA rosters.

It took only until NBA draft night in 2002 before Dickau got a foreshadowing of what was to come. He was taken by Sacramento No. 28 overall, at the end of the first round, and traded to Atlanta – a team for which he hadn't worked out.

Atlanta should have been a good landing spot, but if Dickau grew to learn one thing over his career, it was: What seems and what is are two vastly different things.

His first coach, Lon Kruger, got fired the day after Christmas, replaced by Terry Stotts.

"His philosophy then was night-and-day different from what it is now with Portland," Dickau says. "Now, he wants to do all this shoot-the-three, space-the-floor, pick-and-roll stuff. Then, his mantra to me was, 'You're a rookie, I don't need to talk to you.' And his other thing was, 'I don't need my backup point guard to shoot.'"

Even more ominous for Dickau was a torn meniscus cartilage in his knee, something he says he played with his senior year at Gonzaga.

"I battled knee stuff the whole [Gonzaga] year," he said. "We never took an MRI, anything. I knew it was an issue. I [didn't] want to know. It was after a game against Eastern Washington. I woke up, took one step out of bed and fell on the ground. I figured out how to work through the pain."

Shortly into the season in Atlanta, the pain had grown so intense that Dickau finally had an MRI, and surgery on the knee.

Not that the marriage with Stotts would have worked anyway, but an Achilles problem requiring a procedure early in his second year led the Hawks to trade him to Portland.

The good news: It was the team nearest Dickau's hometown of Brush Prairie, Washington. The bad: "That team was a mess," he says. "Holy cow."

Dickau struggled through a season with Ruben Patterson, Rasheed Wallace and Bonzi Wells as teammates. Then: Traded again, this time to Golden State, along with Dale Davis, for Nick Van Exel.

About then, the lot of a fringe player in the NBA was dawning on Dickau. Playing time for a deep reserve was, at best, minimal. And any misstep might weigh more heavily on the coach's mind than a positive contribution.

"I would play a three- or four-game stretch, be the backup point guard playing 16 minutes, and I think I'm playing well," Dickau says. "Well, you can have one bad possession or one bad defensive rotation, or you make one big mistake in the eyes of the coach, and all of a sudden you don't see the floor again for the next four games. It is what it is. For a third-string point guard in the NBA, that's what you deal with."

So it was on to Golden State. Or so it seemed. Dickau flew to the Bay Area and lined up a rental house in nearby Walnut Creek. Two days from flying south for the season, he was back home in Vancouver, Washington, barbecuing with friends in the backyard, when the news came across the crawl on ESPN: ". . . Golden State trades Dan Dickau . . ."

And another NBA fact of life hit home: A player's salary sometimes means more than his trade value. If the numbers fit, you could be a trade throw-in, outbound on the next flight.

Ergo, Dallas, which was in the process of raising the character quotient on a team whose nucleus was Dirk Nowitzki and Michael Finley. "I knew I wasn't a part of their future when they had a press conference with all their newcomers," Dickau recalls with a self-deprecating laugh, "and I wasn't in it."

The deck there was stacked against Dickau, a team laden with guaranteed contracts. But he had a knockout training camp and one night, at a team meal, he experienced one of the fulfilling moments of his career. Avery Johnson was a player-coach then, and he got up and said, "I'm retiring. I don't think it's fair to take someone else's roster spot who deserves it."

"He was looking right at me," Dickau says. "I'm sitting there, like, 'Wow! I want to burst out crying. I want to give the guy a hug.'"

So Dickau stuck, and he came to know that just as there are good and bad NBA teams, there is camaraderie and there is poison.

"I got to know Dirk fairly well," Dickau says. "There are so many differences, college or pro, between a good team, a good organization, and a bad one. The good teams, they'll go out to dinner together, spend time together, or hang out on the plane, play poker. On bad teams, they don't do any of that."

It was Dallas' team chemistry that one night found the Mavericks boarding taxis for a dinner out in South Beach before a game at Miami. Dickau and Nowitzki were the last two players to get in a van cab. Dickau slammed a rear door shut and got in the front seat.

"Dan, open the door," Nowitzki said, and he repeated it.

Dickau, desperately trying to play for a second contract in the league, had just shut the door on the fingers of a future NBA most valuable player.

"I open the door," Dickau says, "and I think, 'I just finished my NBA career.'"

At dinner, Nowitzki iced his fingers and Dickau was too stricken to talk. Naturally, the next morning, as Dickau got on an elevator to go to shootaround, there was Don Nelson, the coach.

"Hey, anybody hear what happened to Dickau last night?" Nelson called out to nobody in particular. "We cut the little [bleep]."

Suffice to say, Dickau felt a lot better when Nowitzki went out and scored 41 that night and the Mavericks won by 20 over the Heat.

Early in December 2004, he and Heather were going to go out and get a Christmas tree. Instead, he arrived home to tell her he'd been traded again, to New Orleans. That made it four teams – Portland, Golden State, Dallas and New Orleans – since July.

So he went from Dallas, one of the league's best organizations, to a team that was 1-13 when he got there. But Dickau was a revelation, starting 46 games and averaging 13.2 points and the runaway leader in assists.

Allen Bristow, the coach, took Dickau aside at the end of an 18-64 season and told him they loved how he played. And then two months later, New Orleans took Chris Paul No. 4 in the 2005 draft.

Within months, New Orleans dealt him to Boston, coached by Doc Rivers, and Dickau found himself on his sixth NBA team. From the start, it didn't go well; bothered by an Achilles tendon, he played poorly in training camp, and the Achilles ruptured in Chicago.

Rehabbing, he flew every few weeks from Portland to Boston to get the splint changed out. One day in Boston in late January, just as Heather was going into early labor with their son, Luke, he was rushing to join her back home when he was intercepted by an emissary from NBA security – he had been selected for random drug testing. His protests went for naught, so he submitted hurriedly to the test and made it home hours before the birth.

So the 2005-06 season was scuttled. But he worked tirelessly to rehab the Achilles, and that brought Dickau to his bete noir, draft day. Three times in a six-year NBA career, that was the occasion when he was traded.

Draft day, 2006: The Dickaus were headed with friends in a four-vehicle caravan to Sunriver Resort in central Oregon. As usual, there was the whiff of possible trades in the league, but by this time, Dan and Heather Dickau knew better than to let it rule their lives.

They were driving south on State Highway 97 when a friend in their party began peeling down the "suicide" lane, going about 90 miles an hour, waving at them to pull over.

"Of all the times Dan was going to be traded, that was one of the times Dan knew it was possible," Heather says. "He didn't tell me, knowing I would be disappointed."

Indeed, it happened. Their buddy had heard the deal on the radio: Dickau was going back to Portland. The first order of business: Find a grocery store outside the central Oregon town of Madras.

"I'm pretty sure we went in and bought some beers and toasted," Heather says.

Once again, they were coming home. That was the good part, and Dickau could take pride in the fact he recovered fully from the Achilles surgery, never to miss a game again because of it. But again, Dickau's playing time was sporadic and his contribution accordingly spotty; he shot a career-low 26 percent on threes.

As always, then, in 2007 Dickau eyed warily a certain late-June date. "Draft day, I'm a little concerned," he says. "I don't know if I necessarily want to watch the draft."

But he had played some pickup ball at the University of Portland with a Blazers teammate, guard Freddie Jones, and they had agreed that most of the trade scuttlebutt they were hearing didn't include either of them. This was the momentous Greg Oden-Kevin Durant draft of 2007, and the rumor (it would become fact) was that Blazer Zach Randolph might be outbound, perhaps with young Martell Webster.

So naturally: "Next day," Dickau says, "Freddie and I are both in the trade to New York."

There appeared no future with the Knicks. They were in the middle of a nine-year streak of losing seasons, general manager Isiah Thomas was embroiled in an ugly sexual-harassment lawsuit and there was nothing to suggest New York needed Dickau. So he pressed his agent for a better fit, was waived, and a couple of days later, reached his final NBA destination with the Los Angeles Clippers.

On a team that finished 23-59, he appeared in 67 games and had a solid finish in The League. Given the see-the-world nature of Dickau's career in the NBA, it figures that he'd eventually catch up with Richie Frahm, the Zag standout on the 1998-2000 teams and his old sixth-grade classmate at Laurin Middle School in Vancouver, Washington. And he did.

From there, Dickau knocked around a couple of NBA training camps, teams in Italy and Germany, even the Fort Wayne Mad Ants of the NBA Development League. Along the way, he continued accumulating an ever-bulging suitcase of wacky experiences.

One of them happened on an endless flight from Milan to Chicago, as he attempted to hustle a roster spot at Golden State. Somewhere over the Atlantic, two-year-old Luke Dickau turned toward his dad and threw up all over him. Dan turned his sweatpants inside out, wrapped himself in a blanket to try to deodorize himself and became a sweaty mess by the time he'd reached American soil.

He made a final, valiant stab at the NBA with a productive but unrewarded training camp in Phoenix, and after a forbidding bout of plantar fasciitis, he asked himself the inevitable question: "What's next?"

What was next was a year (2011-12) as a player-development assistant with the Trail Blazers. After that, it meant TV analysis for Pac-12 Networks and the Gonzaga network, the occasional hoops clinic and owner-operatorship of three Spokane franchises of the chain The Barbers.

That seems fitting. In the grand tradition of barber shops and conversation, Dickau has a lot of stories to tell.

Matt Santangelo

His world is baskets. Baskets everywhere, from Spokane Falls Boulevard to Sprague, from Bernard to Monroe. As Santangelo says, you have to see it to believe it.

I saw Spokane's three-on-three gala known as Hoopfest on a late-June weekend in 2015 when the temperature rose to 105 degrees, and ESPN featured the event as part of a series on under-the-radar summer events.

"Fourteen thousand games," says Santangelo over a salad before a midseason 2015 Zag matchup with Saint Mary's. "Last year we put up 456 or 458 courts. It turns into Basketball City."

Since 2014, Santangelo has been executive director of this extravaganza, following a few years in business, which came on the heels of a six-year European career marked by the serial weirdness and head-scratching happenstance that seems to accompany the paths of American players who venture there.

Santangelo was one of the originals, a point guard whose direction and fearlessness marked the first Zag teams that began the current run of NCAA tournaments. Much of the lore around Santangelo and Gonzaga has been entwined in the story that Stanford took Arthur Lee, leaving Santangelo to the Zags, but there was also heavy Oregon subtext around the Portlander.

The Ducks, then under coach Jerry Green, offered Santangelo a scholarship when he was a sophomore at Central Catholic High. He sat on it until he was a senior, when Mark Turgeon, assistant then to Green and now Maryland head coach, made a declaration born either of program self-interest or extreme consideration for Santangelo.

"Turgeon pulled me aside and said, 'We have this scholarship for you, but I don't think it's the best situation for you,'" Santangelo recalls. "I was like, 'Thanks, coach.' Apparently they had a couple of junior college transfers coming, and didn't want me and that was their way of letting me down easy."

Meanwhile, Gonzaga coach Dan Fitzgerald was using his "A" material on Santangelo. "I remember coach Fitz came into our living room with coach Few," says Santangelo. "He said, 'No one is bigger than the program, no one. But if I had a ball, I would hand it to you and say, 'We're going to go where you take us.'

"I love that stuff. I'm all about team, yet I had control over my own destiny."

After the breakthrough Elite Eight in 1999 and a Sweet 16 the next year, Santangelo signed a "guaranteed" three-year contract to play in Greece with Iraklis Thessalonaki. "That lasted five months," says Santangelo, "which is pretty typical."

They paid for his housing, they paid for his car, and "I got paid for the first month, and that was it."

If the finances were an eye-opener, so were the arenas. "We sat in this little dugout so people couldn't throw things at the back of our heads," Santangelo says. "Everybody smoked. You'd come out at halftime, and you could barely see the other basket. You'd go to the locker room and smell like you'd been in the bar all night long."

Before the year was out, he was off to Cantu, Italy, and a restorative experience on a team run on a shoestring that became local heroes because it spared its fans the ignominy of relegation to Italy's second division. Not that those fans weren't sometimes skeptical. There was the night the Cantu team played at rival Milan, and down 22 at half, returned to the floor to find its contingent of about 500 fans gone.

"Where are all our fans?" Santangelo asks rhetorically. "They're in the parking lot, throwing rocks at the bus."

He moved on to Poland, where his team made a historically deep run in the Euro League; then for three years to Seville, Spain, and what is widely considered the best league in Europe; and finally to a couple of Italian teams, the latter the powerhouse Benetton Treviso club that won an Italian championship.

"It was an adventure," Santangelo says. "I never got paid once on time."

Fortunately, the checks from Hoopfest are more punctual.

Casey Calvary

The man who made the most famous shot in Gonzaga basketball history looks lean, fit and able to play still, even though he's in his late 30s. He's still calling it as he sees it, full speed ahead, and damn the sensitive feelings.

Quentin Hall penetrated, put up a 13-footer that was long, and Calvary charged down the lane. He didn't tip the ball so much as flailed at it, and it rolled around and went in with 4.4 seconds left, putting the Zags ahead of Florida, 73-72, in the 1999 NCAA regional semis in Phoenix.

"My guy, I don't remember who it was," Calvary says, "he didn't box me out at all."

In part, that was because Florida went zone on that last possession, and when Hall's shot went up, Calvary took the fast lane to the hoop, unaccounted for. After he converted, what he remembers is "running back on defense, trying to make sure they didn't get a good look – which they did. That'd have been a dagger."

Florida's Eddie Shannon cast up the jumper that threatened to make Calvary's tip academic, and on CBS, Gus Johnson took up the moment: "Shannon, from the cor-naaaahrrr! And it's over ... Gonzaga!! The slipper still fits!!"

Calvary was a tireless, athletic force, even as a sophomore. Two years later, he would cap his GU career by being a part of seven NCAA-tournament wins, averaging 19 points in 2000-01 and being named WCC player of the year.

He was always a no-nonsense, no-frills kind of guy, and when the NBA didn't give him a sniff, he didn't beg for one.

"I didn't really pursue it very hard," he says. "I was pretty young and naïve. I assumed scouts came and watched you, paid attention to what you did in college. At that point in time, what you did in camps was how they made their evaluation on you. I didn't do a good enough job taking any of that seriously. My attitude when I didn't get drafted was, [screw] it, I'm going overseas, I'm not going to deal with these guys."

He went to Japan and liked it, though he didn't feel immersed in the culture. Next came Chalon, France, and he found that to be less than satisfying.

"I did not like France as a country," he says. "That's a place I would never bother to visit. I found the people to be quarrelsome and rude, very inhospitable. Every other place I traveled, you can walk into a restaurant and not feel, like, open hostility. I felt that pretty much everywhere I went."

It got better, if no more glamorous. He did a stint in the Continental Basketball Association, playing under Larry Krystkowiak with the Idaho Stampede. Loved it. Then he went to Townsville, Australia, where he found the people "fantastic," and finally, a fulfilling couple of years in Spain.

Like seemingly every other player who competes overseas, Calvary can recite horror stories about not getting paid. He says it's especially problematic at less competitive levels.

"They think, 'So we don't pay the Americans. How are they going to get back at us? They're going to sue us,'" he says. "First, you're going to have to find a lawyer, then you're going to go into a courtroom where the judge is probably a booster of the small-town team you're playing for and the jury is full of people who know other guys on the team. Good luck winning that lawsuit."

It was so much more simple that night in Phoenix, when he slapped at the ball and it responded favorably, and Gonzaga rose to an epic height.

"A lot of effort," he says of the tip, "and a lot of luck."

Ronny Turiaf

The most popular Zag in the history of the program is sitting up in an empty McCarthey Athletic Center, wearing a designer hoodie, jeans and brushed burgundy sneakers, outlining his next move in vague terms.

"It's an ongoing journey," he says, "of discovering who Ronny Turiaf really is."

Spokane already has an idea. Turiaf brought an exotic Caribbean mix of curiosity, impetuosity and raw, genuine emotion to the floor and to the city. He seemed impossible not to like, and that's how fandom embraced him. There was nobody quite like him.

When I asked him if he felt the love, Turiaf took it a step further. "Not that I felt it," he says. "It was that I was in it. It never appeared to me any other way."

He was back in Spokane early in 2016, quietly making contacts at Gonzaga to begin graduate school, not ready to say basketball is unequivocally behind him, though it appears it is. (Turiaf announced his retirement late in 2016.) Nor was he able to say definitively what the next step is.

"Where I am now, I'm living life to the fullest, man," he says. "I'm living life to the fullest, with the mindset that I want to live this life of service to others. I want to be able to empower other people to go for their dream. And to help dreams come alive every single day."

He grew up poor on the island of Martinique, developed his game in France, and had a dynamic career with the Zags as a quick, explosive 6-feet-10 player with a face-up jumper and a capacity to block shots. His last three seasons, he averaged in the neighborhood of 15 points, and, combined with an average of 9.5 rebounds in 2004-05, he was named WCC player of the year. Much of it occurred with dreadlocks flapping while he toggled between scowls and smiles.

The Lakers took him in the 2005 draft, 37th overall, but then shocking misfortune seemed to strike. Turiaf's heart was found to have an enlarged aortic root, and doctors laid out the options: He could have open-heart surgery, with the possibility of complete recovery, or he could merely take medication, which would mean he would be done with basketball and have to live a more sedentary life.

He didn't even have insurance. Turiaf had taken out the routine insurance policy protecting him during his senior year at Gonzaga, but not yet having signed an NBA contract, he was uncovered. The Lakers generously picked up the tab for the surgery.

Turiaf hardly had time to be scared. He knew immediately he

would have the operation, and he went about it fatalistically, businesslike.

He was hardly alone. Assistant coach Tommy Lloyd accompanied him through the entire crisis. He was joined at various times by all the coaches, plus senior associate athletic director Steve Hertz and Gonzaga booster Bob Cross.

"Of course it was difficult," Turiaf says. "Of course it was crazy. But I was lucky."

Lucky, in that the Lakers were there for him. Lucky, in that the aorta valve was completely sound.

"If that valve was not fine, I would not have been able to play basketball again," he says. "So my golden star is there for me. It's steering me the right way."

Four months later, he was back on the floor with the CBA Yakima Sun Kings, getting in shape. At the thought, Turiaf turns playful: "They ended up being CBA champions. I should actually call them for that. 'Can I get a ring, please? Size 11. Thank you very much.'"

He returned to play 23 games for Los Angeles in 2006, and then settled into what would be mostly a backup role (though he started 88 games over four seasons in his mid-20s).

Turiaf would play with eight NBA teams. He saw great organizations and bad ones, champions and losers. He spent three seasons with the Phil Jackson Lakers, which, in combination with the heart surgery, "was such a profound moment in my life, probably the best experience of my professional career."

Turiaf signed a free-agent deal with Golden State reported to be worth $17 million over four years. He calls it bittersweet: He was able to take care of his family financially, and felt even more a part of a team than he had in LA, playing for Don Nelson, "as powerful in his own way" as Jackson. But it wasn't easy leaving his first NBA team, and the Lakers would win the championship the next two years.

After Golden State, Turiaf knew a nomadic existence. He went to the Knicks, where they got New York excited with a playoff appearance after nine straight losing seasons. Among his last four teams was Miami in 2012, where he joined the LeBron James-Dwyane Wade-Chris Bosh Heat and played 13 games for an NBA titlist.

"We had a joke back in Miami that it was the Big Three and the Little Twelve," Turiaf says.

Somehow, despite the odds-on predisposition everybody had about Miami's title chances, Turiaf says there was no feeling of the Heat carrying a burden.

"Zero," he says. "We just played basketball. All that extra stuff, that's your job. For us, we just felt we had a chance of making something special happen."

When the ride ended with the Timberwolves in 2014-15, Turiaf had played 10 seasons. He had been teammates with the best, with Kobe Bryant and Carmelo Anthony and LeBron James.

But now he's on to a new chapter, and it makes sense that the chilly, faraway place that embraced him madly would be a part of it.

"From the support I got here, from the administration office, the coach's wife, from the support I got from the community after my heart surgery, everybody signing all those things, it was just so overwhelming to me," he says. "That's why this holds such a special place. I felt I was a part of them and they felt they were a part of me. It was a step further than love."

Mike Hart

You can't pin this one on Mike Hart. When the top-ranked and No. 1-seeded Zags fell to Wichita State in the round of 32 in 2013 – surely among the top two or three most devastating defeats in program history – there were multiple other suspects.

Not Hart. For the rest of his life, he'll carry with him the incongruity of a night when he climaxed his improbable collegiate story with the best game he ever played, framed by one of the program's hardest moments.

"It's kind of crazy," he says over a lunch-time wrap near campus.

At 6-feet-6, Hart grabbed 14 rebounds that night, when nobody else on the floor reached double figures. Seven were offensive boards. A player who often seemed reluctant to shoot took two threes – he had made only 11 all season (on just 20 tries) – and hit both. He didn't commit a turnover.

In the world of big-time college basketball, Hart was an extreme rarity. He went from walk-on – not invited walk-on, but a guy from the student body who had averaged eight points in his only year of starting at Jesuit High in Portland – to starter on the No. 1-rated team in college hoops.

His senior year, assistant coach Ray Giacoletti seemingly paid him the ultimate compliment. Talking about Hart's intangible contribution and how Gonzaga might seek to cover for him after his graduation, Giacoletti said, "I don't even know where you go to find a guy like that."

Indeed, when you check out the advanced metrics from that 2013 team, there's a stat called "Box plus/minus," which measures how many points per 100 possessions a player contributed to his team above a league-average player. And, at 13.5, the top one for Gonzaga that season wasn't Kelly Olynyk or Elias Harris or Kevin Pangos, but Hart.

He felt he owed it to himself to take a fling at playing overseas, and Lloyd hooked him up with a small club in Germany. But because he wasn't on the top team, he didn't have day-long access to the gym, and practice wasn't until the evenings. Hart was bored and knew almost immediately it wasn't for him.

"I would have had to do the same thing I did at Gonzaga – grind and grind for three or four years," Hart says. "But this would have been making a thousand dollars a month or whatever, grinding and grinding. In my mind, just like Gonzaga, I could have done it, I could have made it to the top level. But I didn't want to do that over there again. I'd already done it here for what I think was the bigger prize. Over there, I don't think the reward would have been the same, and the journey wouldn't have been as fun."

So he came home quickly, still unsure what he wanted to do with his life. He huddled with a lot of acquaintances at Nike and worked the shoe giant's skills academy in New Jersey. He had a stint as a product tester, playing basketball and offering feedback on shoes.

He returned to Gonzaga and took on a do-it-all (or at least most of it) role of video coordinator and camp administrator. He had a hand in the organization of all camps for the program – summer camps, winter camps (Winter camps? Who knew?), team camps, little kids' camps. That means handling logistics like housing and food.

Hart was the video expert, charged with knowing software technology and being able to accommodate coaches' on-the-fly requests for tape. And he was liaison between coaches and players, their day-to-day conduit for ever-changing practice times, weightlifting times, meal times.

One thing he didn't do: Coach on the floor. And without a foreseeable prospect for doing that at Gonzaga, one day in the summer of 2016 he called up a coaches website, took a swing at an assistant's job at an NCAA Division III school and landed it. He's now at Colorado College, an academically stiff institution in Colorado Springs, where, he says, "like 15 percent of applicants get in."

He has a strong sense coaching is what he wants to do, rather than athletic administration or business. "This is just to prove if I'm right," he says.

He's just figuring out the recruiting dynamics at a school without athletic scholarships. "You either have to be very smart and get a lot of aid," he says, "or be really smart and have a lot of money."

So he needs to be resourceful. But Mike Hart learned how to do that years ago at Gonzaga.

Richie Frahm

Few used to recall how Gonzaga's deadly three-point shooter would pour his soul into the game, endlessly curling around imaginary screens in an empty gym and flicking long jumpers until he was drenched in sweat.

It probably figures, then, that Frahm would do the same with his post-basketball passion: Competitive bike racing. As in, some 10,000 miles a year gripping handlebars, and as of late 2015, six wrecks, several ghoulish cases of road rash, a dislocated shoulder and a torn labrum.

"My wife kind of says my crash card is all filled up," says Frahm, nursing a cappuccino at a Spokane coffeehouse.

Frahm was a major part of the Zags' burst to national prominence, shooting .423 from three-point range in four seasons and twice helping the program get to the second weekend of the NCAA tournament. Then he fulfilled a dream by playing in the NBA, albeit more sparingly than he wished, over five seasons.

He was left to this cold conclusion: "I wasn't good enough."

Nor, when basketball was all over, were his competitive juices sated. In 2011, after a knee began balking on him and he had returned home to Spokane following a career-ending stint in Japan, he bought a heavy bike from REI. It was going to be recreational, a way to become more familiar with the town where his name became golden.

He signed up for a 50-mile charity ride and when it was over, promptly threw up. As baptisms go, it wasn't auspicious.

Back in his hometown of Battle Ground in southwest Washington, his brother Rob prodded him to take a Cannondale road bike at the closing of a shop there owned by Rob's father-in-law. Then he had a chance meeting in Spokane with a regular rider from a local club – a former junior road cyclist with Lance Armstrong's team – who encouraged him to join them for their weekly ride. That Saturday, there were 30 riders in cycling outfits, warily eyeing the 6-foot-5, 210-pound guy in Nike shorts and a tank top.

But Frahm was hooked. Soon he went out to the 2.5-mile track at Spokane County Raceway for a nine-lap event. The competition was mostly 40- and 50-year-olds – easy pickin's, Frahm thought. About the seventh lap, Frahm stood up and sprinted and hit the dreaded wall. The peleton – the tight group behind him – blew past, leaving the gassed Frahm in its wake.

He hung in there, retreated to the Internet and read up on rules, etiquette and tactics. He got better quickly, rising in four years from a Category 5 novice to a Category 2 expert regularly winning events. He figures that's his ceiling, what with the requisite time commitment and a brisk real estate business consuming him and his wife.

"I haven't touched a basketball in three or four years," Frahm says. "And I love basketball."

Frahm debuted in the NBA with the Luke Ridnour-Nick Collison-Rashard Lewis Seattle SuperSonics of 2003-04. He bookended that with a one-month tour in 2007-08 with the Clippers, reuniting him with his sixth-grade teammate, Dickau. "Just surreal," Frahm says.

It turns out Gonzaga can thank Frahm not only for his marksmanship in the 1999 and 2000 NCAA-launch years of the program, but for his salesmanship as well.

"He had a huge part to do with me actually transferring to Gonzaga," says Dickau.

About the time Dickau was becoming disenchanted with Washington his sophomore year, he was spending time on the phone with Frahm, his old boyhood chum. Then came early December 1998, and a meeting between the Huskies and Zags in Spokane. As Dickau tells it, he and Frahm worked out for about an hour on the eve of the game – in the Kennel. Dickau was peppering Frahm with questions on whether Gonzaga would be a good fit for him.

Then a friend walked in, and Frahm introduced Dickau as "Gonzaga's next point guard."

"I'm like, 'Hold on, I'm starting against you guys tomorrow,'" Dickau says.

Soon enough, Dickau would be Gonzaga's next point guard. Before that, Frahm would average 14.4 and 16.9 points, respectively, his junior and senior years. Then, as now, it was a good ride.

Cory Violette

The Zags' reliable forward of the early millennium (2001-04) kicked around Italy and Turkey, did his best to impress NBA decision-makers in camps, and soldiered through the D-League. But it was his last stop in Japan that left the biggest impression on him. And it really had nothing to do with basketball.

Violette was playing for the Toshiba Brave Thunders in 2011 when the deadly 9.0-magnitude Tohoku earthquake hit northeastern Japan, creating a massive tsunami. Little remained in the season and the nation's infrastructure was such a mess that the balance of the schedule was cancelled.

Violette decided to stay for a couple of weeks to see if he could help. What he saw was people coming together instead of taking advantage. Signs in grocery stores would implore customers to take only one loaf of bread, not 10, and they complied. Violette saw stores where proprietors couldn't adequately tend cash registers, but customers would leave small piles of money they owed on a counter.

"I was thoroughly impressed with how the Japanese deal with a disaster like that," Violette says. "It was unbelievable."

It shouldn't be a surprise, then, to know the Toshiba club made good on the contracts, despite the truncated season. That was exactly in keeping with Violette's three years there.

"They treated me with a lot of respect, and they did what they said they would do, which was not normal in other countries," Violette says. "If you signed a contract [in those nations], you'd get 75 to 80 percent of it, and that was considered all of it. In Japan, they expect you to be on time for everything, but they're on time for everything. And they pay you exactly what they say."

Violette's attempts to find his way onto an NBA roster never quite lined up. Once, John Stockton helped him get an invitation to Utah's veterans camp, and Violette performed well. But he got cut on the next-to-last day before he would have to sign, so he hooked on with a club in Istanbul, Turkey.

A couple of days later, his agent called to inform him that Robert Whaley, who had been one of his competitors at forward for the Jazz, had been suspended for two games by the league for punching a Laker during an exhibition game. A week after that, Carlos Boozer pulled a hamstring. Those were Violette's openings.

"If I had waited, maybe, you never know," he muses, "maybe I would have gotten that call to be the 13th guy on the bench."

His last real brush with an NBA team was with Seattle in 2008. It asked if he wanted to try out for the Sonics' summer-league team. But Violette was beyond the point of groveling for any crumb. He had played for Seattle's D-League affiliate, he had played college hoops in the state. He figured they should have known him.

"If you know how that works, it's kind of a slap in the face more than an opportunity," Violette says. "At this stage of your career, if you're playing for nothing, you're risking a lot."

It was during his time overseas that Violette began to put his finance degree to work. His teammates wondered why he paid attention to the stock market, and he puzzled over some of their dubious choices with their cash.

"I help people make intelligent decisions with their money, and how to build wealth," he says, sitting behind a desk in a downtown-Spokane bank building. "It's not something you build in a day; you chip away at it."

He was workmanlike as a player, too, averaging eight rebounds each of his last three years, and 14.2 points as a senior. As for his own decision to go to Gonzaga, he's convinced that was wise in the same manner as he guides his clients: "I'd do it every time."

Derek Raivio

Somehow, even in a career in which he twice made the all-conference team and was the WCC's co-player of the year in 2007, Raivio seemed underappreciated. Maybe that had something to do with playing alongside the inferno that was Adam Morrison and the flamboyance of Ronny Turiaf.

But he had a way of rising to the occasion. There was the night in December 2004, when Gonzaga fans gulped at the prospect of their team, badly outclassed at Illinois days earlier, facing unbeaten and 14th-ranked Washington. Raivio responded with 21 points, eight assists, four steals and nary a turnover in 38 minutes in a rousing victory.

Seventeen days later, Gonzaga was facing No. 3-ranked Georgia Tech, and Raivio found himself pretty much bereft of teammates on a fast break. Instead of challenging the Yellow Jackets at the rim, he pulled up by himself and hit a long jumper. He scored 21 that night, too.

"Looking back on it," he says, recalling that moment when he flew solo, "it was probably a little crazy."

He would finish at Gonzaga as the NCAA's No. 2 free throw shooter both for a season (96.1 percent in 2007) and career (92.7), and then settle into a comfortable existence in Europe. Comfortable, in part, because the Belgian-born Raivio lived his early years overseas – his dad Rick had been a player in France – and he was receptive to the new lifestyle rather than intolerant of it.

"We love living in Europe," he said over the phone from France in late 2015. "My dad is always like, 'Play as long as you can. You can get a regular job when you get home.'"

Raivio has played in Germany, Belgium, the Czech Republic and France. Along the way, he married former GU soccer player Lori Conrad – not in the United States, but in Prague – and they've flourished overseas, regularly doing postseason trips to new countries.

"Once you start to appreciate the culture and immerse yourself, it makes it more enjoyable," Raivio says. "We love it."

Clearly, the Raivio of today is a more expansive one than that of his playing days, when, he admits, he was almost obsessively focused on basketball.

"I'd kind of escape," he says. "Now that I've seen more things, I've definitely become well-rounded."

Early in 2016, when Washington-to-Gonzaga transfer Nigel Williams-Goss was unable to carry out scout-team duties because of ankle surgery, the guy who sometimes stepped in for him was Raivio – himself rehabbing from an ankle problem sustained in France.

If they asked, Raivio could tell the Zags about a lot of life experiences. And a little about shooting free throws, too.

Blake Stepp

Fitzgerald, the longtime former Zag basketball coach, once called Blake Stepp "the best player ever to play here." This, from a guy who coached John Stockton in the early '80s.

Turns out we never really saw the best of Stepp, either.

You get a sense of his physical liabilities as he cools down from a pedestrian game at Hoopfest on a blistering June day in 2015. It's a slow, slow process, befitting a guy who, at 33, knows his body's limits. He averaged 13 points in four seasons (2001-04) at Gonzaga and was WCC player of the year his final two, yet there could have been more.

"I was actually very athletic in high school," he says. "I could windmill [dunk]. I could '360' off two feet. Then I got to Gonzaga and started getting hurt."

He counts 10 knee surgeries, seven on his left. Doctors told him it's probably genetically related. He figures he has the knees of a 70-year-old.

"People see me as kind of a heady, good-passing shooter," he says. "In high school, I was actually a very athletic kid."

Mostly, the injuries went unnoticed by Gonzaga partisans, because Stepp did a lot of teeth-gritting. He had knee surgery after his freshman season, and it still wasn't right, and if he could do it all over again, he says he would have redshirted his sophomore season, when backcourt mate Dickau was a senior.

The opening game at Illinois, a thumping administered by the Illini, "I literally had practiced maybe a total of two hours and I started."

Indeed, in that 2001-02 season, Stepp averaged his fewest points (9.2) and shot his poorest (.356) of four years from three-point range.

Good health, seemingly, was never his bedfellow. Out of Gonzaga, he and his agent, Mark Bartelstein, lined up perhaps 20 pre-draft workouts. Just before the first one, he sustained a bad ankle sprain and "could basically barely move. My draft stock really fell."

He went late in the second round, No. 58 overall, to Minnesota. He landed in Europe, in Serbia and Spain, but the knees kept intervening. He came home and, through some buddies, began to dabble in, of all things, online poker.

"I was almost making more money playing online poker than I was overseas," says Stepp, who took part in the World Series of Poker.

He played for a few years before the lifestyle got in the way. Online or at a casino, he'd call it a night about 2 a.m., then unwind for a couple of hours. His wife would be up to go to work at 5:30.

It figures that a guy who grew far too familiar with doctor's offices would end up back in Spokane selling medical vascular devices. And married to a nurse.

Erroll Knight

The worst night of Knight's life might have been the best.

He was a year out of Gonzaga, where he had been a defensive specialist on teams that highlighted Adam Morrison. He went overseas to Israel, where he was the only American on his team. It included a couple of Palestinians, but it worked – basketball as peacemaker.

Knight, whose offensive game was understated at Gonzaga, was able to unleash it in his new clime, averaging about 17 points. He had a couple of games in the 40s.

But not on this night. His team was busing up a hill to Nazareth, home of Jesus' youth. Deeply spiritual, Knight was clutching a Bible. He wore a sort of glassy look and somebody asked him if he was OK.

"All of a sudden, the game starts, and I can't move," says Knight, sharing his remembrance at a downtown Seattle coffee shop. "I'm in slow motion."

He was guarding an opponent from Team Nazareth who was a generation older, but it didn't matter. He was too plodding to defend. Knight describes a performance almost too despicable to qualify for a boxscore: A 1-for-17 shooting night, five or six straight misses from the foul line and eight turnovers.

"You kind of had a bad game," his Yemeni coach said.

Knight took it to be a sign of God's presence, and a message not to make basketball his reason for being. As usual, he called his mother after the game.

"Erroll, it sounds like a spiritual embodiment," she said.

Indeed, playing basketball wouldn't be his calling very long. Like Stepp, he had bad knees; Knight's problems started in high school, continuing at Gonzaga – he missed games early in his senior season of 2005-06, including the memorable Maui Invitational – and beyond. He had a significant microfracture surgery that sidelined him for a year after his days at GU, and he counts nine arthroscopies.

"If I could have stayed healthy," says Knight, who played less than two years overseas, "I might have honestly had a chance at the NBA."

Instead, Knight has had jobs in sales in Seattle, as well as a couple of roles in what he envisions as his dream job – coaching.

Demetri Goodson

The possibilities seemed so bright on that March Saturday night in 2009. With the crowd at the Rose Garden in Portland coming unhinged, Demetri Goodson – "Meech" to everybody around Gonzaga – took the ball up the left side of the floor, ignoring Jeremy Pargo's entreaties to pass, flicked up a little runner inside the final second, and all of a sudden, he owned Spokane.

Pushed to the limit by Western Kentucky, Gonzaga survived, 83-81, on Goodson's six-foot bank shot, a mere nine-tenths of a second before the buzzer to claim a berth in the NCAA Sweet 16.

Alas, that was as good as it got for Goodson in basketball. He would go on to start 68 games at GU, but he wasn't really a fit for Few's system. The Zags loved his athleticism and defensive chops, but he shot a mere 20 percent on treys in his three seasons, and his assist-to-turnover numbers were nothing special. He left after the 2011 season, his junior year, with what seemed like a cockamamie plan: He was going to play college football.

He had been a cornerback, wide receiver and running back until he gave up football for hoops his sophomore year of high school. But now he was on to a high-level program at Baylor.

"Oregon wanted to take a look at me," Goodson told me in spring 2016. "I just didn't want to go anywhere big like that. I knew they had their set corners. I wanted to go to a program that wasn't too small, but that needed me. I felt Baylor was a perfect fit."

He had plenty to discourage him there. In 2011, mere months after he had left Gonzaga, he injured an ankle early in the season. A year later, at the same juncture, he broke an arm.

"It was like my bones weren't used to that contact," Goodson says.

Finally, he put in a full season in 2013, benefiting from the quality of the Baylor receivers. "Baylor has the top wide receivers in the country," Goodson says. "I'd be locking them up [in practice]. The games were easy."

His ceiling impressed Green Bay, which took him in the sixth round of the 2014 draft. He made the team, got in six games in 2014 and 14 the next year, increasing his worth with his special-teams play. And he grew to love the smallest city in the NFL.

"Talk to anybody who plays for us," he says. "There's nothing to do here. I feel that's why we're so good; we can just focus on football. Other teams [their cities] have clubs and stuff. That's cool. I'd rather win the Super Bowl than be out clubbing."

But Goodson's future hit a snag in April 2016, when he was flagged by the league for use of performance-enhancing drugs and hit with a four-game suspension. It would seem the sort of thing that could have imperiled his position in the league.

"I'm not worried about it," he says. "Everybody here knows I didn't do it on purpose." As for a cloud over his future, he says, "I don't think about that. If it's going to happen, it's going to happen. There's no reason to dwell on it. All the coaches think very highly of me here. They know I'm a good person, and the one thing that separates me from a lot of corners is I'm a really good special-teams player."

Baylor was not only his landing spot for football, it's also where he met his future wife. He is due in March 2017 to marry former Bears softball player Linsey Hays. "I actually met her in a bar," Goodson says, laughing. "It was over after that. We just couldn't live without each other."

Goodson keeps in touch with former Zag teammates like Marquise Carter, Rob Sacre and Pargo. The player who had a modest career at Gonzaga will always own one of the program's most famous shots. And just as he did that night in ignoring Pargo's call to pass, Demetri Goodson proved again in 2011 he had a mind of his own.

– 12 –
STRIKE UP ALICE COOPER
("...'CAUSE I'M EIGHTEEN...")

ON THE MORNING OF MARCH 9, 2016, after Gonzaga had thwarted Saint Mary's to win the West Coast Conference championship on the heels of a fretful, fits-and-starts season, here's how Jim Rome addressed the Zags on his national radio show:

"Hey, look, I don't care if these guys have to go through Saint Mary's or the Golden State Warriors to win that thing, they were going to rip a ticket; you knew it. You can't have the NCAA tournament without the Zags. It's like having the AFC playoffs without the Pats or having the top five picks of the NFL draft without the Jags . . . just like every freaking year, Gonzaga is going to be in the field and I don't care how bad it looks in any given year, they'll be there. They always are."

Seemingly, yeah, they always are. A look at those 18 straight March odysseys:

1999

The course of history has brought Mark Few to this conclusion: That the confounding, out-of-the-blue run to the Elite Eight in

1999 – Gonzaga's very first whiff of NCAA-tournament success – is evidence of how the events of March often tilt on random, capricious occurrences that might not have a lot to do with the fundamental strength of a basketball team.

In other words: Stuff happens.

He knows that's a slippery slope. To some Zag fans, that 1999 team is the gold standard by which all the others must be measured; those were Gonzaga's first NCAA conquests, after all, and no GU team has ever gone further. And he might agree that for sheer indomitability – the willingness to lay it all out there, unafraid, and see where the chips fall – that 1999 outfit could be unmatched.

But Few is a big-picture, full-season guy, and the Zags of March 1999 weren't always the ones of November and December.

"People always say, 'Well, that's the best team they've ever had at Gonzaga,'" he says, taking on a faux fan voice, " 'and I'm never gonna acknowledge anybody's better.'"

He begs to differ. The Zags lost early, by 15 at Purdue, and they dropped a snoozer to University of Detroit, 49-48, on a neutral floor. Lee Nailon strafed them for 44 points and TCU beat them in Fort Worth over Christmas break. Two nights before that, Gonzaga won at Pan-American, 74-73, on a night that to Few, proved how fragile victory can be.

"One of the biggest miracle finishes ever," recalls Few, who was in his final year as an assistant coach. "We just played horribly. There were like 200 people at the game. We fouled their little point guard, who was like an 85-percent free throw shooter, and he misses both. We were down one, maybe two, and the rebound came out and we didn't even go for it. We were just so lethargic. Finally, Casey [Calvary] dives on the ball and throws it to Matt [Santangelo] and he shoots a three at the buzzer. They were literally like the 328th-best team in the country."

But the '99 Zags happily co-opted whatever serendipity came their way, and in combination with steely resolve, rode it all the way to the doorstep of the Final Four before eventual champion Connecticut denied them entry.

First, Gonzaga, a No. 10 seed, was sent to a friendly site at Seattle's KeyArena for first- and second-round games. Then, on the eve of a game with Minnesota, came the shocker broken by the St. Paul Pioneer Press, alleging systemic academic fraud in the Gophers basketball program. In short order, Minnesota suspended four players, including two starters. (One wonders how, if the story had come a week earlier, the basketball committee might have analyzed the Gophers.)

"In their second turn around the Dance floor," wrote John Blanchette in the *Spokane Spokesman-Review*, "the Bulldogs have caught more breaks than a surfer at Waimea Bay."

Coach Dan Monson had concocted a triangle-and-two defense to deal with Minnesota, but the suspensions forced a change on the fly – to a box-and-one. The "one" was 5-foot-8 dervish Quentin Hall, who pestered 6-7 Minnesota star Quincy Lewis into a 3-for-19 shooting day. In a 75-63 victory, Richie Frahm was the offensive star with 26 points on 5-for-11 three-point shooting. Until they faced UConn, the Zags were dynamite from distance, hitting 32 of 63 treys over three games.

Stanford fell next, 82-74, as the Zags stood up to a brutish team led by Mark Madsen and again led most of the way. The KeyArena crowd fell madly in love with Gonzaga, Santangelo had 22 points, six rebounds and six assists, and Stanford coach Mike Montgomery said he rued the matchup, perhaps more for Gonzaga's aggressiveness than the partisan house.

"I was hoping Minnesota would beat Gonzaga, I really was," he said.

Of course, what came next was Calvary, or so the condensation of time has it. In Phoenix, the Zags were down 72-71 to a 22-8 Florida team. Frahm had again led them with 17 points, making five of eight threes. And with the final seconds ticking down and Florida in possession, the ubiquitous Hall was supposed to foul, but something inside him said no. He and his team were rewarded when, seconds later, Gator forward Brent Wright traveled in backcourt, and the Zags drew up a final play with 14 seconds left.

"Quentin passed the ball to me," Calvary would remember 16 years later. "I passed the ball right back to him. I was pretty sure he was gonna shoot it, because that was his personality."

Hall's 13-footer missed badly but here came Calvary, unimpeded down the lane, to slap the ball up and in, and seconds later, the Bulldogs created a dog-pile.

Few, weighing the plan to have Hall foul and the good fortune of the Florida turnover, calls the victory "crazy-improbable."

Gonzaga's maniacal March ended with a 67-62 loss to UConn, but only after GU led 32-31 at halftime; only after Hall had harassed the Huskies' touted point guard, Khalid El-Amin, into an unspeakable 0-for-12 day from the field; only after Connecticut made free throws to seal it down the stretch. The shots that fell throughout the tournament were denied by UConn's grudging perimeter defense, as Gonzaga hit only five of 21 threes.

Years later, when John Stockton was inducted into the Naismith Basketball Hall of Fame, he invited along one of the defensive stoppers on the '99 team, Mike Nilson, and his father. They ran into Rip Hamilton, the star of that Connecticut squad.

"Oh, man, you guys were the toughest game we played in the whole tournament," Hamilton told Nilson.

It wasn't as though the '99 team didn't already have Nilson's seal of approval.

"I love that team," he says. "We were really about 10 guys deep. To be a starter, giving up minutes to that seventh, eighth, ninth, 10th guy, you've got to be a pretty special person that values the team. A lot of times, I think there are guys on the bench hoping the starters don't do well. But we all liked each other."

Naturally, the outside perspective on Gonzaga was: One-hit wonder.

"The coaches did a good job reminding us, that's a program-changing effort," Calvary would say years later. "That this doesn't have to be a one-off deal."

Guess the coaches knew what they were talking about. And the guys they were addressing listened.

The takeaway: Given Gonzaga's near-empty history in the NCAA tournament, the inaugural run was one of the most stirring surprise surges in the annals of the event.

2000

By the time Gonzaga opened its next season, it had a new coach – Few. Monson, romanced for the job at nearby Washington State in the spring, succumbed in midsummer to the lure of a power-conference job only after the personal agony of a hiring process that left him in knots.

The longtime attorney for both Monson and Few, Brad Williams of Spokane, remembers a negotiating process in which Minnesota raised the ante from $400,000 a year over five years to $750,000 per, plus a guarantee that covered the four years of NCAA probation the school was about to endure for one of the most unseemly academic scandals in history.

Williams took a couple of things from that negotiation that he would pass on to Few: First, if you're interested enough in another job to visit that campus, you'd better be prepared to take the job.

"They're not going to let you off, because of the embarrassment factor," Williams says. "People knew we were on campus when we got there. The media had picked it up."

Williams' second cautionary note might seem surprising.

"Another thing I tell people, I wouldn't move to a place where there's two competing newspapers," he says. "They're always trying to scoop each other. A columnist will come out: 'I think they should fire Monson.' They're always looking for the story that a lot of times wasn't there."

Few recalls the dueling emotions of his colleague of the past 11 years departing: Deep sadness – "Dan and I had been together so long; you were losing a buddy" – coupled with the realization, in July, that he was a Division I head coach. "How crazy is that?" he says at the recollection.

Whoever was coaching them, the Zags were self-motivated. Says Frahm, "Since that Elite Eight run, we basically didn't stop all summer long. That was our first summer, where I think guys really figured out how to train, how to take care of themselves. Our focus was not to be a one-year fluke. We wanted to come back and make some noise again."

Done. In Tucson, Frahm was again nails with 31 points, hitting nine of his 14 field-goal attempts, as Gonzaga scuttled Louisville, 77-66. The Zags, a 10 seed once more, then schooled a 2 seed for the second straight year, beating St. John's, 82-76, despite trailing by nine late in the first half. Santangelo was the driving force, hitting six of 10 threes among his 26 points on a day when he also had five assists while playing 40 minutes.

That brought the Zags to Albuquerque, where, in an ugly 75-66 loss to Purdue, the loss of Nilson was a factor. Nilson had suffered a torn Achilles tendon in the WCC tournament, and in an unusual opening against the Boilermakers, the first dead ball for a media timeout didn't happen until the 12:40 mark, leaving both teams gassed in the high altitude. Purdue had a 20-7 run to end the half and controlled it thereafter.

The takeaway: It was the end for the glorious Santangelo-Frahm backcourt, but an auspicious start for the Few regime. Nobody knew then how long and how decorated it would become.

2001

For the first time in its NCAA history, something new and different happened to Gonzaga, albeit as a No. 12 seed. It found itself the villain, not the darling.

In the second round in Memphis, the Zags were paired against Indiana State, which had upset Kelvin Sampson's Oklahoma team in the first round. The Sycamores led GU into the second half before Gonzaga's 19-3 finishing run doomed ISU, 85-68. In his last college victory, Calvary scored 24 points and had seven assists.

Afterward, Few recalled how after the 1999 run, legendary Al McGuire warned the Gonzaga coaches to try to keep expectations tamped down, because results would never match them.

"You guys will never get back to the Sweet 16," McGuire said, according to Few. "You know how hard that is. Some of my best teams never made it."

The Zags had advanced with a first-round victory over Virginia on a putback by Calvary with nine seconds left, 86-85. Dan Dickau, the transfer from Washington, scored 29 points, including six threes, a couple of which drew heavy iron before re-routing themselves into the net. Calvary, Zach Gourde and Alex Hernandez combined for another 43 points.

"He'd be way out, shoot a Scud, hit the rim, hit the backboard, go in," Pete Gillen, the Virginia coach, marveled of Dickau. "He was on fire."

The Zags thus became the first program to make the Sweet 16 three straight years as a double-digit seed. Michigan State coach Tom Izzo, whose team was next up for Gonzaga in Atlanta, said, "It's like somebody said on TV: Why don't they just make those guys a No. 5 or 6 seed, because that's how they play."

For the second straight year at this juncture, Gonzaga was ousted by Big Ten brawn, as Michigan State had a 49-29 rebounding advantage in a 77-62 victory. The Zags would dedicate themselves – successfully – to becoming a better rebounding team.

The takeaway: The three-year run of seven NCAA-tournament victories stands as the greatest introductory in history by a program with no pedigree.

2002

At the Red Lion Hotel in Spokane, maybe a thousand people gathered on Selection Sunday for the unveiling of Gonzaga's latest tournament escapade. The Zags had pieced together a 29-2 regular season and Few wondered privately whether his team might be capable of a No. 2 seed. Then came the bracket on big screens over CBS TV, and as the hour wore on, it became obvious this wouldn't be a signal occasion in Gonzaga's growing hoops history.

Gonzaga drew a No. 6 seed, and if that weren't enough, it was matched against the Mountain West's 21-8 regular-season champion, Wyoming – at mile-high Albuquerque, which meant the Cowboys would actually be going downhill in the thin-air comparison. The long faces and strained comments of the Zags were palpable.

Four days later, the Zags simply couldn't get shots to fall – Dickau, in his final game, and Blake Stepp combined to make eight field goals in 37 attempts – and the Cowboys prevailed, 74-66.

"It's hard to say we were underrated, but after playing that team, there's no doubt in my mind Wyoming was," forward Cory Violette said in 2015. "They would shoot these fadeaway jumpers that they had worked on and worked on. We were taught not to shoot fadeaway jumpers. They could just hit 'em and it was tough to guard."

Violette says the Zags should have routinely run more in the break leading to NCAA-tournament week, and he would have preferred a four-day arrival before a game played at high altitude. In any case, the week was the first real downer in Gonzaga's expanding tournament portfolio.

The takeaway: There were two lessons learned from Selection Sunday, 2002, followed to this day: First, schedule harder. And second, choose a small, private gathering without TV cameras for the bracket announcement.

2003

The Zags' stay in Salt Lake City was nothing if not memorable. On Thursday, in a game pitting 8-9 seeds, Gonzaga eliminated Cincinnati, 74-69, a day distinguished by the fact that not only did Cincy coach Bob Huggins get ejected with 16 minutes left for prolonged argument of an official's call, so did Bearcats radio color man Chuck Machock. Chris Dufresne of the Los Angeles Times wrote that Machock screamed at official Mike Kitts, "That's a terrible call, you SOB, terrible!"

Picture Hugs in the locker room by himself, where he said he drank "a Cranapple" and, with no TV to watch, claimed he was unaware of what was happening on the floor.

Perhaps the Bearcat scouting report was really the source of Huggins' ire. Gonzaga guard Winston Brooks, a 30-percent three-point shooter, hit three of four against Cincinnati – including one that was supposed to be a lob pass.

Next came one of the Zags' all-time valedictories. Gonzaga and a top-seeded Arizona team laced with six future NBA players – including Channing Frye, Luke Walton and Andre Iguodala – warred through two overtimes before the Wildcats staggered home a winner, 96-95, when Stepp's leaning bank shot from astride the key misfired at the buzzer.

People would compose sonnets about the game. In its year-end edition, Sports Illustrated rhapsodized about it as example of what sports could be.

"It was unbelievable to be a part of that," says Violette. "It was an interesting end-of-game environment, too. Arizona knew they had just survived something. It looked like they felt they had won the coin flip on that one."

A picture of Stepp putting up that shot hangs in the GU basketball offices. But to this day, he hasn't watched the second overtime, just the first. "I never had the balls to watch all of it," he says.

Situation, and urgency, made it a more nuanced shot than it looked.

"That last shot was tough," Stepp says, noting that 'Zona guard Jason Gardner was rushing at him and the horn was about to sound. "I still can't make it to this day. Any kind of leaning shot, especially off the glass, is tough."

He needn't apologize. In 47 minutes, Stepp had 25 points, eight assists and no turnovers. Teammate Tony Skinner was the only player to see all 50 minutes, scoring 25 points. So exquisite was the game that the teams combined for only 20 turnovers.

A postscript: The epic game was in its latter stages after another NCAA sub-regional ended at the Spokane Arena. A few thousand fans there stuck around to cheer – and ultimately, lament – what they saw on the big screen.

The takeaway: It's possible to lose, and you don't really lose.

2004

You could call this the NCAA tournament of Gonzaga's lost innocence. Until now, the Zags had either performed famously, or, in the case of 2002, seemed to be at least partly victims of circumstance.

Not so much in '04, although Gonzaga partisans have wondered what might have happened if Ronny Turiaf had been on the floor the whole day. He wasn't, and the second-seeded Zags were bludgeoned by No. 10 seed Nevada, 91-72. The Wolf Pack built a big early lead, was up 47-32 at halftime and wasn't really threatened.

At the site where its post-season success was christened in 1999, KeyArena in Seattle, Gonzaga opened the tournament with a lopsided win over Valparaiso. The Zags, at 28-2, had lost only to a pair of No. 1 seeds, St. Joseph's and Stanford. For the first time, there was widespread recognition of Gonzaga's place in college basketball – which made the Nevada loss that much more difficult to stomach.

"It feels as if someone took your life away, almost," Adam Morrison, a freshmen, said then. "This is all we've got, this is all I've got – basketball."

The overarching message here: Looks can be deceiving. The Wolf Pack had big-time talent. Swingman Kirk Snyder was the 16th pick in the 2004 NBA draft. Bigs Nick Fazekas and Kevinn Pinkney each played in the NBA.

"If you go back and watch it, it'd really make you mad," says Violette, who had 16 points and 11 rebounds. "Turiaf had two phantom fouls."

Around Gonzaga, the game will be remembered for how the officials sent Turiaf to the sidelines with three fouls in the first nine minutes. He played a mere 15 minutes – and scored 13 points.

"I have a hard time dealing with the Nevada [loss]," Turiaf told me in 2016. "I felt like Nick Fazekas, they bailed him out. I'm a physical player; I should have made a little bit better choices as far as not using my strength and so on and so forth. But I felt they bailed him out."

The takeaway: It would be the first of three straight crushing exits from the tournament for Gonzaga.

2005

Donny Daniels, now an assistant coach at Gonzaga, was on the staff at UCLA, which made it to GU's sub-regional in Tucson. The Bruins lost to Texas Tech, while the Zags struggled past first-round opponent Winthrop. Daniels had the scouting assignment on the Gonzaga-Winthrop game as UCLA's next opponent if it had won.

"Wow, there was Morrison, [J.P.] Batista," Daniels says, recalling the GU-Texas Tech matchup. "Second-round game . . . that should have been an Elite Eight game."

That figures as small consolation to the Zags of '05, who saw a 13-point second-half lead melt into a 71-69 loss to Texas Tech, where coach Bob Knight had resurrected his career after being fired at Indiana.

The particulars: Erroll Knight, known more for his defense, shot seven for eight from the floor for 14 points in an unexpected offensive contribution. The Zags pounded Tech on the glass, 44-32. But they couldn't get stops in a zone defense early in the second half, surrendering points on eight straight possessions.

So it condensed into plays at the wire. Ronald Ross, Tech's leading scorer, shook loose for a three in the left corner with 70 seconds left to put the Red Raiders up for good, 68-67. Turiaf, who made only three of nine free throws – he was a 71.5-percent shooter in his career – missed a one-and-one with 49 seconds left. Jarrius Jackson got the benefit of a foul call that Batista contested and made a free throw for Tech.

Down by two, the Zags were left with a final telling possession. Morrison, who scored 25 points, got the ball on top off a high ball screen, and when Turiaf's defender didn't show, Morrison found himself in no-man's land, putting up a three-pointer that missed.

"Right when I went up to shoot, I was in two minds, whether to drive or shoot," Morrison said in 2015. "Right when I released it, I was like, 'Shit, halfway in-between.'"

Morrison was part of the Gonzaga staff when GU visited Arizona in December 2014. He couldn't help but revisit the spot on the floor and wonder why he didn't take two dribbles and try to get to the rim.

"But I loved that season," he says. "The young guys from the year before got an opportunity to play."

In the end, it was Gonzaga's inability to impose itself inside that made the difference. Morrison's 22 shots were exactly as many as Batista and Turiaf took combined.

The takeaway: Call it an opportunity lost, as Gonzaga would have faced seventh-seeded West Virginia in the Sweet 16. As for the Winthrop team the Zags ousted in the first round, Gonzaga would see that coach, Gregg Marshall, far down the road.

2006

UCLA. To any long-standing Gonzaga fan, the reference roils up an old wound, like the name of a significant other in a relationship gone bad.

UCLA, in Oakland, in 2006, where the Zags sustained the most gut-stabbing defeat in their history. They led by 17 once, and they led 71-62 with 3:27 remaining, and then they went 0 for 7 from the field with three turnovers and didn't score again. And they would cause Bill Walton to say on TV years later, "We walked out as fans, and we looked at each other, and we said, 'Did that just happen?'"

Make no mistake, this was a gifted Bruins team. If it didn't have a superstar, it had rich talent across the board; six players made the NBA, and five of them – Arron Afflalo, Jordan Farmar, Luc-Richard M'bah a Moute, Ryan Hollins and Darren Collison – had extensive careers in the League.

That doesn't remove the scab that seemingly will always be there to remind the '06 team that the Elite Eight was right there. And that in Memphis – the next game's opponent that wasn't – there was a team the Zags had played evenly in Tennessee in December before the game slipped away late in an 83-72 defeat.

"It was just devastating," David Pendergraft says over lunch a decade later. "We knew, situationally, 'This is when we have a chance to do it. Like this is one of the chances of a lifetime. This team has the ability to get where we want to go.'"

The third-seeded Zags had opened with a hard-fought win over Xavier and then converted a trip to the Sweet 16 by dispatching a smaller Indiana team.

"That team we had was a pretty loose team," says Sean Mallon. "I think we were pretty confident."

Nothing that happened early should have dissuaded the Zags. UCLA got a horrendous start, going – hard as this is to believe – its first 14 possessions without a field goal. On the CBS broadcast, analyst Len Elmore said, "I think they're embarrassed. They should be."

Nor did Gonzaga start quickly. But the Zags discovered some rhythm and nudged a lead into double digits. On the UCLA bench, Donny Daniels watched Morrison curl off a screen, rise over the shorter Afflalo and score with seeming ease.

"Oh my God, this is going to be a long night," Daniels thought. "How we gonna defend this guy?"

When Batista hit a jump-hook over M'bah a Moute to make it 31-16, UCLA coach Ben Howland called his third timeout with 6:42 left in the half. Later in the half, Morrison lost Cedric Bozeman on an inbounds play and hit a left-handed layup and Gonzaga had its biggest lead of the game, 37-20. The Bruins got it back to a 42-29 deficit at half.

Recalling the halftime locker room, Pendergraft says, "Fewie came in and said, 'OK, one more half and you guys are the greatest team in Gonzaga history.'"

UCLA nosed back as Gonzaga made three silly turnovers in the first three minutes after the break. Quickly, the Bruins got the game back to single digits, but the Zags steadied and when Morrison took Afflalo – who was playing with four fouls – for a 15-foot jumper, Gonzaga led 64-51 with seven minutes-plus left. On TV, Gus Johnson was preparing his audience to be taken elsewhere, saying, "We're going to ping-pong you back and forth between this game and Texas-West Virginia, but we'll definitely get you out to the finish."

While Afflalo survived his foul trouble, Gonzaga's Knight did not. He got two quick ones with 10:53 left, on a single UCLA possession, and then he fouled out at 3:27 on a seemingly chippy call defending M'bah a Moute.

"Coach," Knight implored Few, "what did I do wrong?"

Surely, Knight didn't entertain the notion that he was leaving a collegiate floor for the final time. But everything was going south for the Zags. As more than one in their program will put it, if 10 things needed to go wrong to lose, 10 things did. One of them was the officials, who seemed to execute poorly – both ways – down the stretch. Collison didn't get the benefit of a possible and-one opportunity with 1:29 left, and at an even more critical time, Batista was whistled for a phantom rebounding foul with 20 seconds left, allowing Hollins (a 61-percent free throw shooter) to go to the line and make it a one-point game. He hit both.

Two days later, against Memphis, Hollins was two for 11 on free throws.

In the last moments, Derek Raivio missed an open look from the corner; Morrison had a mid-range jumper pop in and out; and Farmar got a high pick against Raivio, dribbled to the right side and kissed in a difficult bank shot to make it a 71-68 game with 52 seconds left. Few called timeout with 41 seconds left. Morrison dribbled the ball up, handed it to Raivio and got it back, and on a UCLA switch, had Farmar on him rather than the Bruins' best defender, Afflalo. But Morrison chose a tough, left-side 17-footer rather than drive Farmar inside, and that's when Batista was called for fouling Hollins, whose free throws made it 71-70. If anything, Morrison might have shot it too quickly; there were 24 seconds remaining and eight on the shot clock.

Then came the sequence that endures in Zag infamy. Gonzaga inbounded and got the ball to Batista, who held it aloft in backcourt as Raivio faced him near the low block maybe 15 feet away. Bozeman flicked the ball out of Batista's hands, Farmar rushed it to

M'bah a Moute underneath and he scored to give UCLA a 72-71 lead. M'bah a Moute then hurtled downcourt and, from behind, slapped away the ball from Raivio, leaving the TV tandem – and anyone else who saw it – in disbelief.

Elmore: "Unbelievable!"

Johnson: "Oh, what a game!"

Elmore: "Unbelievable!"

Johnson: "What a game!"

Elmore: "Unbelievable!"

Johnson: "Unbelievable!"

Elmore: "Are you kidding me?"

Elmore: "Holy mackerel."

In the minds of more than one Zag, their fatal mistake was in becoming too conservative offensively. Says Raivio, "We played not to lose instead of playing to win that game. Towards the end, we weren't aggressive. We were more concerned with running the shot clock down. They were the aggressor."

Morrison agrees, to a point, saying, "Any basketball-IQ person would say you need to eat clock. I think we got caught in that, and couldn't get our rhythm back when we had to score."

Dissenting, Pendergraft says, "We got shots we got all year long. You're talking about some of the best shooters, the best scorers in the history of our program."

Daniels, on the other side then, appreciated what a challenge Gonzaga was. Morrison and Batista combined that season to average a robust 47 points. Raivio was a deadly shooter, and when he got fouled, next to a lock at the free throw line.

"They had a *team*," Daniels says. "That was a Final Four team."

It hardly made the Zags feel any better when, after returning home, they saw the regional final. UCLA and Memphis staged an absolute atrocity won by the Bruins, 50-45. UCLA made 14 field goals and missed 19 free throws. Memphis was two of 17 from three-point range. The teams collaborated for 12 assists and 35 turnovers.

A decade later, the UCLA game is discussed around Gonzaga only when a media member has cause to bring it up. It's the family incident of long ago that can be revisited, but never reconciled.

"We had no business winning that game," Daniels says.

It's left to Gonzaga to accept the converse of that reality.

The takeaway: The final game at Gonzaga for Morrison, Batista and Knight was as bitter as they come.

2007

Few will always preach the value of the journey over the destination. Well, anybody around the Zags would agree the year 2006-07 was about the journey.

The destination was Sacramento and an NCAA first-round game against Indiana, the program's ninth straight Big Dance. But the road map to that site, that was something else.

Gonzaga upended No. 2 North Carolina in the NIT Season Tipoff in New York, and after routing Washington in the final game of a series truncated by the Huskies, rose to No. 16 in the Associated Press poll. But early February brought the Josh Heytvelt revelation involving possession of hallucinogenic mushrooms, and his season-ending suspension presented formidable challenges.

First, there was his 15.5 points a game, and then, the altered rotation and chemistry that inevitably follows a departure.

"We were thin that year as it was," Few says. Recalling his message post-Heytvelt, he adds, " 'This is who we are now, it's over [Heytvelt's participation]. Every one of us has to make adjustments – staff, management, players, everybody.' I just kept telling them, 'We'll figure it out as a staff, you've just gotta bring it every day.'"

Finally, the Zags had to come to grips with the betrayal they felt that a teammate had apparently trivialized the mission.

Seven days after the Heytvelt bombshell, the nine-loss Zags hosted No. 8 Memphis in what loomed as a possible statement game for NCAA selection. But in an overtime thriller at Spokane Arena, the Tigers prevailed, 78-77, as Chris Douglas-Roberts shuffled across the key and coaxed home a shot with seconds left.

"We were devastated," Pendergraft says. "That was our NCAA at-large bid."

There was thus one avenue: Win the WCC tournament in Portland.

"We were a motley crew out there," Raivio says. "We were very undersized. I remember telling myself, I didn't want to be part of the team that like ended the streak."

Clearly, that was powerful motivation. In the semifinals, the Zags routed San Diego, 88-70, as Pendergraft went for 22 points, hitting four of Gonzaga's six threes. And in the final, Gonzaga came from nine points behind in the first half in a 77-68 triumph over Santa Clara, whose coach, Dick Davey, had announced his retirement. Raivio scored 28 points, hitting eight of 12 field-goal attempts and all 10 free throws, bisected by a second-half visit to a courtside garbage can to throw up. Raivio was the MVP, joined by Pendergraft and Micah Downs on the all-tournament team.

"That was the biggest, most fun accomplishment I've had in my basketball career," Pendergraft says today. "No question about it. It was just fun. No one believes in you, so you have nothing to lose."

The actual NCAA appearance was an anti-climax, as the 10th-seeded Zags lost to Indiana, 70-57. The Hoosiers were led by big man D.J. White, who a year later would be the Big Ten player of the year and a first-round NBA pick.

With the passage of time, Pendergraft can afford to be candid about the loss.

"We played hard," he insists. "It was one of those, 'We made it, who cares?' There wasn't this focus like in years past. We didn't have the talent. It was just making it."

The takeaway: The stretch run was an affair of the heart for Gonzaga in a season as fragile as any in its 18-year NCAA streak.

2008

For want of a rebound, the Stephen Curry story was launched.

Davidson and Gonzaga were tied, 74-all, with 70 seconds left in their NCAA-tournament game at Raleigh, N.C. The Wildcats put up a trey that missed, and the ball bounced to the right of the basket. Zags guard Jeremy Pargo went to pick it up. On the bench, Gonzaga assistant coach Ray Giacoletti looked upcourt, assuming the possession was the Zags'.

"Nobody was stopping anybody," says Few. "We would have gone down and scored."

Somehow, Pargo and ball never quite intersected. He attacked it too casually, and Davidson forward Andrew Lovedale snatched it from his grasp.

"Curry was at half-court," Few recalls. "He flipped around, they threw it out to him and he hit a three."

Gonzaga couldn't reply, and seconds later, Davidson had an 82-76 victory that ignited a run to the Elite Eight and burnished Curry's name, while sending the Zags home for the second straight year without a victory.

"He'll remember that," Few says of Pargo. "We spent the whole next year talking about rebounding."

Entering that game, of course, Curry wasn't yet mega-star, more like curiosity. He was a willowy guard who averaged 25.9 points in '08 – fourth in the nation – but he played for a small private school in North Carolina that hadn't yet done anything in the postseason. As a freshman in 2006-07, he led the Wildcats into the tournament, where they lost to Maryland despite his 30 points, and Terps coach Gary Williams would say – pretty prophetically, as it turned out – "He's for real. I told him after the game, 'You could play anywhere.'"

Painfully enough, the Zags discovered for themselves. The scouting report underscored it – shooter, shooter, shooter – but Curry outdid himself, making eight of 10 threes and scoring 30 of his 40 points in the second half. He wasn't the ball-handler he is today, but he had a magical feel for pace and space, and the same hair-trigger release.

The Zags led most of the way, and if they had survived, the story would have been their own Stephen – or Steven. Freshman guard Steven Gray hit seven of 12 treys for the Zags. But it was his fate to be guarding Curry much of the afternoon, and that was a discouraging assignment. Curry would go on to score 25 of his 30 points in the second half of a close win over Georgetown; 33 in a 17-point Davidson waltz over Wisconsin in the Sweet 16, and 25 in a loss against eventual champion Kansas, albeit on 4-of-16 three-point shooting.

"We're so set into what a prototypical best player in the world looks like," Pendergraft muses today. "Michael Jordan, LeBron, Kobe . . . freak athlete, whatever. Steph comes up and looks like a little boy. Your mind won't let you go there. He breaks all the norms."

The takeaway: Two of them: Yeah, Steph Curry turned out to be pretty good. And once you get beyond the preferred top four or five seeds, the bracket is a geographic grab-bag. The Zags were a No. 7 seed and were shipped three time zones to play a No. 10 seed whose campus is just 158 miles from Raleigh. Then again, GU had a similar benefit in Seattle when that gilded run began in 1999.

2009

"We had a lot of mouths to feed that year," Few says.

There was Heytvelt, the leading scorer at 14.9. There was Austin Daye, about to jet off to the NBA following his sophomore year. There was the fiery Pargo, and Matt Bouldin, and Downs, in his second home after Kansas.

"We were like a top-five team, I thought," Few says, "and then Sacre broke his foot."

The Zags had once envisioned Heytvelt as a low-post factor, but it never really materialized. So when Robert Sacre suffered his injury early in the season, it turned them into a finesse outfit. That carried them to the Sweet 16, but at that stage, their No. 4 seed pitted them against North Carolina, and they were torched, 98-77. That Carolina team had three players averaging 15 points or more, led by Tyler Hansbrough, and it captured the national title without ever being truly tested.

In a 28-6 season, three of the Gonzaga losses came consecutively. In the Battle in Seattle, the Zags kicked away a would-be victory against a No. 2-ranked Connecticut team (it would be No. 1 in mid-season) and lost in overtime. Then they came home and were ambushed by Ken Bone's Portland State team.

"We kind of pouted," Few says, recalling the UConn aftermath.

Following a one-point loss to Utah, the Zags won in overtime at Tennessee – oddly, their second win over the Vols. But, typical of the undulating nature of this team, it was thrashed, 68-50, at Spokane Arena by a 14th-ranked John Calipari Memphis team.

Even its run to the Sweet 16 against double-digit seeds was edgy. In Portland, it trailed Akron by six with 15 minutes left before bursting free, and it booted away a late lead against Western Kentucky and ultimately needed Demetri Goodson's running bank shot near the buzzer to move on, 83-81.

The takeaway: Few wouldn't call this his most selfless, cohesive outfit. Still, it might have won another game had it not matched up against the extravagantly talented Tar Heels.

2010

A season is a kaleidoscope of moments, some poignant, others merely meaningful, some mirthful.

Picture Few and Giacoletti, walking the streets of Manhattan late on the night of Dec. 19 in a snowstorm, wondering where all this was leading. The Zags, good enough to win the Maui Invitational that year, had been brutalized by Duke, 76-41, that afternoon at Madison Square Garden, marking the fewest points Gonzaga had scored in 25 years. Nobody had more than three field goals for the Zags, who made 15 baskets on 54 shots and hit 10 of 21 from the foul line. Bouldin, who had missed a game with concussion symptoms, picked a bad day to return, shooting one of seven and making five turnovers.

Thus, the walk, amid swirling snow and the bonhomie of the Christmas season, which might have been lost on Few and Giacoletti.

"He needed some time to get it all together and process it," Giacoletti says. "It was pouring down snow."

Few and his closest coaching friends have a term for it: "Season-on-the-brink moments."

"You have 'em every year," Few says. "We probably walked three hours."

The season was a roller-coaster. In the eight weeks after that snowy trudge, Gonzaga would lose only once – in overtime at San Francisco, when Gray saved a rebound on the end line and threw it back in – directly to Dior Lowhorn, who hit a tying trey with 10 seconds left in regulation.

Gonzaga won the WCC regular-season title, but was throttled rudely in the league-tournament title game by rival Saint Mary's, 81-62.

The Zags' two days in the NCAA tournament turned out much like the rest of the season. On a Friday night in Buffalo in an 8-9 seeding matchup, Gonzaga stumped Florida State, 67-60, shooting 50 percent against the No. 1 team in the nation in field-goal percentage defense. In fact, it was the first time in 68 games an opponent had hit at least half its shots against the Seminoles.

That won Gonzaga a date against No. 1 seed Syracuse, which was 150 miles from its campus. The Orange, who had spent the week of

March 1 ranked No. 1 in the country, manhandled the Zags, 87-65, in a game that wasn't that close. It probably didn't make GU feel any better when, a week later, 'Cuse fell to Butler as the Bulldogs began their first Final Four run.

The takeaway: This was a roster infused with a lot of new faces after the '09 Sweet 16 team. But several – Bol Kong, Manny Arop, G.J. Vilarino, Grant Gibbs and Andy Poling – would later transfer.

2011

Jimmer.

In Denver after the 11th-seeded Zags riddled St. John's, 86-71, the coaches spent the usual hard night in a film room. They were joined by one of the cagiest minds in school history, John Stockton.

"That was the only time in six years I can remember him coming in the film room," says Giacoletti, referring to his tenure as an assistant coach.

The coaches were huddling, brainstorming ways to deal with Naismith and Wooden Award winner Jimmer Fredette, and Stockton threw in his two cents. Alas, none of it worked for Gonzaga, which went down hard to Brigham Young, 89-67.

The plan was to make Fredette work as hard as possible, make him guard at the other end. But both Marquise Carter and Goodson, who had had terrific games in the St. John's victory, had off-days. Neither had a basket. And as Few recalls, the Zags weren't a premier team at attacking a zone that year.

Fredette had a monster day, scoring 34 points and hitting seven of 12 three-point shots. On one unforgettable launch, he caught the ball about 25 feet from the basket not even facing it, corkscrewed his body into alignment in mid-air and threw down a trey.

Making matters worse, says Few: "You couldn't touch him if you were in the vicinity. We knew he was getting the benefit of the doubt on any contact he had."

The game before, the slight-underdog Zags had blistered St. John's, winning the rebounding battle 43-20. The Johnnies' leading board man, D.J. Kennedy, was out after injuring his knee in the Big East tournament. Goodson handled the St. John's full-court pressure adroitly, and Carter scored a career-high 24 points.

In a 25-10 season, there were pockets of real struggle for Gonzaga. It was 4-5 a month into it, and later, there was a rare three-game losing streak to WCC opponents. But GU thumped Saint Mary's, 75-63, to avenge the previous year's tournament loss to the Gaels and win the WCC automatic bid.

The takeaway: "In retrospect," says Few, "that was one of those years you felt pretty good about tapping out. We had reached our ceiling pretty good."

2012

One was a white kid from outside Toronto. The other was an African-American product of suburban Seattle. And the summer before they began a golden four years together, Kevin Pangos heard Gary Bell Jr. issue a challenge they could embrace together: To be the best backcourt in Gonzaga history.

By the time they were done, they had combined to start 257 games and be a part of 122 victories, or more than 30 a year. And Few would laud them for never having a bad practice, never taking the game for granted, always bringing the best they had to bring.

Pangos announced his arrival loudly. In his second game in a Zag uniform, he drilled nine threes against Washington State to tie a school record. Down the road, he would become GU's career leader on treys.

Their worker-bee personalities joined a figure with a different sort of mien: Sacre, the booming senior center from outside Vancouver, B.C.

"An awesome, incredible individual to be around," says Few. "Funny and gregarious, but yet tough and resilient. He brought it every single day. Right when he walks in those double doors, you can feel it and hear it in here."

Gonzaga lost at home to a Draymond Green-led Michigan State team, and was 13-3 after getting drubbed 83-62 at Saint Mary's, the Zags' worst loss to the Gaels since 1989. After the teams split the season series, Saint Mary's, keyed by Matthew Dellavedova, won in overtime in the WCC-tournament final.

That put Gonzaga in one of those how-did-this-happen notions of the NCAA basketball committee, a No. 7 seed playing 10th-seeded West Virginia in Pittsburgh, 78 miles from the WVU campus. That only added to the stunning nature of GU's 77-54 victory, one in which Mountaineers All-American forward Kevin Jones had a season-low four rebounds, and West Virginia didn't string four points together until the final four minutes.

"What Mark's done is a great job of recruiting guys who can play basketball," said West Virginia coach Bob Huggins. "Sometimes you get caught up in guys who can run and jump but have no clue about how to play basketball."

Alas, a game effort against No. 2-seeded Ohio State went for naught. Gonzaga once led by seven in the first half, fell behind by 10 with nine minutes left and came back five minutes later to tie it behind Bell's heroics. But Jared Sullinger, who would be the 21st pick in the NBA draft in a few months, leaned on Sacre for two important baskets down the stretch, and Gonzaga had five straight dry possessions as the season ended at 26-7 with a 73-66 loss.

In the locker room, Sacre wouldn't let the moment be morose. Somebody laid a stuffed rodent on his shoulder, and the atmosphere was surprisingly light. As Bell explained, "With Rob, if he's in a good mood, we're in a good mood. He's our leader."

Sacre's college career ended there. Not so for the program's good times.

The takeaway: The West Virginia victory is part of a tradition of Gonzaga's rousing first-round NCAA-tournament games. But a footnote: The leading rebounder in that game was a Zag freshman playing his final weekend for GU. Ryan Spangler would transfer home to Oklahoma following the season.

2013

To most Gonzaga fans, the year 2012-13 will forever conjure two memories, one celestial, the other gruesome.

This was the season the Zags ascended to a No. 1 ranking. The school that used to celebrate mere winning seasons, that used to bunk up in hotel rooms for free with fellow assistants of more well-heeled programs, had climbed a mountain that was once unimaginable.

I won't forget the quote from Monson, Few's predecessor, who recalled their days together as assistants at Gonzaga: "Even as cocky, young and brash as we were, we never thought we could be No. 1. We had a lot of beers together, but we never had that many."

This was the team with a newly redshirted and reconstituted Kelly Olynyk, who would be a first-team All-American. Elias Harris was an athletic senior at forward. The sophomore guards, Pangos and Bell, had started two years by season's end. Mike Hart was a glue guy at the "three" spot.

Gonzaga began the year 21st-ranked in the Associated Press poll. Indiana started the year No. 1, but the honor would be ping-ponged between the Hoosiers, Duke, Louisville and Michigan. Then, on the night of Tuesday, February 26, No. 1-rated Indiana lost at Minnesota and the possibility was sitting there for Gonzaga, ranked No. 2. The Zags were 27-2 at that point, having dropped a home game to an explosive Illinois team and lost a one-point thriller at Butler in January.

The Zags had to squeeze out a tough game at Brigham Young – it was tied with less than five minutes left – and then routed Portland in the home finale, setting up the poll vote. At precisely 9 a.m. Monday, upon release of the AP ballot, GU president Thayne McCulloh got the news via text in his office, calling it "wonderful." On campus later that morning, Gonzaga's food-service provider put out a 21-foot sheet cake with blue frosting in a "1" configuration, free to student passersby.

Not so wonderful was what came on the heels of the momentous occasion. As if to presage Gonzaga's challenge of being on top, Loyola Marymount trailed by a mere point at halftime in the WCC semifinals, the Zags' first time on the floor as a top-rated outfit. They won that game and beat Saint Mary's for the title, but never really hit full stride after the rush of the No. 1 ranking.

Gonzaga went to Salt Lake City, where Stockton had won hearts for so long, and where the Zags had played an unforgettable game with Arizona in 2003. No matter. The crowd panted for history's first upset of a No. 1 seed by a 16, and nearly got it, but Gonzaga pulled away from a tie with Southern University inside the four-minute mark to win, 64-58.

"That arena flipped on us just like that," Few says, snapping his fingers. "That was shocking to our guys."

Speaking of Shocking . . . two days later, Gonzaga confronted Wichita State. It's fair to say that the Shockers – then as now – played with an edge and had a psychological advantage, while Gonzaga seemed to be burdened with the ranking and the seed. Yet some of the events of that night are lost to sound logic, like the dog 500 miles from home who somehow finds his way back.

That season, Wichita State made 33.9 percent of its three-pointers. In its previous six games, it had gone 29 of 112 (25.9 percent). Against Pitt in its first-round victory, the Shockers made exactly two of 20 three-point shots.

But Giacoletti recalls something telling.

"We talked to a lot of people leading up to that game," says Giacoletti. "Marshall [Gregg Marshall, the Wichita State coach] kept allowing them to shoot the ball, and instilling confidence in them."

Indeed, even though the Shockers were generally lousy three-point shooters, they took a school-record number of them that season – 765. (They did play an elongated, 39-game schedule.)

You know the rest of the story: In 28 tries, Wichita State made 14 from three-point range, one off the school record. Gonzaga's adjusted defensive rating that season was 37th, not spectacular, but nothing to suggest the roof was about to crumble upon its head, either.

The Zags began, naturally, with a plan to deny driving lanes, but had to adjust when the Shockers kept raining threes. Of course, that became tougher when Gonzaga's best defender, Bell, couldn't play in the second half with pain resulting from a stress fracture in his ankle.

"It's hard to say; maybe one or two of those he could have prevented," says Hart. "I thought the world of Gary, but I don't know if it would have mattered in that half, just because of the way they played."

After trailing by double digits in the first half, Gonzaga seemed to have taken control inside the 12-minute mark with a 49-41 lead. But Wichita State kept banging threes and the Zags made uncharacteristic mistakes down the stretch, including a key, late miscommunication between Harris and David Stockton on an inbounds pass. Gonzaga's glorious season ended, 76-70.

Shortly, the Shockers would prove they were no fluke, taking out Ohio State to get to the Final Four, and then getting eventual champion Louisville down by 12 points before succumbing. Sour as the night was for Few, he found it as nettlesome that the game, for some, became the yardstick by which to measure Gonzaga.

"Wichita is just a really, really good team," he says. "I mean, it's taken people years to figure that out and get over it. So many people use that as their source of identification for us, in regards to, 'Oh, they can't win the big one,' or 'Chokers . . .'"

But Few concedes that the Zags violated a code he talks about all the time. The goal is to remain the aggressor rather than act the victim, no matter the adversity. "We played," he says, "like we were a victim."

And ultimately, on one of the darkest nights in program history, they were.

The takeaway: Had the Zags survived, they had an excellent shot at the Final Four. Underdog – but outmanned – La Salle would have been next in the Sweet 16, followed by an Ohio State team that wasn't the equal of the one that ousted Gonzaga in 2012.

2014

You could call this a bridge year: It came between the national breakthrough of 2013 and the Elite Eight march of 2015. By those standards, it wasn't a boffo season, but Few won't remember it that way. "As a team, we reached our highest, fullest potential of any team," he insists. "We hit the 99.8 percentile. That team was limited."

For a good part of the season, it was also injured. Shortly after Pangos bedeviled Arkansas for 34 points in the Maui Invitational, he developed a painful, persistent case of turf toe that would dog him the rest of the way. Late in the calendar year 2013, injuries to Sam Dower (back) and Bell (broken hand) overlapped.

Gonzaga won the regular-season and WCC tournament championships – punctuated by some bipolar games within a week. The Zags devoured Saint Mary's in Moraga, 75-47, leading by 31 with 10 minutes left. But in the WCC quarterfinal, against an 18-loss Santa Clara team, they needed Stockton's driving layup with two seconds left just to stick around for the rest of the tournament in a 77-75 victory.

Then they inflicted some of their first-game NCAA-tournament magic on unsuspecting Oklahoma State, a Keith Smart-driven team that had shown well in the Big 12, the No. 1-rated RPI conference.

Gonzaga led virtually the entire way before it got bruising down the stretch. Oke State opted to try to lengthen the game by fouling, and the two squads combined for a staggering 37 free throws in the final 3:52, stirring boos from some fans in San Diego's Viejas Arena before it ended, 85-77, Gonzaga.

The season expired with a thud two days later against a gifted Arizona team that would fall two straight years in Elite Eight games to Wisconsin. This one had Aaron Gordon, soon to be the fourth pick in the 2014 draft; Rondae Hollis-Jefferson, a first-round pick in '15; forward Brandon Ashley and leading scorer Nick Johnson.

Pangos turned an ankle early, went to the locker room and returned moments later, but his availability was nowhere near enough. Gordon was unguardable, Bell went scoreless for the first time that season and Gonzaga made the first 11 turnovers in the game – 20 in the first 34 minutes. It added up to an 84-61 Arizona win that ended the Zags' season at 29-7.

Pangos' resilience was underscored by a postseason stretch of about three months in which he stayed idle to cure the troublesome turf toe. Few called his effort as courageous as any he had been around, saying, "He literally couldn't walk after games. It was totally frustrating, especially for a point guard."

The takeaway: It was the third time in the 18-year run the Zags tried to emerge from an 8-9 seed matchup to make a deep March run. Again, they found it not to be the preferred route.

2015

The Zags had just dispatched UCLA, 74-62, at NRG Stadium in Houston, and the coaches began the ritual, long night that coaches put in peering at video between weekend games in the NCAA tournament. They were in the Elite Eight for the first time under Few, and the generation's most irrepressible team, Duke, stood in the way of Gonzaga's first Final Four.

They debated what to do against Duke's freshman big man, Jahlil Okafor: Double him or let Zag center Przemek Karnowski try to contest him one-on-one?

"I should have gone with my original gut feeling," Few would say a couple of months later. "We were not gonna double Okafor because Przemek is so good. Then I got caught up with, 'Nobody's-shooting-in-the-dome,' so I'm like 'Ah, what the heck, let's double Okafor then.'"

Surely there was a case for the decision to double Okafor. They were playing in a massive football stadium and in Friday night's Sweet 16 games, nobody had shown an ability to hit an outside shot. The Zags had somehow won by 12 despite making three of 19 threes. UCLA had connected on three of 13. In the other game, Duke was three of nine and Utah four of 16.

It gnaws a little at Few that the strategy backfired. Duke's Matt Jones made half his team's threes, hitting four of seven, and the Blue Devils pulled away down the stretch for a 66-52 win on the way to Mike Krzyzewski's fifth national title. It wasn't long into the game before the Zags decided to single-cover Okafor, but by then, as Few says, "It got Jones on board. He got rolling."

At the other end, a Duke defense that had been maligned much of the season denied the Zags consistent good looks. This was a defense that had allowed opponents to shoot 50 percent or better five times since the calendar turned to 2015, but it surrendered just 38 percent in its six NCAA-tournament games.

"Duke improved so much from their league, and their league tournament, defensively," Few says, "because they were not a very good [defensive] team, from what we saw on tape. I don't know if they were just not into it, or what their deal was. They were not giving great effort [previously]. Yet, they climbed up into our guards. Maybe they just needed something to be playing for."

Still, the Zags shot 44 percent, best of the six Duke NCAA opponents. And if you knew that, and that Duke shot only 37.5

percent, and that Gonzaga had a slight rebounding edge, 35-31, you might have guessed that Gonzaga was moving on to Indianapolis. But the Blue Devils committed a mere three turnovers – 10 fewer than GU – and it was the Zags left to wonder what might have been.

GU led by four early in the second half, fell behind by eight, and was ultimately poised to tie it at 53 on a layup by Kyle Wiltjer inside the five-minute mark. He missed, and Gonzaga seemed to have nothing left.

"It was just one of those things," Few says, exhaling deeply as he remembers Wiltjer's miss, "it just kind of took you down, for whatever reason."

There wasn't much else about the season to lament. Gonzaga lost a 66-63 overtime grinder at Arizona in early December, then clicked off a school-record 22 straight victories, all the way to a Senior Night upset loss to Brigham Young, 73-70. Then came a wide, revenge victory over BYU in the WCC tournament final, a No. 2 seed in the NCAA tournament, a rugged, not-so-easy 86-76 first-round win over North Dakota State and a 19-point throttling of Iowa at Seattle's KeyArena.

If there was a message to Gonzaga's journey, it might have been this: It belonged. It was good enough to beat Duke, it just didn't. The Final Four was elusive, but attainable.

The takeaway: Gonzaga finished with a school-record 35 victories, a number that would have left Dan Fitzgerald dizzy. The Pangos-Bell era ended and Byron Wesley's one season was done, leaving the 2015-16 team with challenges it would meet in its own unique manner.

2016

When I first saw Gonzaga live in the 2015-16 season, it was against Montana December 9. Gonzaga won, 61-58, in hairbreadth fashion, and afterward, Few was as down as I've ever seen him. The

Zags were a mess then. Eric McClellan didn't seem to understand the offense. Josh Perkins was throwing no-look passes when looking was the wise option. Kyle Dranginis wasn't making the transition from complementary player the year before to key player now.

"That NCAA-tournament streak . . . I don't know," Few muttered grimly. "This might be the year it doesn't happen."

Karnowski had fallen hard on his back in practice and his return was uncertain. Three days before the Montana game, Gonzaga had led Arizona by double digits, but fell in the late stages.

"We really got after 'em after that Arizona game, and it backfired," said assistant coach Tommy Lloyd. "They tried too hard, or got too timid. We probably overreacted, challenging them. Then UCLA beats us, and it's 'Holy shit,' and we're just thinking, 'It's all caving in.'"

It was the oddest season, one unlike any other at Gonzaga. Karnowski underwent surgery and was declared out for the duration, and without him, the Zags failed time and again to pick up a quality win. Whereas the staple of Gonzaga's string of NCAA-tournament runs was amassing resume-building victories outside the conference, this year, post-Karnowski, saw none of that. To make matters worse, the Zags kicked away games at Saint Mary's and against Brigham Young – losing double-digit leads well into the second half – that might have served as equity on Selection Sunday.

Nor, however, were the blemishes unsightly. The Zags had a mere two losses to teams below the Ratings Percentage Index top 50, meaning even as they toiled without prize victories, they weren't turning in clunkers, either – save for those late-game giveaways. As a unit, they were just sort of . . . there.

"We've had teams that – even last year – that went on the road and struggled, didn't play well," says assistant Brian Michaelson. "And this team never really did that."

It was a team in search of itself. Early, Lloyd saw signs of what he called "splintering – 'I want us to be good, but I want to be one of the main reasons we're good.' Somebody would break away from the herd. We'd be up 10 or 12, and 'I can do my thing.' Guys would be competing for who was going to make the play or be the guy. It was Wiltjer, it was [Sabonis], it was Josh, it was Eric. It wasn't just those two guards."

As February melted toward March, the chance of returning to another NCAA tournament was growing dimmer. That apparently wasn't a motivational hammer the coaches brought out of the toolbox.

"No, no," says Michaelson. "Coach Few is great at that. He keeps them in the present. It was about the next game."

Finally, the next game was at Brigham Young, and they won that for a piece of the WCC championship. Then they won three more in the league tournament, over Portland, BYU and Saint Mary's, and celebrated the 18th successive trip to the NCAA field. An 11th seed, they shut down No. 6 Seton Hall, the Big East tournament champ, 68-52, rendering the Pirates' lead dog, Isaiah Whitehead, completely ineffective. Then came a masterpiece against third-seeded Utah, 82-59, and a shutdown of the Pac-12 player of the year, Jakob Poeltl. Given the circuitous route, Few called it the "sweetest" Sweet 16 of his six.

Six days later in Chicago, it would all come full circle. Moments from a consecutive Elite Eight appearance, the Zags' guards coughed up a couple of nasty turnovers down the stretch and lost to Syracuse's desperate comeback, 63-60. Two days later, the Orange were at it again, pressing top seed Virginia into oblivion in coming from a 15-point deficit midway through the second half to steal the Final Four berth.

The takeaway: Chalk this one up to the culture. In a season that seemed ripe for fracture, Gonzaga instead persevered and found a stunning reward at the end. The 2016-17 team would have a much different makeup, but like its predecessors, would have a tradition to uphold.

– 13 –
EIGHTEEN QUESTIONS

HEREWITH, SOME QUESTIONS deserving of answers, or at least exploration. Imagine: There are 18 of them.

1. Did HBO abscond with any state secrets last winter?

No, but in airing "Gonzaga: The March to Madness," the network got away with a despair-to-deliverance saga that was precisely the kind of narrative it would have hoped for.

The Zags weren't approached about the possibility of a reality show until September 2015. It would be patterned after the popular annual HBO series "Hard Knocks," chronicling life inside an NFL team.

Initially, athletic director Mike Roth and basketball coach Mark Few were against the idea (which is a bad place to start). Were they really going to pull back the curtain and show what they do behind the scenes?

"Right now, people think we do something special," Few fretted. "We probably do the same things everybody else does. We just get better outcomes."

Associate athletic directors Chris Standiford and Kris Kassel loved the idea. So did the assistant coaches. They'd be the first college basketball team featured by HBO.

"It's not my cup of tea," Few says. "I'd much rather keep our program private."

Reluctantly, the Zags agreed, after Roth called fellow AD Jack Swarbrick at Notre Dame, where Showtime had done a similar look at Irish football. Roth watched an episode and was smitten.

The Zag version was going to be an 11-installment series, fleshing out the entire season. TV cameras followed them down waterslides in the Bahamas in November. Then there was a shakeup at HBO Sports, president Ken Hershman resigning, and the series was slimmed down to five parts, starting well into the West Coast Conference season.

By then, the season appeared to be unraveling. In January, BYU thwarted Gonzaga with a comeback from a 13-point deficit in Spokane, and a week later, Saint Mary's came from 10 behind late to win at home.

"We're in the freakin' Greek tragedy," Roth mumbled to somebody about then. Instead of a documentary on Gonzaga's steady success, this was going to be about the end of its tournament streak.

Few squirmed and swallowed hard. He refused to be mic'ed up during games, but "then they started getting tricky. There were mikes on the floor, underneath the clipboard. Imagine, everywhere you go . . . you go to walk the dogs, you get mic'ed up."

Each episode was previewed by GU compliance, for propriety or potential violations. The production company filmed youth-league games of Few's three youngest kids, but the one featuring his seventh-grader, Joe, was flagged – because the NCAA deems seventh-graders to be recruitable athletes.

Ultimately, the Zags found themselves at season's end, and even as he remains skeptical of the recruiting value, Few admits he got tons of positive feedback at the Final Four in Houston.

As stories go, it was perfect. At least that's what the production-company sound technician must have concluded. He was bawling his eyes out the night Gonzaga won the WCC title.

2. Are WCC teams gaining on Gonzaga?

Not so you'd notice. The 2016 NCAA tournament brought more of what the conference has been seeing virtually since Gonzaga began its March insurgences. The Zags were the only WCC team in the conference to make the Big Dance, and in the NCAA's format of "unit" payouts to conferences, Gonzaga made about $3.2 million for the conference over six years with its two victories.

Nothing new there. According to a Bloomberg News analysis in 2015, over a 25-year period starting in 1991, Gonzaga made $34.33 million for the WCC, while earning only $6.82 million from other WCC members' work in the tournament. Tellingly, the gap between breadwinner and No. 2 contributor was larger in the WCC than in any other conference. (Since the 2000 season, a WCC team other than Gonzaga has earned an at-large bid to the tournament only eight times, which means it happens every other year.)

Bill Grier, the former Gonzaga assistant who went on to coach at San Diego, told me in 2014, "I don't know how schools are going to close the gap on them. We've taken some boosters on that trip (to Gonzaga) and they're blown away. They have no idea what resources they have."

3. Did Few get a rise out of the WCC?

Few took the occasion of Selection Sunday, 2016, to criticize WCC members for failing to invest in facilities improvements, even as they continue to cash checks derived from Gonzaga's victories in the NCAA tournament. His point was touched off when Saint Mary's was snubbed in the '16 bracket, ostensibly because of the overall weakness of the conference below Saint Mary's, Gonzaga and BYU.

WCC commissioner Lynn Holzman points to a heavy turnover in league presidents in recent years, and says she has sensed an increased urgency to upgrade facilities since late 2015. Said Holzman in June 2016, "We didn't have the presidents nearly as engaged as they are now. We just came off a meeting in which they're sitting there, talking about men's basketball and how important it is. They can't put so much pressure on the league to take care of things for them."

There are signs of life. San Francisco just began a $15-million renovation project, to be followed by a planned final phase to construct a practice gym. Portland's new recreation facility that opened in August 2015 includes a practice floor used by visiting NBA teams. When Santa Clara hired Herb Sendek, it did so with the promise of new locker rooms, an increased budget and what athletic director Renee Baumgartner called the mindset of a "top 20" program.

Pepperdine has explored a possible replacement for 3,100-seat Firestone Fieldhouse with a 5,000-seat building, getting approval from Los Angeles County and the California Coastal Commission. The next question: How to pay for it? That's a problem personified by Saint Mary's, which, even as it has been a consistent force under Randy Bennett, continues to play in 3,500-seat McKeon Pavilion.

Spring of 2016 brought four coaching changes on the men's side of WCC basketball. But that could be interpreted two ways – as a sign of commitment, or a failure to understand some of the underlying reasons for losing.

Holzman says she's optimistic, but the reputation of many WCC programs isn't exactly dynamic and forward-thinking. "I'm also a realist," she says. "We need to see how it actually plays out on the court."

The cold facts are that four programs – Portland, Santa Clara, San Francisco and Loyola Marymount – haven't been to the NCAA tournament this millennium. And it's inevitable Gonzaga, even as it has funneled millions to those schools, has had something to do with crushing hopes.

"One of the big challenges we continue to have in the league is, very few programs in the last 15 years have tasted it," says Holzman, "not having that opportunity to energize boosters."

4. Is there a better landing spot for Gonzaga?

In a word, no. The Zags haven't had football since World War II days, and that means they don't fit a conference like the Mountain West.

Since the Big East splintered, leaving a collection of Catholic schools, Gonzaga has pushed the idea of a conference that would cover times zones from East to West. But as Roth says, it was a major step for the Big East to expand to Omaha, which for some administrators, was as distant as the moon.

"Well, we're on Mars," Roth says.

Two things that might make outer space work: Another expansion in the Big East, and a divisional alignment that would, for instance, keep Gonzaga playing mostly in Central time zones rather than on the East Coast. And second, somebody of Gonzaga's institutional and basketball ilk that would be a West Coast partner. Saint Mary's would be an obvious candidate, but the Gaels seem satisfied playing in a gym that would be an impediment.

"We need peers," says Roth.

For better or worse, right now Gonzaga seems peerless.

5. Is Gonzaga's facilities edge actually growing larger?

Against its competitors in the WCC, it is. Late in September, 2016, the Zags broke ground on a $24-million building adjacent to the Martin Centre, with a target opening in late 2017. The Volkar Center for Athletic Achievement will house an academic center for all GU athletes, a basketball practice floor, a strength-and-conditioning facility, nutrition space and a hall-of-fame component. As ample as

Gonzaga's basketball brand has become, there's precious little access to the McCarthey Athletic Center and no touchstone display to describe to visitors what it represents.

Roth calls the fund-raising effort "almost mind-boggling." It included one $3-million gift, plus the benefaction of Pat and Sandy Volkar, whose contribution included multi-acre waterfront property on the east side of Lake Coeur d'Alene that the university intends to sell.

The hands-on players are familiar – the same Spokane architectural firm, the same Spokane construction company that collaborated on other major Gonzaga athletic projects. Says Roth, "As I told people, we've got the band back together. We don't have to 'learn' each other."

His excitement is palpable. "This is ground-breaking, a game-changer for us,"

Roth says. "Schools like us aren't doing things like this."

Apparently, they are now.

6. Did the Zags politick against Seattle U.'s campaign to join the WCC?

If they did, it was done in unobtrusive fashion. Back in 2007, when Seattle U. was beginning to transition from NCAA Division II to I, it lobbied for inclusion into the WCC, and former Gonzaga president Robert Spitzer supported the move at the league meetings. (The Zags insist they are bound to do that for other such schools in their Jesuit province.)

Seattle U.'s push fell flat; it didn't prove it had the financial commitment to athletics just yet. And the Redhawks eventually were annexed into the ungainly, reconfigured Western Athletic Conference. It has to be vexing for old-line Seattle U. faithful. Institutionally, the school is a perfect fit for the WCC – Jesuit, formidable academically, urban – but it's competing in a league against teams from Illinois, Missouri, Utah, Texas and Arizona.

But thems the breaks. Seattle U.'s unremarkable basketball since then seems to reinforce that taking in the Redhawks several years ago would have been a mistake for the WCC, a cart-before-the-horse move. If Gonzaga was privately stuffy about beckoning Seattle U., it might have been well-founded.

"Mike has always told us he's supported us," says former Seattle U. athletic director Bill Hogan, referring to Roth. "You always hear rumors [about Gonzaga opposition] but I have no reason not to believe that."

Seattle U.'s stiffest challenge is not having a suitable campus arena. It plays at KeyArena, usually in front of about 2,000 people. Hogan, who said in 2007 fund-raising was taking place for a new building, told me in the spring of 2016 that nothing like that is in the works, that the Redhawks are trying to build the fan base off-campus first, then push for a new arena.

With Brigham Young's future in the league uncertain – the Cougars are always on the prowl for a more football-friendly home – that 10th spot in the WCC could someday be up for grabs. The last time it came open, the league welcomed Pacific, for reasons that have never been entirely clear – particularly to supporters of Seattle U.

7. How might history have been different if – gulp – Gonzaga basketball had been given a postseason ban in 1999?

The question stops Roth, who says, "I've literally never thought about it until you brought it up."

Who knows what sort of machinations were rattling in the minds of the NCAA committee on infractions when it dealt with the Dan Fitzgerald improprieties back in 1998? Maybe a one-year ban in '99 was a real possibility, maybe it was never broached. But you had an athletic director who had also been the basketball coach, misguiding funds and bringing about a finding of lack of institutional control. Not that anybody was particularly obsessed with it at the time, given Gonzaga's sparse postseason history, but it wouldn't have been a major upset if the Zags had been ordered to sit out March 1999.

All of which, of course, would have meant no program-changing weekend at KeyArena, no Casey Calvary tip-in against Florida, no electrifying run to the Elite Eight.

So go ahead and speculate. It's safe to say that Dan Monson wouldn't have been squired by Minnesota for its vacant job, so he's back for the 2000 season. It seems reasonable that the Zags would have found their way to the NCAA tournament that year (as they did in Few's first season), but would they have made the sort of splash to pull Monson away? If Monson had hung around a few more years, would Few have been tempted to uproot for another head-coaching job? Might all of that have tilted the scales to Grier, the other longtime assistant coach, if Monson had eventually left?

Delicious, but ultimately futile, conjecture.

8. What to do about retiring numbers?

Like a lot of schools, Gonzaga has been haphazard about retired numbers, doing so for John Stockton (No. 12) and Frank Burgess (44). That means nobody's number from the past three decades has been retired, owing mostly to an absence of policy on how exactly to do it.

"We haven't done a good job with that," says Few. "It's really hard. I'd like to retire 50 of them, but you can't do that."

Even Stockton's selection reflects a fluid debate on how it ought to happen. He is far and away the NBA's career assist leader, but in his four years at Gonzaga (1981-84), the Zags went 27-25 in conference games and had one top-three finish.

Few posits that "maybe the retired jersey is kind of archaic," and that instead, hall-of-fame recognition might be based on team achievement.

9. What's the 18-year all-star team?

Few won't go there but here's a stab:

Guards: Kevin Pangos and Dan Dickau. Let the debate rage (and the slings and arrows be launched).

Dickau's first-team All-America honor in 2002 speaks powerfully. Pangos was unusually consistent, never shooting below 40 percent on threes or less than 80 percent from the foul line. He was a capable, but not uncanny, passer, ranking No. 5 on the school's assist list. And he led a team that became ranked No. 1 in 2013. He gets the nod here over Matt Santangelo, Blake Stepp and Richie Frahm. Santangelo is the Zags' career assist leader, but his shooting tailed off his last two seasons. Stepp is the only Gonzaga player in history to win back-to-back WCC player-of-the-year awards and the late Fitzgerald said he was the best guard in school history. A terrific passer, he had enigmatic shooting problems in the NCAA tournament. Frahm, like Pangos, was a picture of shooting consistency, but not as accomplished a playmaker.

Bigs: Casey Calvary, Adam Morrison and Ronny Turiaf.

Calvary's teams won seven games in the NCAA tournament, he's on several school top-10 lists and he hit the biggest shot in Zags history. Morrison doesn't really qualify as a "big," but his incandescent 2006 season wins him a spot nevertheless. Turiaf is the pick here over Elias Harris (top four in school scoring and rebounds), on the strength of his 2005 conference player-of-the-year honor, a long pro career and his most-favored-Zag status in Spokane. Kelly Olynyk contends as well with a first-team All-America year in 2013 but his brilliance was limited to a single season.

10. What's continuity worth in the GU athletic department?

In a word, plenty. The tenure in key spots at Gonzaga is mind-bending, possibly unequaled in college athletics today.

Roth, the athletic director, has been on the job 19 years, but has had roles at Gonzaga dating back three decades. The average tenure of today's WCC AD outside Spokane is eight years. Deputy AD Chris Standiford has had that title (or associate AD) for 14 years, he's been a full-time employee since 1993 and a GU student before that. Few arrived as a graduate assistant in 1989, and at 53, has spent more than half his life pulling down paychecks from Gonzaga.

There's also Steve Hertz, Gonzaga baseball coach for a quarter-century and now associate AD for major gifts. Associate director for compliance Shannon Strahl has been in the department since 2000, after she ended her soccer days there with the Bulldog Club's female athlete-of-the-year award.

Longevity is no guarantee of success, but if you have competent people in place, they know where the bones are buried and how best to get things done. It's probably no coincidence that the three most successful men's basketball programs in the league are at Gonzaga; Saint Mary's, where Randy Bennett has worked for 15 years; and Brigham Young, where Dave Rose has 11 years' tenure.

Roth comes in for major props among those he's overseeing. Says Few, "He's one of the heroes of this whole story. He's always been willing to keep growing the product, the one that's got to explain to the powers-that-be. He always gave us as much as he could possibly give us."

Standiford is similarly grateful, saying, "The magic in Mike is his humility. He always does the work and never puts himself out front. He's freakin' amazing at what he does."

11. Did Fitz do the Zags wrong, or was it the other way around?

Almost two decades have passed since Fitzgerald stepped aside as basketball coach, followed by the discovery of improprieties in the way he dispersed money as athletic director. That got the Zags on NCAA probation and stirred a rancorous debate on his proper place in the school's history.

Publicly, the school mostly fell silent on the wrongdoing – after forcing him out – and Fitzgerald's supporters were vocal and vehement about a perceived cold shoulder to him. Indeed, Fitz didn't come around and there was no real recognition of his service by the school.

His supporters insist he hired all the young lions who turned Gonzaga into the force it is today. Others will tell you he merely lured Dan Monson, who attracted Few, who enlisted Grier, while Fitz rubber-stamped.

Surely in a new support-services building, in a display of Gonzaga's hoops history, there will be a tasteful way to recognize Fitzgerald's energetic, frenetic 15 years as head coach – without a need to render judgment on the propriety of the actions that put the Zags in the NCAA crosshairs.

12. Is Few underpaid?

Tough to say with certainty, because, as a private school, Gonzaga isn't required to furnish salary figures. USA Today's annual survey in spring 2016 put Few's earnings – as reported on 2013 federal tax returns – at $1,374,811. But that figure is outdated, and according to Roth, "He gets paid top-25 money."

Twenty-fourth on the list is Oregon's Dana Altman, at $2,000,100.

If Few is indeed at $2 million, he probably is underpaid, at least by the overheated standards of today's college marketplace. He has taken six teams to Sweet 16s, and among current coaches, that's bettered only by Mike Krzyzewski, Roy Williams, Rick Pitino, Jim Boeheim, Bill Self, Tom Izzo, John Calipari, Tubby Smith and Bob Huggins.

Among those trailing Few in that metric: Ben Howland (5), Lon Kruger (5), Jay Wright (5), John Beilein (4), Tom Crean (4), Mike Brey (3), Jamie Dixon (3), Scott Drew (3), Gregg Marshall (2), John Thompson III (2), Mike Anderson (2), Altman (2) and Ernie Kent (2).

Of course, Sweet 16s are only one measure, and several of those coaches have gone to Final Fours (and in Wright's case, won a national championship) while Gonzaga hasn't.

Crean's resume presents a question of intrigue for Zag fans lusting for their first Final Four: Would you take his portfolio over Few's? They began as head coaches the same year (1999-2000), and Crean took a Marquette team fueled by Dwyane Wade to the Final Four. But in his 17 seasons, he has failed to make the NCAA tournament five times, including a period when he had to rebuild Indiana.

Seems like a debate best entertained over an IPA at Jack and Dan's, spiced by the fact that Few was a target of the Hoosiers in two different searches, one when Crean was hired.

13. Can Few make the Naismith Hall of Fame?

Given that the selection committee's thresholds are only slightly less mysterious than those for choosing popes, it's open to question, and surely subject in part to the eventual length of Few's career. In terms of name familiarity, he's long-since distanced himself from the novelty stage and become a household name on the coaching scene.

If nothing else, the sheer volume of wins – 466 entering 2016-17 – will begin to get him into the discussion. A Final Four would certainly aid the cause. But two Northwest icons – Marv Harshman and Ralph Miller – both made it without a Final Four.

I ran the question by John Akers, veteran editor of Basketball Times. He views two coaches who made it in – Lou Carnesecca of St. John's (1992) and John Chaney of Temple (2001) – as "comparables." Carnesecca had a Final Four in 1985, Chaney never went.

Both had the benefit of the attention of the Eastern media. Carnesecca was seen as a beloved figure, and Chaney was recognized partly as a mentor of inner-city kids in Philadelphia. Similarly, beyond the yardstick of wins or tournament advancement, Few ought to score points for the building and sustenance of a program that came from far off the radar.

14. Is Gonzaga playing better defense?

Verifiably, yes. Stat analyst Ken Pomeroy has been tracking offensive and defensive efficiency since 2002, and his numbers speak loudly – even surprisingly – about improved defense at GU.

In the first six years of KenPom's stats (2002-07), which account for strength of opponents and measure points per possession allowed, Gonzaga averaged a tepid No. 99.5 ranking nationally in adjusted defense. In the nine years since, the average ranking has been 39.3, or a quantum jump of 60 places.

Few's calling has always been offense, and still is. But over time, he's come to terms with defense. On any given defensive drill, says assistant Tommy Lloyd, "You look around, and he's in the bathroom. But his deal is, we're going to get guys to play with great effort, intelligence and hold them accountable to sticking with the plan."

15. Whither Coaches Versus Cancer?

Before we address that one, first picture Keith Urban, doing a hastily arranged mini-concert for a gathering of unsuspecting but appreciative donors in the backyard of a Spokane South Hill home in the summer of 2015.

Now the back story: In 2002, Spokane's iteration of Coaches Versus Cancer, the American Cancer Society's campus-centered fund-raising arm, took flight under executive director Jerid Keefer, and heavily supported by Mark and Marcy Few. Marcy would become one of the event's driving forces.

In 12 years, Keefer says the event raised $6.5 million, putting it near the top of Coaches Versus Cancer efforts nationally.

"It had a huge impact," says Mark Few. "It was really impressive, how the community came together and made it happen."

Some $1.2 million of that $6.5 million went to fund Camp Goodtimes. That's an annual event at YMCA Camp Reed in north Spokane, which for a summer week hosts young cancer patients and a companion free of charge. Gonzaga basketball players annually join them for a day.

American Cancer Society changed course after 2013, mandating that all money raised from its Coaches Versus Cancer events would go to research. That imperiled funding for local charities like Camp Goodtimes and the Ronald McDonald House.

Enter the Community Cancer Fund, again with Keefer at the helm. It raised some $2.4 million in its first two years of existence, with the freedom to distribute the proceeds locally. When Urban owed somebody a favor, here came the country singer/songwriter, springing his talent on a cozy gathering of 200 people, many of whom thought they were merely showing up for a wine-tasting event.

The Fews aren't as directly involved with the new organization, but they remain supportive and the momentum is unmistakable. Says Mark Few, "This Community Cancer Fund is killing it."

16. Has the Kennel Club lost a step?

The student rooting group sprang up in the mid-1980s as a rogue and rabid part of Gonzaga home games. For much of a generation, it was a social heartbeat on campus, combining two important ingredients – basketball and beer.

Tomson Spink, Gonzaga's manager of facilities, maintenance and grounds, recalls his role as co-president back in the mid-'90s: Put up flyers around campus offering a T-shirt and a party before all home games for $30; play host in a house on Desmet Avenue; shut down the keg a few minutes before tipoff; and hide the taps – otherwise, a good many revelers would never make the game.

"The point was to be social, have beers, hang out, laugh and go to a basketball game," says Spink, recalling a Kennel Club of 150-175 regulars.

About a decade ago, the Kennel Club officially moved under university aegis. But don't count Spink among the old-days-were-better crowd.

"I would say it's a lot better now," he says. "Less vulgar, maybe. Definitely more organized."

You might also call it more sophisticated, if that means picking its spots. Perhaps because of the basketball team's success, students sometimes pass on less-attractive opponents, and the passion level of those in the house is often a topic on message boards and sports-talk radio.

"I would say they're getting spoiled a little bit," says Spink. "It was the opposite for us, where we didn't win as much."

Adam Morrison had as good a view as anybody. He played in the first game of consequence in the McCarthey Athletic Center, against Washington in 2004, and sat on the bench as a student assistant a decade later.

"The atmosphere in the Kennel was amazing," he says, recalling a victory over the UW. "Nobody wants to say it, but the atmosphere was way better back then than it is now. I just think it was a little more raw."

17. Spokane: What's the allure?

Whether it's the pull of old college ties, the city-without-urban-suffocation, or the appeal of outdoor pursuits, an inordinate number of former Gonzaga players have settled in Spokane, hard winters be damned. A few, like J.P. Batista and Ronny Turiaf, own homes and return on occasion, but a horde of others, many from the west side of the Cascades, have put down roots there. Here's the list, especially heavy with new-millennium grads (and apologies for any omissions):

Ken Anderson (1980-81), J.P. Batista (2005-06), Eric Brady (1992), Jim Bresnahan (1969-71), Winston Brooks (2002-03), Jeff Brown (1992-94), Casey Calvary (1998-2001), Jeff Condill (1984-86), Dan Dickau (2001-02), Colin Floyd (2003-06), Ryan Floyd (1997-2000), Richard Fox (2003-04), Richie Frahm (1997-2000), Zach Gourde (2000-03), Mike Hart (2010-13), Alex Hernandez

(2001-02), Josh Heytvelt (2006-09), Bret Holmdahl (1989-90), Sean Mallon (2004-07), Jim McPhee (1986-90), Brian Michaelson (2002-05), Adam Morrison (2004-06), Mike Nilson (1997-2000), David Pendergraft (2005-08), Brad Pinney (1990), Derek Raivio (2004-07), Robert Sacre (2008-12), Matt Santangelo (1997-2000), Tony Skinner (2003-04), Scott Spink (1991-94), Blake Stepp (2001-04), David Stockton (2011-14), John Stockton (1981-84), Ronny Turiaf (2002-05), Paul Verret (1988-89), Cory Violette (2001-04), Mike Winger (1987-90).

Richie Frahm remembers his mindset as a student-athlete, flying south to the Bay Area or Los Angeles and mild winter temperatures: "After college, I'm going to move to California. I don't know how expensive it's going to be, but I'm going to do it."

Frahm's post-collegiate passion, of course, was pro basketball. Meanwhile, his wife, whom he met as a student, is from the Spokane Valley, so it was natural to return for the summers, "to stay young and motivated. We'd be gone for nine or 10 months, and I'd get re-motivated with the youth of Gonzaga.

By the time he was done with basketball, more than a decade had passed. The Frahms got into residential and commercial real estate, and Richie, who had come from Vancouver, Washington, realized this was home.

"I've grown to appreciate it since I retired," he said. "Once you get in the real world, you've got to fall back on your connections and resources, and I think it's easier to do that here in Spokane than it might be somewhere else."

18. What does Jud think?

For years, of a winter Tuesday, Jud Heathcote would come into town and have lunch with Few at Jack and Dan's. The sandwich or bowl of soup was always secondary to Heathcote's signature, acidic critique of whatever might have been lately ailing the Zags (even if nothing was).

Now Jud is 89 and he doesn't get out much. But, then and now, he says Gonzaga has usually surprised him.

A generation ago, he says he and his wife went to their first Gonzaga game. It was over Thanksgiving vacation, so the crowd wasn't much.

"I still remember, my wife said, 'Is this Division I basketball? We had more people at high school games than this,'" Heathcote says. "Then they started to play. They had Paul Rogers, the seven-foot center and Scott Snider, the 6-8 forward, and then [Kyle] Dixon, the guard. They could play on any of my teams. They've always been blessed with better players than you'd think would end up at Gonzaga."

Heathcote just passed 20 years as a Gonzaga season-ticket holder since his retirement from Michigan State, where he won the 1979 national championship and coached Magic Johnson.

"Every year, I say, 'Well, it can't be as good as they were this year,'" Heathcote says. "And each year, it seems like they're better. It's remarkable, unheard-of. At a small school like Gonzaga, it's almost unreal."

ACKNOWLEDGMENTS

GLORY HOUNDS is my first foray into the arena of self-publishing, and I owe thanks to Pete Tormey for helping me negotiate the process and avoid the pitfalls.

For his cover photography and terrific design work, props to Rajah Bose.

Thanks to the people of Gonzaga for their willingness to allow a deep dive into the program, in particular Mike Roth, Chris Standiford, Mark Few and Tommy Lloyd.

For inside photographs, a nod to Todd Zeidler at Gonzaga and from the West Coast Conference, Ryan McCrary and Jeff Tourial.

For legal counsel, thanks to George Brunt. For editing help, a tip of the red pen to Bill Reader.

And for her (frequent) tech support, and the occasional shoulder to cry on, my wife Velvet.

CPSIA information can be obtained
at www.ICGtesting.com
Printed in the USA
FSOW01n0716131216
28523FS